C000181441

Mayhem

THE LEWIS WALPOLE SERIES IN EIGHTEENTH-CENTURY CULTURE AND HISTORY

The Lewis Walpole Series, published by Yale University Press with the aid of the Annie Burr Lewis Fund, is dedicated to the culture and history of the long eighteenth century (from the Glorious Revolution to the accession of Queen Victoria). It welcomes work in a variety of fields, including literature and history, the visual arts, political philosophy, music, legal history, and the history of science. In addition to original scholarly work, the series publishes new editions and translations of writing from the period, as well as reprints of major books that are currently unavailable. Though the majority of books in the series will probably concentrate on Great Britain and the Continent, the range of our geographical interests is as wide as Horace Walpole's.

NICHOLAS ROGERS

Mayhem

POST-WAR CRIME AND VIOLENCE

IN BRITAIN, 1748–53

Yale UNIVERSITY PRESS
New Haven &
London

Published with assistance from the Annie Burr Lewis Fund,
and with assistance from the foundation established in memory of
Amasa Stone Mather of the Class of 1907, Yale College.

Yale University Press books may be purchased in quantity for educational,
business, or promotional use. For information, please e-mail sales.press@yale.edu
(U.S. office) or sales@yaleup.co.uk (U.K. office).

Set in Sabon type by Keystone Typesetting, Orwigsburg, Penn.
Printed in the United States of America.

Library of Congress Cataloging-in-Publication Data
Rogers, Nicholas.
    Mayhem : post-war crime and violence in Britain, 1748–53 / Nicholas Rogers.
        p. cm. — (The Lewis Walpole series in eighteenth-century culture and history)
    Includes bibliographical references and index.
    ISBN 978-0-300-16962-1 (cloth : alk. paper)
    1. Great Britain — History — George II, 1727–1760. 2. Great Britain — Social
conditions — 18th century. 3. Violence — England — History — 18th century.
I. Title.
DA500.R64 2012
364.10941′09033 — dc23   2012019519

A catalogue record for this book is available from the British Library.

This paper meets the requirements of ANSI/NISO Z39.48–1992
(Permanence of Paper).

10 9 8 7 6 5 4 3 2 1

For John Beattie

Contents

Acknowledgments

I began thinking about the demobilization crisis of the mid-eighteenth century some twenty years ago and wrote an essay about it in a collection of essays entitled *Stilling the Grumbling Hive* in 1992. I returned to the subject after writing on naval impressment, convinced that it could be embellished and amplified through the series of interlocking narratives that finally made up this book.

My early explorations owed much to microfilm collections at the Robarts Library at the University of Toronto, and I would like to thank the librarians in Microtext (now Media Commons) for their help over the years. More recently, the book has benefited from the online collections that are now available to scholars, especially those of the eighteenth century. I was fortunate to be able to use Eighteenth Century Collections Online and the Burney Newspapers Online in conjunction with the Old Bailey Proceedings Online to round out my study. My thanks in this regard to Tim Hitchcock and Bob Shoemaker for making the Old Bailey records available to scholars and for providing helpful linkages to cognate sources such as the Ordinary of Newgate's *Account*.

Much of this book draws on printed and online sources, but for some chapters and subthemes, manuscript sources have been essential. I would like to thank the archivists of the National Library at Kew, the Metropolitan London Library, the East and West Sussex Record Offices, for the help they have given me.

Aspects of this work were presented at a number of seminars: the Toronto Legal History seminar; the Greater Toronto British History seminar; the Eighteenth Century seminar at the University of Toronto; and, more recently, the British Studies seminar at the Harry Ransom Center, University of Texas, Austin. In March 2011 I offered a synopsis of some of the central arguments to the Pacific Coast Conference on British Studies at Seattle. I appreciate the useful comments I have received from those audiences.

A special set of thanks must go to Roy Ritchie, the former William Keck Director of Research at the Huntington Library, San Marino, California. He offered me a long-term fellowship at the library in 2009–10 to complete the work on this project, and the fabulous setting of the library and the conviviality of the other fellows inspired me to finish much of the writing and final research. Aspects of the project were presented to the University of Southern California Early Modern British Institute at the Huntington, and to the joint Huntington/Caltech seminar organized by the Division of Humanities and Social Science at Caltech. I thank the participants for their encouragement and support. I would particularly like to thank John Brewer, Kristine Haugen, and Kevin Gilmartin for the interest they took in my work and the insights they offered.

While at the Huntington, I sounded out editors at Yale University Press regarding the possibility of publishing my work. They responded quickly, and I am especially appreciative of the guidance and help I have received from Laura Davulis and Christina Tucker, and from my copy editor, Eliza Childs, in getting the manuscript to press. My thanks also to the anonymous readers who pushed me to expand the introduction and conclusion.

I would like to thank a number of scholars who have offered advice and sources relating to this project over the years. They include Donna Andrew, whose book *Philanthropy and Police* was a critical guide to the mid-century; Bob Harris and Joanna Innes, whose conversations on eighteenth-century social policy and politics have prompted me to ask new questions of my material; Doug Hay, who provided me with important information regarding the Staffordshire riots of 1750 and whose knowledge of eighteenth-century criminal law is vast; Paul Craven, who loaned me his microfilm copy of the early council minutes of Nova Scotia; and James Oldham, who kindly offered me material from the Dudley Ryder MS regarding the 1746 smuggling act. The chapter on Halifax would have been poorer without the help and advice of Julian Gwyn and Bill Wicken, both experts in the history of Maritime Canada. The introductory chapter also benefited from a scrupulous reading by Brenda McComb. Anita Szucksco helped me get my graphs in order and has selflessly provided me with technical support for this and other projects. Elaine Stavro gave me love and support in the final stages of this enterprise.

Finally, I would like to thank two younger scholars, Andrea McKenzie and Simon Devereaux, for sharing their knowledge of eighteenth-century criminal justice with me. They were among the last students that John Beattie supervised at the University of Toronto. I was among the first. It is a special honor to me to acknowledge John's generosity of spirit and friendship over the years and his formidable contributions to the field of criminal justice history in the eighteenth century. As a small token of my appreciation for all he has done, I would like to dedicate this book to him.

Introduction

"We have at last celebrated the peace," wrote Horace Walpole to Horace Mann on 3 May 1749, "and that as much in extremes as we generally do everything, whether we have reason to be glad or sorry, pleased or angry."[1] He was referring to the peace that concluded the War of Austrian Succession, or King George's War as it is often known in America, and to the predominantly elite events that commemorated it. These included a masquerade at Ranelagh and a massive fireworks display at Green Park. The latter was fashioned by a Florentine, Giovanni Niccolò Servandoni, who had made a name for himself as the director of stage design at the Paris Opéra and as the principal painter and designer to the Académie Royale de Musique. Servandoni had contributed to the festivities celebrating the birth of the French Dauphin in 1729; consequently in 1748 he was invited to choreograph the London fireworks display celebrating the Peace of Aix-la-Chapelle.

Servandoni began work on his structure in November 1748, a few weeks after the peace was signed. He completed it five months later. It resembled a Doric temple, 114 feet high and 144 feet long, to which were attached two pavilions. The structure, stretching over 800 feet, featured a huge musicians' gallery over which presided a figure of Peace attended by Neptune and Mars. A bas-relief depicted King George handing a peace treaty to Britannia, the symbolic queen of the country. Predictably the king himself visited the site before the actual thanksgiving and distributed a few gifts to the carpenters. Their work would sit a large crowd. A large gallery was built to accommodate the nobility and chief citizens of London, and a stand was erected for the thousands of spectators who were expected to throng to the event.[2] Everyone awaited it in breathless expectation.

The hype of the event was captured in the print *The British Jubilee* (figure 1), which depicts fireworks emitting from the Doric structure in awesome symmetry. In the foreground men celebrate the Peace with a barrel of beer amid the cacophony of marrow bones and cleavers. Although one man is crushed by the press of the throng that has gathered to receive free beer, the celebration is hearty and amiable. It is presented as a triumph, a sociable occasion fit for women, clergymen, and all classes, a genuinely popular Jubilee.

In fact, the Green Park festival was a glorious flop. Its only lasting legacy was Handel's *Music for the Royal Fireworks,* which was rehearsed at Vauxhall Gardens before twelve thousand people, six days before the celebration.[3] George Frederic Handel's music actually opened the celebrated event, interspersed with brief cannonades, but the pyrotechnics were less impressive. The rockets soared, but the other fireworks spluttered on the damp April day. Workmen had to clamber up the structure to reignite the serpents and wheels. The crowd of ten thousand grew impatient. And then, to cap everything, the left wing of the edifice caught fire, requiring three engines to put out the flames and a party of carpenters to sever the smoldering pavilion from the main edifice.[4]

The man officially in charge of the proceedings, Charles Frederick, the MP for Shoreham and the Controller of the Woolwich depot, was not amused. Nor was the Chevalier Servandoni. They quarreled, Servandoni drew his sword and was promptly dispatched to a lock-up to cool off and probably sober up. According to one account, he was released the following morning after apologizing to the Duke of Cumberland, who had watched the unspectacular event from the Queen's Library. According to another, the Italian choreographer was bailed by Henry Fielding, the Bow Street magistrate, to answer the charge of assault against Frederick.[5]

Horace Walpole was relieved that the fireworks went off with only minor casualties. The French celebrations in February 1749 had generated an altercation between the Italian and French pyrotechnicians, which resulted in an explosion that took forty lives. Yet few were as urbane as Walpole in believing that the pitiful pyrotechnics of Green Park would not prompt further comment. The fact that the giant sun atop the temple shone for only fifty seconds and that King George's bas-relief crashed to the ground led some to remark that an imperfect celebration mimicked an imperfect peace. The *Chester Courant* believed the

Fig 1: Robert Sayer, *The British Jubilee*, 1749. © British Museum.

event had always been intended as a ruse to deflect attention from the peace; now the "dazzling blaze" poorly reflected on Britain's "happier days." One anonymous pamphleteer thought the £40,000 expended on the fireworks an absolute scandal when "our disbanding Soldiers and Sailors are starving, or robbing in the Streets for Want of Bread."[6] More sardonically, the *London Evening Post* commented that the celebrations were a fitting finale to a "long, bloody and taxing war" that had increased Britain's debt by more than £30 million (to £76 million) and had left so many grievances outstanding.[7]

Those grievances were troubling. Contrary to the terms of the treaty, Dunkirk remained fortified after the peace. Much blood and energy had been expended on capturing Louisbourg, the French fort on Cape Breton, only to return it and leave Britain strategically vulnerable along the North American coast and on the waterways to the Ohio valley. The neutral islands in the Caribbean, moreover, were neutral only in name. The French showed little interest in abandoning either Tobago or St. Lucia. They wanted to add to their already formidable sugar industry, which was slowly but surely outpacing that of Britain. Saint-Domingue (later Haiti) produced more sugar than the British islands combined, and more cheaply as well. Whatever advantages accrued to Prussia and Hanover by the Peace of Aix-la-Chapelle, British transatlantic interests had not been protected, and they had been among the casus belli in the first place. After all the effort, Britain was essentially back to the status quo ante bellum, awaiting a return to arms against a nation (France) three times its demographic size and by reputation the most powerful in Europe. The peace was only an intermission, a hiccup between wars; in some parts of the world nothing more than "a continued warlike Peace."[8] In India, for example, where rival East India companies battled for trade and territory amid a declining Mughal empire, the French officer Charles Bussy remarked that "neutrality between the two nations is a pipe dream."[9]

The uncertainties of the peace form the conjuncture of this book, which is principally concerned with the demobilization crisis of 1748–53 in England and the social reforms that were developed to deal with it. In some ways it might seem odd to characterize the demobilization after the War of Austrian Succession as a "crisis." When I was an undergraduate, the mid-century years were quintessentially the years of Sir Lewis Namier, who cast them as fundamentally elitist and deferential, marked only by a few patrician bickerings amid a bedrock of political stability. From this perspective, electoral clientage and compromise connoted the placidity of the lower class, whose entrance to the Namierite theater of politics was typically as the corruptible voters of large open boroughs. Even Namier's rival J. H. Plumb, who was never happy about the elision of the political nation in his opponent's interpretation, saw the mid-century political structure as one of "adamantine strength and profound inertia."[10]

We have come a long way since then. As soon as one broadens the political terrain beyond the hustings to consider lower-class actors as "stakeholders" in a social formation characterized by emergent forms of capitalist enterprise and a fiscal-military complex geared to war, the whole prospect changes. The aftermath of this mid-century war may have been situated between two general elections that epitomized Whig oligarchy, but it also generated fears of a leveling disposition among the plebeian classes, or at the very least a truculence that did not gibe with patrician conceptions of a deferential, paternalist order. The demobilization of some 80,000 soldiers and sailors, most of them in their twenties and most of them unable to find work, sparked a rise in property crime and particularly of robberies that carried with them the threat of violence. As I shall show in chapter 5, this crime wave occurred at a time of social unrest — of striking keelmen in Newcastle and artisans in London and of riotous colliers and rural laborers protesting against the introduction of turnpikes in the West Country. It occurred when the government was struggling to suppress smuggling, which had become endemic on the south and east coasts and had escalated into a veritable war between customs officers and smuggling gangs. Those gangs astonished contemporaries with their brazen defiance of authority and brutal assaults on government agents. To further complicate matters, these smuggling fraternities were in league with France, Britain's traditional enemy and major international competitor. They harbored Jacobite sentiments that contemporaries had hoped would die with the Forty-Five, the final rebellion against the Hanoverian monarchy by a Stuart prince, whose army had marched within 120 miles of London. Cumulatively the mid-century era was not one of patrician confidence or Georgian calm: it was one of deep anxiety, if not panic, about the state of the country and its capacity to continue a war that everyone feared had been abandoned only temporarily.

I have endeavored to track the anxieties of the period and the tensions caused by demobilization through a series of cascading, overlapping narratives. In the tradition of "incident" history, each story is intended, in the words of Pierre Nora, to be a "tangled event which illuminates more than the story itself, a narrative that generates others, radiates out of itself to explore larger frames of reference."[11] The book begins with the colorful career of Admiral Charles Knowles and his confrontation with Don Andres Reggio off the coast of Havana in what was the very last battle of the war. This inconclusive engagement between a British and Spanish squadron generated frustrations among the officer elite that eventually resulted in courts-martial and duels, episodes that illustrate how recriminatory relations within the officer elite could become over matters of prize money and honor. In these bitter disputes one officer was killed and another sentenced to be hanged, although the offender in question, Captain Edward Clark, was too well connected to swing at

Tyburn. Despite the fact that he did not observe the gentlemanly proprieties of the duel, Clark was exonerated by his friends and pardoned on account of his war record and his contacts in high places.

War records were not much solace to the lower-deck sailors who were demobilized in 1748. They left their ships without full pay or the windfalls of prize money. They often had to wait around to receive their money from the Pay Office or the naval commissioners of the outports, and as young, reckless men in their twenties, they were vulnerable to the dubious pleasures of the town and to the con men and women who sought to take advantage of their momentary affluence. Chapter 2 charts their predicament, as victims and predators, in the sprawling, imperial metropolis that was London. Enviable targets when they were flush, they targeted others when they were not. As the evidence from London's central criminal court reveals, there was a conspicuous upsurge in property theft by demobilized sailors and soldiers in the years after 1748 and a very noticeable rise in robberies accompanied by violence. Contemporaries sensed this, and the newspapers of the day played upon it, construing the rise in theft as an attack upon the rich. The demobilization crisis in turn generated a discussion of how best to handle this rise in crime and what calculus of punishment could best deter it. Various options were mooted, including imprisonment in the hulks and galley servitude. The preferred option — more exemplary hangings, with the additional ignominy of dissection — was complicated by the troubling appearance of demobilized sailors at the gallows to claim the bodies of their friends. Indeed, the Tyburn riots against the surgeons threatened to undermine the solemn theatricality of public hangings and required some careful negotiations by sheriffs to sustain the credibility of these executions.

Among those executed at Tyburn in fall 1749 was a young journeyman wigmaker named Bosavern Penlez. He had been indicted for helping to pull down a bawdy house on the Strand, part of a series of reprisals against whores and whoremasters who had cheated sailor-clients. Many thought Penlez marginal to these sailor-dominated protests and some even suspected he had been framed, yet the government was determined to make him an example to deter such wrecking excursions in the center of town. His controversial hanging occurred just prior to a by-election in the populous City of Westminster. Because the incumbent, Viscount Trentham, had not intervened on Penlez's behalf, he came under heavy criticism. The Penlez affair, and Trentham's sponsorship of a troupe of French actors at Drury Lane, curiously and unpredictably cast him as an arrogant, aristocratic Francophile out of step with the popular mood of the constituency. It required all the interest of the Court and his father-in-law, the Duke of Bedford, to get him reelected. The third chapter reveals, in fact, the fragility of the clientage of the big houses in popular boroughs such as Westminster and the brazen coercion of dependent voters when the big houses came under pressure. The eruptive power of demotic politics caught the Whig oligarchs off guard and revealed how seemingly minor incidents could have cultural and political purchase.

While scrutiny for the Westminster election was conducted, London experienced two earth tremors, one on 8 February and one on 8 March 1750. The possibility of a third and final earthquake a month later generated a widespread panic in which hundreds of people left the metropolis for safer ground. Sermons and pamphlets quickly sought to explain the causes of the quakes, in terms of natural science and also in terms of divine judgment. They offer a unique window into the religious tenor of the age, particularly on the issue of whether providential arguments were tamed by Enlightenment thinking. They also enable the historian to consider whether the public sphere of discussion and debate had shifted from a religious to a more secular mode of reasoning in which science and empirical observation prevailed. In chapter 4 I argue that the substantial clerical intervention in this debate did not confirm the hegemony of religious discourse, as has sometimes been argued; rather it stemmed from a fear that sermons and religious tracts were being upstaged by journalism and by the new fad of natural science that was present in the monthly magazines. It also demonstrated that clergy were not always in step with contemporary anxieties. Clerics were preoccupied with moral laxity, whether blasphemy, profanity, Sabbath-breaking, or religious indifference or skepticism. They were troubled by popular amusements such as the masquerade, which was seen as a tonic to immorality, and by the ubiquity of prostitution in the metropolis. Their diagnosis of what was wrong with London, or Londoners, echoed the preoccupations of the Reformation of Manners movement earlier in the century. The clergy had relatively little to say about such topical issues as the gin epidemic or the demographic implications of national degeneracy. They were completely silent on the question of law and military honor that consumed the contemporaneous trial of Edward Clark. And, with one or two notable exceptions, they were reticent on the problems of social reform that would engage the attention of magistrates or legislators, such as the bad effects of "luxury" upon family stability and crime, or the inability of the current poor laws to inculcate habits of industry and respectability. They replicated the standard fare of old-style moral reformers, not the social issues that emerged in the period after the publication of the *Fable of the Bees* by Bernard Mandeville, when commentators began to rethink the relationship of work, leisure, and international competitiveness.

The relationship of work, leisure, and international competitiveness did emerge, however, in the long debate over the gin craze, which preoccupied a rich variety of commentators in the two decades before 1750. This is addressed in chapter 6. The popularity of rot-gut gin among the urban poor sparked fears that British labor power would falter at a crucial moment of imperial expansion and consolidation, when Britons aspired to commercial supremacy in the transatlantic trades and New World markets. It generated fears of demographic degeneracy at a time when Britain needed the requisite manpower to confront its enemies in Europe and the West. It raised issues about the leisure preferences of the poor and whether these might be rechanneled into more productive paths. It also posed problems of governance, not simply in terms of law enforcement, which was highly dependent on the unpopular mediation of informers, but also in mapping the dimensions of gin addiction and assessing its social significance. The desire for what Michel Foucault would have called "biopower," the need to coordinate the human resources of the nation for commerce and empire and to understand the actual dimensions of the gin malady, gave rise to demands for a national census in 1753 to chart more accurately the trajectories of age-specific mortality and the parameters of economic growth and dependency. Historians have sometimes suggested there was a decline of interest in statistical mapping of this kind from the heyday of political arithmetic in the late seventeenth century to the age of the early census, but in fact the application of numbers remained potentially part of social investigation throughout the eighteenth century.[12] This was particularly the case with gin regulation, where cost-benefit analyses proved attractive to resolve the issue of whether the taxes derived from gin were outweighed by the disadvantages, as measured in terms of lost consumption or labor.

The debate on gin was part of the postwar assessment of national capacity in the face of another impending war, for few seriously thought that the Treaty of Aix-la-Chapelle would be anything more than a hiatus in the continuing rivalry between Britain and the Bourbon powers. The aftermath of war also forced politicians and administrators seriously to ponder the current status of social regulation in Britain. This involved not simply strategies to combat the crime wave, and very specifically the violence that accompanied it; it entailed a quite comprehensive review the general state of social welfare and philanthropic enterprise as it existed in the middle of the eighteenth century. The intensity of this quest can be measured by the continuing demands for a parliamentary inquiry into the causes of crime and the inadequacies of welfare administration and by the agenda of the committees that were actually struck to deal with them. That agenda involved the regulation of disorderly houses, the form of capital punishment, the future of convict labor, and the revisions to the Elizabeth legislation on which the eighteen-century Poor Law and the cognate laws on vagrancy were based. Although such social legislation is sometimes seen as a peripheral to parliamentary business, and if not peripheral, then intensely local in import and inspiration, in the years 1751–53 it was very much center stage.[13] There was a high-level engagement with the fallout from war, which some legislators experienced first- or secondhand in the shape of London theft or robbery. But there was also a more generalized assessment of the problems of social regulation at a moment when patrician-plebeian relations, hitherto moderated by decades of peace and a spate of good harvests, were encountering new pressures.

Some of those pressures are addressed in chapter 5. Despite the defeat of the Jacobite rebellion in 1745, popular disaffection survived in the leading towns of Lancashire and the West Midlands, enough to unnerve a Whig government whose political support in Parliament was unassailable. At the same time that the leading Whig patrons were tracking down Jacobite rebels and revelers, they were encountering plebeian recalcitrance in their very own counties of the southeast, this time in the shape of smuggling gangs who openly and stridently challenged troops and customs officers in their efforts to contain the trade in contraband. It took extraordinary legislation and some reckless, brutal behavior from the gangs themselves, behavior that alienated them from the local communities, to bring them to heel.

These episodes revealed that however politically powerful governments might be at Westminster, they needed community support to root out troubling incidents of plebeian dissidence. The same was true of the turnpike riots in the southwest, where country protesters proved able to mobilize the local muscle of the region, destroy tollgates and houses, and win considerable sympathy from local juries. As with Midland Jacobites and Sussex smugglers, governments found they could not try cases before local juries. They had to send them to London or to neighboring counties, and then with mixed success. The smuggling affrays of the southeast revealed how difficult it was for the fiscal-military state to police its own boundaries and sustain the tax base so necessary for war. The turnpike riots illustrated the strength of customary economies in the face of new market opportunities, again a problem that the state had to confront if it was to retain its cost efficiency and competitive edge in international markets.

Some commentators believed these episodes connoted a sea change in patrician-plebeian relations; among them Henry Fielding, then an active Bow Street magistrate. In chapter 7 I investigate this mid-century moment through his conservative eyes and offer some reflections on the achievements and failures of the legislative activity that accompanied the aftermath of war. Although some new legislation was launched, most notably the Murder Act of 1752, which sought to recalibrate the dynamics of judicial terror, these busy years were noteworthy for their tentative probing of new forms of containment and surveillance, including stipendiary magistrates, policemen, penitentiaries, and large workhouses. These would form part of the new regime of governance in the nineteenth century.

The final chapter of the book returns to the sailors who were cut adrift in 1748 and 1749 and were the continuing subject of social inquiry. In keeping with the general character of this work, which is principally concerned with how demobilized sailors handled the predicament of peace after a decade of war, it charts their fortunes in one of the few ventures that was launched to accommodate their jobless status. As I shall show, there was an inherent tension, if not contradiction, in the desire to offer seamen land in the new colony of Nova Scotia and to mobilize their services in what was really a continuing war zone. In the uncharted landscape of Nova Scotia, fraught with danger and with a bewildering mix of players, the mariners coped as best they could. Theirs was not a progress from sin to grace in the Bunyanesque mode; nor, in the manner of Hogarth's harlot, was it a slide from innocence to damnation. It was a matter of surviving the first of Britain's eighteenth-century colonial wars and taking advantage of the small opportunities afforded seamen along the North American littoral.

Probing the links between war, politics, and social policy in the eighteenth century is not in itself a new venture. In her recent collection of essays, Joanna Innes has done much to establish such links and to show that long before the so-called administrative revolution of the nineteenth century, a "revolution" that among other things transformed the Poor Law, introduced new Factory Acts, and regulated urban sanitation, there was an ongoing connection between high politics, public debate, and social reform.[14] The site of this interest in social reform was more often than not Parliament, but it was also to be found on the bench and among the committees of voluntary trusts, and it was publicly aired in pamphlet and newspaper. Indeed, local agendas for social reform often framed parliamentary inquiry rather than vice versa. Diffuse as this activity might seem, it is nonetheless clear that the Hanoverian state was not without a notion of national social policy. Such a policy was not discovered by the Victorians, whatever moral earnestness and anguish they brought to the process.

Bob Harris had recently developed some of these insights in his admirable and wide-ranging discussion of mid-century Britain, in which he develops the concept of "national revival" in the context of politics, commerce, and social reform.[15] His interests run very close to mine, although I have chosen to focus on the passions of one particular moment, the immediate aftermath of the War of Austrian Succession, and to do so through a series of interlocking episodes that capture many of the issues and challenges contemporaries faced amid the uncertainties of demobilization. I have also chosen to delve into the fortunes of those who experienced the demobilization crisis firsthand, whether as victims or as administrators, whether sailors down on their luck or magistrates bewildered with the seeming ubiquity of crime and hamstrung by the machinery to deal with it. Whereas Harris maps the "attitudes, interests, hopes and projects, of the upper and diverse middling ranks of society,"[16] I look out from Bow Street or the governor's lodge in a wooden-shacked colonial port at the immediate problems confronting a "national revival," and especially to the soldiers, sailors, and street folk who strove to scrape together a living in the uncertain times that demobilization brought with it. Mine is more of a history from below that charts the fortunes of men (and it is principally men) caught up in the business of war and its sudden dissolution as they decamped in London and elsewhere. Figuratively, Bob Harris's book captures the spirit of a Jonas Hanway, merchant, philanthropist, projector. I have been more inspired by William Hogarth, whose paintings and engravings depicted the urban squalor, violence, fashion, and luxury that made his contemporary London a metropolis of such glaring contrasts, contrasts that were framed by a sharper debate over Britain's commercial and imperial destiny.

I

The Trials of Admiral Knowles

As he drove to Deptford in December 1749, Admiral Charles Knowles must have wondered how he came to be in such a pickle. He had been charged by four of his subaltern officers of botching a battle off Havana some fourteen months earlier. In their estimation, Knowles had made an "un-officer-like Attack" on the Spanish squadron of Admiral Don Andres Reggio, allowing four ships to begin hostilities while others straggled behind. He had also not switched flagships when his own, the *Canterbury*, was severely disabled, which meant that he had virtually abdicated his command in the heat of the battle. Whether through "cowardice, negligence or disaffection," his subaltern officers claimed, and they left it very much to the court-martial to decide which, Knowles had failed to engage the enemy in a manner befitting his rank and responsibilities.

These charges were humiliating to a man like Knowles, an ambitious seaman with more than a chip on his shoulder by virtue of his illegitimate, yet genteel origins (figure 2). The son of Charles Knollys, the titular fourth earl of Banbury by a relatively obscure actress, he was, like his father, anxious to make his mark. Whereas his father spent much of his life petitioning for an official recognition of his noble status, Charles Knowles strove to cut a figure in the navy and to reap the harvests of war. Like so many of his contemporaries, Knowles had entered the navy as a teenager, initially as a captain's

Fig 2: John Faber the Younger, *The Honourable Charles Knowles Esquire*, when governor of Jamaica, engraving, 1755–56. © British Museum.

servant. As part of the crew of the *Lyme* frigate under Lord Vere Beauclerk, then based in the Mediterranean, he had picked up a working knowledge of French and a sound grounding in mathematics and mechanics. These skills were put to advantage in the wars of the 1740s, when Britain's raid-and-destroy missions on Spanish ports and privateering centers required the rapid demolition of military fortifications. After Admiral Edward Vernon's famed descent on Portobelo in November 1739, a victory which transfixed a war-hungry public at home, Knowles was sent in to destroy the fort and spike the guns. In Vernon's second successful venture, the attack upon Fort Chagre, Knowles was given command of the bomb ketches and fireships. On the sur-render of this privateering station, he was temporarily made governor of the castle until its defenses were destroyed.

These tasks he accomplished efficiently, and his esteem in the eyes of his imposing admiral grew. At the fateful expedition to Cartagena in March 1741, Knowles was the principal surveyor and engineer of the fleet. It was he who reconnoitered the approaches to the inner harbor and cut the boom across the Boca Chica. He also played a critical role in the reduction of Fort St. Joseph at the entrance to the harbor, and then of the Castillo Grande, before the town of Cartagena, which he reputedly accomplished with a "cool and determined valour."[1] There he cut a passage past scuttled ships and began bombarding the town, notwithstanding the heavy fire of the enemy and the damage to his mainmast.[2]

As part of the advance naval party before Cartagena, Knowles was in a position to view the army's fateful assault on Fort St. Lazar and to judge who was responsible for the eventual failure to raise the siege of Cartagena. Indeed, he was an important intermediary between the two commanders in their dis-cussions of how the assault should take place and how much cover the navy might provide General Thomas Wentworth's troops.[3] As a protégé of Edward Vernon, Knowles predictably took the admiral's side in the subsequent debate over Cartagena, especially on the question of whether the army or the navy was primarily responsible for the failure of the expedition. Knowles did not leak information to the press in the manner of a partisan officer; when he returned to Britain with the prisoners and the sick on the Weymouth he penned his own account of the expedition.[4] In this pamphlet, published anonymously, Knowles castigated the army for its indecision and incompetence. He accused General Wentworth, its commander in chief, of landing his troops in dense, vulnerable clusters, "so closely crouded," Knowles wrote, that "scarcely one Man could have used his Arms" against enemy sharpshooters.[5] He also blamed the general for unnecessarily exposing his troops to the inclement climate from the mo-ment they landed, sowing the seeds of destruction that followed.[6] And he lambasted army officers for their tardiness in erecting a battery at Boca Chica, leaving the navy to bear the brunt of Spanish resistance at the narrow passage to the lagoon. In Knowles's opinion the army was feckless and undisciplined, full of raw recruits, and captained by rakes and salon officers who knew nothing of tropical warfare. "Working," he sneered, "was no Part of their Trade."[7] Because many of the troops were unseasoned for the tropics, the indecision of the army officers and the slow advance to Cartagena was aggravated by malaria and yellow fever. At a critical moment in the campaign, the troops flubbed the landing at the Isla de Gracias in the inner lagoon before Cartagena and botched the approach to St. Lazar, from where they might have been able to bombard the town effectively. The British troops were brave enough in Knowles's estimation; they were simply "raw" and "undisciplined." The same could not be said for the American auxiliaries who also participated in the disastrous assault on the fort and fled before scaling ladders could be placed on the walls. He thought even less of them than the ragamuffins brought from England. In his eyes they were a bunch of rum-swigging adventurers, led by amateur officers composed of "Blacksmiths, Taylors, Shoemakers, and all the Banditti that [the] Country affords."[8]

Intemperate language aside, Knowles's pamphlet struck a chord with a public starved of news about the catastrophe of Cartagena and fed on conflicting rumors of victories and disasters. As a writer in *Old England* remarked, "Tho' the Author of this Performance has not thought fit to put his Name to it, yet the facts contain'd in it are so new and so perspicuously stated, that it well deserves the publick Attention."[9] His shilling pamphlet ran through three editions in two months and was given a good airing in the *Gentleman's Magazine* as well as in some provincial papers.[10] It certainly bolstered the case of Vernon in his continuing recriminations against Wentworth and against the ministry, for Knowles's comments about the raw character of the troops fed suspicions that the Walpole administration had held back its crack troops for the continental campaigns in which George II had a very personal interest.[11] Certainly the ministry did little to ensure that the troops sent to reinforce Vernon's squadron were free of the dysentery and typhus, which was ravaging the southern ports of embarkation. They started out with compromised immune systems, and the heat, humidity, and rum of the Caribbean destroyed many of them. Seventy-four percent of the British-based troops on the Cartagena expedition died, and even among the American rangers, who were likely more accustomed to the heat and humidity, the death toll reach 65 percent.

Knowles himself did not personally witness the ongoing debate over Cartagena that filled the British press in the spring and early summer of 1743. He was back in the Caribbean, working under Vernon's staunch friend and ally Sir Challoner Ogle, who assigned him new duties as a squadron commander. In February 1743 Knowles planned a raid upon two Spanish privateering stations, La Guira and Porto Cabello, on what is now the Venezuelan coast southeast of the Dutch islands of Aruba and Curaçao. These ports had been targeted earlier in the war, albeit ineffectually, and this time Knowles was resolved to succeed. With a squadron of five ships of the line and some smaller craft that housed 2,300 seamen and marines and 400 regular troops, he probably dreamed of emulating Vernon's early exploits. This was not to be. The main objective was Porto Cabello, but Knowles had issued orders to the captains to take whatever prizes they found in La Guira road, with the result that the squadron deviated from its main task and tried to take La Guira by surprise. Unfortunately, in their enthusiasm the ships fired their broadsides too early and erratically amid the swell of the road and had to face the guns of a surprisingly well-fortified port. The squadron consequently suffered high casualties. Knowles's flagship, the *Suffolk,* sustained ninety-seven shots to its hull that left thirty men dead and eighty wounded, approximately 25 percent of her working crew.[12] The *Burford* and *Eltham* suffered similarly, and although the squadron did manage to force a landing when the bomb ketches played on the west part of the town, the third lieutenant of the raiding party was too preoccupied with plundering to accomplish much. The result was that the descent on La Guira was thwarted, and so, confronted with the death of one of his captains and considerable confusion among his squadron, Knowles repaired to Curaçao to refit and regroup.

At Curaçao, a Dutch port that was an entrepôt for slaves and did business with almost everyone in Atlantic waters, Knowles had to haggle for extra men. He hoped to recruit about 250 volunteers, but the governor allowed him to depart with only a hundred, mainly blacks and mulattoes. Meanwhile the governor was conspiring with Knowles's adversaries, supplying the Spanish at Porto Cabello with extra gunpowder. These deals left the governor of Carracas time to send 4,000 Amerindians, mulattoes, and blacks to reinforce the fort. Knowles's negotiations for additional men lost him the element of surprise, and a strong lee current to Porto Cabello only added to his woes. Eventually he resorted to a beach landing at nighttime in an attempt to create a second front of attack. Unfortunately his advance troops came across a Spanish patrol and in attempting to restrain it, alerted the enemy with gunfire. The troops in the rear of Knowles's column thought the van had engaged the enemy; they panicked and opened fire, sometimes on their own men. Chaos broke out. Knowles reported that "no-one knew at what they fired, some cryed out they were all cut off, and the most fearful frightened the rest till at length they all betook themselves to Fly as fast as they could." He attempted to draw off the fire of the fascine the next day, but after several attempts to bombard Porto Cabello, he retired with a squadron "so shattered in their masts and rigging as scarce . . . able to sett a Sail to run off."[13]

The expedition to the Venezuelan ports proved a dismal and, in human terms, costly venture. Twenty percent of Knowles's squadron were either killed or wounded in these ventures,[14] twice as many as at Trafalgar and without a figment of glory. In a broader context the expedition demonstrated that although prizes were a tonic to recruitment in the Caribbean, they could be a disincentive to military discipline. It also illustrated why timing and favorable weather conditions were essential prerequisites to successful raids on reasonably fortified harbors. At a personal level, the episode revealed Knowles to be something of a martinet. Just before sailing Knowles had one Irish seaman hanged at the yardarm for desertion, essentially pour encourager les autres. During the expedition itself he cashiered one officer for not obeying orders and moving closer to attack the fascine battery. "I cannot help observing to their lordships that during this behaviour, both officers and men were crying out shame," he wrote to the Admiralty. With respect to this officer's conduct and that of another who had backed off in the battle, Knowles felt himself "cruelly used"; "a negligent performance of duty may bring on as ill Consequences as immediate breach of orders."[15]

Knowles's frustrations with his officers and men were intensified by the drain of his manpower. When his squadron arrived in Antigua in 1743 he was about a hundred men short of his complement and particularly concerned that homeward-bound merchant ships were luring men to desert with offers of rum and high wages. On his return from the La Guira expedition, he was piqued to learn that the merchants of the island were employing a privateer to prevent the Spanish from raiding the local plantations of slaves. Aware that privateers were often at the vanguard of popular opposition to impressment, he thought their visibility around the island would encourage more resistance to navy recruitment. So he proposed to teach the Antiguan privateers a lesson. When the privateer returned to the St. John's road in June 1743, Knowles had Captain Gage of the *Lively* send a lieutenant and his party to impress the boat's crew. The plan badly backfired. The privateering crew took the lieutenant and one of his men hostage. Knowles responded by arresting one of the ringleaders in hopes of detering others from resisting impressment, but the merchant-owners of the privateering vessel protested to the governor that this was illegal as "there was no law for Pressing." This was not technically true, although the previous legislation concerning colonial pressing was controversial and its legality much disputed. In the face of pressure from the owners, Governor

Matthews caved in, released the privateering leader, and allowed Knowles and his captain to be arrested and committed to gaol for false imprisonment. Knowles was able to get out of gaol on a bail of £12,000, an enormous sum even when converted into pounds sterling (£6,000). He then discovered that the owners had procured a habeas corpus for the release of some other privateers who had been taken aboard the *Suffolk* and the *Lively*. Knowles urged the governor to intervene, reminding him that the opposition to impressment had already had a reverberatory effect in St. Kitts, where privateers had forced Captain Abel Smith of the *Pembroke Prize* to release men who had been impressed. Knowles failed to sway the governor; in fact, he was eventually sued for £4,000 for impeding the flow of commerce through his intemperate actions. As he ruefully reflected, naval officers sometimes had to "suffer in their private fortunes" to pursue the king's business.[16]

Knowles was the sort of man who bristled at this kind of legal offensive, believing that the king's business should override the vested interests of merchants and planters. But in the Caribbean there was little he could do. A 1744 statute made it very difficult for naval commanders to impress ashore without the consent of governors and assembly unless they could show there was a dire emergency, and the threat of a £50 fine for every illegal impressment deterred them from testing the act too vigorously. In that year Knowles resorted to impressing at sea, finding seaman on Antigua difficult to catch.[17]

Knowles knew, however, that North American merchants had failed to have the 1744 act extended to their coast, and when he sailed south from Louisbourg for his third turn of duty in the Caribbean in 1747, he was determined to test the waters. In Boston he advertised for a privateer crew, and when men congregated at the keys to enlist in the venture, he swept them up, claiming that he was looking for the thirty-odd seamen who had deserted his squadron while it was anchored for repairs at Nantasket island.[18] The Bostonians were outraged by this sharp practice. It fueled their sense of British injustice over impressment, which in their eyes was illegal under an earlier statute, 6 Anne, even though British legal opinion determined that that particular act had expired.[19] Three hundred privateers and Guineamen mobilized with arms, took several of Knowles's officers hostage, and threatened to burn one of the open boats of the squadron. When Thomas Hutchinson, speaker of the Massachusetts House of Representatives, managed to free one of the hostages, a mob complained to Governor William Shirley about the illegality of the press and threatened to storm the council chamber if their complaints did not receive a sympathetic ear. Governor Shirley found the mob so intimidating that he retired to the castle, but Knowles took his own hostages and threatened to bombard the town if his men were not returned. This hot-headed reprisal fortunately came to naught. An unfavorable wind prevented Knowles from getting close to the town, although the fact that his opponents had manned the batteries probably made him think twice about this reckless course of action.[20] Eventually the militia and the House of Representatives managed to defuse the situation, and the hostages on each side were returned. Even so, Knowles emerged from the crisis with a reputation for intemperate arrogance. The *Boston Evening Post* catalogued his mishaps and failures, including the Antiguan affair.[21] At Louisbourg, the paper asserted, where Knowles had briefly been governor, his energies had been dissipated on trivial matters. He had wasted his time policing the fort and arresting tipplers rather than attempting to thwart the French presence in Acadia and the St. Lawrence. At La Guira and Porto Cavallos his courage was thought to be cosmetic; his seemingly intrepid behavior, it was speculated, flowed from a medical malady that sometimes seized his bowels and fevered his brain. Compared to Sir Peter Warren, a humane "Gentlemen of paternal Estate" who was sympathetic to trade, Knowles was a reckless hothead of distinctly illiberal tendencies. His actions in Boston illustrated this very clearly.

The *Boston Evening Post* painted a damning picture of Knowles's leadership. It completely overlooked his contribution to refortifying Louisbourg and his ability to whip a motley crew of drunks into shape. When Knowles first assumed his responsibilities at the Cape Breton post, he reported that as many as a thousand servicemen were drinking prodigious amounts of rum to protect themselves against the cold, so threadbare were their uniforms amid subzero temperatures. It took some resolution to rectify this state of affairs and bring order to the garrison. Even so, Knowles's career in Atlantic waters was looking decidedly checkered. His early successes at Portobelo, Fort Chagre, and Cartagena had been followed by failure and controversy. True, he had been promoted from captain to commodore to rear admiral of the blue by 1747, and there was no doubting his willingness to serve in the Caribbean, something that other flag officers avoided. Yet there were nagging doubts about his judgment and impetuosity. As the commander of the Jamaica station, he would find himself tested.

Knowles desperately needed another victory and chose Santiago de Cuba as his target. This was a symbolic choice. After the depressing failure at Cartagena, Knowles's mentor, Admiral Vernon had chosen Santiago as a morale booster, only to find that the problems he encountered with the army command at Cartagena continued to frustrate his hopes of victory. After landing the army near Guantanamo Bay, Vernon was disturbed to discover that Wentworth's troops had made little progress toward Santiago de Cuba but were idling in camp in the sweltering heat, compromising the admiral's hopes for a second front on this strategic port. Vernon abandoned the Santiago expedition and laid all the blame on the army. Knowles hoped to succeed where his former commander had failed. He had no General Wentworth to deal with, no prevarications from army officers in the field about poor terrain and ambushes. He had managed to persuade Edward Trelawney, the governor of Jamaica, to back the expedition, and he brought with him a company of 240 men, some volunteers, and, according to the newspapers at least, about 300 maroons.[22] Unfortunately the northerly winds proved unfavorable, and Knowles's squadron headed south for Port St. Louis, a privateering station on the south side of Saint Domingue, which had been a source of trouble for Jamaican trade. On 1 March 1748, Knowles's men of the line went in close to the walls, and after a three-and-a-half-hour battle the governor of Port Saint Louis surrendered. British casualties ran at fifty wounded and twenty dead, the French substantially more. Buoyed by that victory, Knowles headed north for Santiago once more. His men were said to be in "high spirits."[23]

One of the difficulties in attacking Santiago was that the entrance to the harbor was narrow, and in high seas incoming ships were highly vulnerable to attack from the castle that guarded it. Vernon thought this was such an impediment that Santiago could be taken only by organizing a diversionary front, which is why he wanted Wentworth to march on the town from the south. Knowles, remained unconvinced this was the case, and sent his senior officer, Captain Digby Dent of the *Plymouth,* to reconnoiter the harbor. What he learned was not to his liking. Dent discovered there were some sunken ships and a boom across the entrance, held in place by a chain. According to some reports, the sunken objects were full of explosives that would ignite if the chain was broken.[24] Whether or not this was true, Dent's Spanish pilot thought the barrier impossible to breach. Knowles told Dent that he had it on good authority that the entrance was passable: "If your Pilot raises any objections to confuse your People, shoot him or throw him overboard, for we are not to be diverted from the attack."[25] If Dent did not care to break the boom, he would have him replaced. Dent backed off from a confrontation and agreed to take another look. But when the *Plymouth* and the *Cornwall* approached the harbor they were beaten back by gunfire from the batteries and had a few masts shot to pieces. Knowles was frustrated and furious. He blamed Dent for not cutting the chain in the first place and for allowing the sunken vessel to moor up against the western reef. When he later heard that Santiago was undermanned at the time, Knowles resolved to court-martial his senior officer for bad conduct.

Knowles hoped to resume his attack on Santiago in April 1748 but the prospect of a grand victory eluded him. New masts had to be retrieved from Boston, and several ships were leaking badly because teredo worms had burrowed into the hulls. Both the *Cornwall* and the *Lenox* were "very bad," Knowles reported, and others not much better. His seamen, moreover, were in an "almost Naked Condition" for want of adequate clothing.[26] Thus he busied himself trying to rack up a few more prizes to add to the quite lucrative haul he had already made in the Caribbean. In April he planned to intercept a convoy of French merchant ships out of Cap François and to harass the ports of Pettit-Guaves and Leoganne in Saint Domingue, but the weather prevented him. As he reported: "The Breezes have blown so Violent for near these two Months past and the Current run so Strong to leeward that nothing has been able to Beat to Windward."[27] Some of the cruisers had sprung their masts, he lamented, and he now had only one ship available to convoy the next shipment of sugar, rum, and coffee. He was also under the weather. He had also been forced to take the waters at a local spa, he reported, "having been extream ill with my Old Disorder for some time past."[28]

Early in July Knowles received word that the British government had concluded a peace with France, and he realized that his pursuit of prizes would soon be coming to an end. But the war with Spain was not yet over, and so the admiral concentrated his efforts on intercepting ships out of Vera Cruz on their way to Havana. He had five of his ships cruise between the Tortuga Bank and Cape Cartouche looking for such ships and dispatched Captain Drake of the *Towey* to La Guira to capture a Spanish ship laden with cacao and 50,000 pieces of eight.[29] It was during this final quest for Spanish prizes that Captain Holmes of the *Lenox* left his merchant convoy to alert Knowles of Don Reggio's squadron off Havana.

Knowles encountered Reggio's fleet early on the morning of 1 October 1748. The Spanish fleet was to windward. Having made some headway a league northward, Knowles ordered his squadron to move onto a larboard tack in order to take the weather gage. This reversed the order of battle with the *Tilbury* in the van. Knowles tried to close in on his enemy, but the *Warwick* started to fall to the rear, and some confusion over signals left both that man-of-war and the *Canterbury* well behind the others. In his flagship the *Cornwall*, Knowles shortened his sail to allow the stragglers to catch up, but the result was that the leading two ships, the *Strafford* and the *Tilbury*, engaged the enemy before the British line had been formed. For almost an hour Captain Brodie in the *Strafford* bore the brunt of the action, with the *Tilbury* firing ineffectually out of range, but at four o'clock in the afternoon, when the British squadron finally closed on the enemy, Knowles drove the Spanish admiral out of the line yet found his flagship incapacitated by shots to his fore-topsail and main-topmast. He then ordered a general chase to leeward, but Captain Holmes in the *Lenox* appeared slow to respond, perhaps because his ship was so waterlogged. The chase continued all night, until the Spanish ships limped into Havana or were scuttled in a neighboring bay.[30] The next morning a Spanish sloop informed Knowles that the peace preliminaries with Spain had been signed and that the war was over.

The battle off Havana was less than satisfactory to Knowles, certainly a poor substitute for capturing the Spanish treasure fleet that had eluded him.[31] Reggio's flagship, the *Africa,* was burnt off the coast, and the only other available prize, the *Conquistador,* became the subject of a dispute between Knowles and Captain Innes of the *Warwick* as to who had formally captured it. Publicly Knowles put on a brave face about the battle; privately he simmered about the conduct of some of his officers, particularly Captains Powlett, Toll, and Innes. In his report to the Admiralty, he remained convinced he could have taken Reggio's squadron before nightfall, but in the general chase "there appeared too much Bashfulness, to give it no harsher Term."[32] At this point he made no formal complaints. "I have much ado to prevail with myself not to make an Example of them here," he confided to Lord Vere Beauclerk. "If I live to see another War," he continued, he hoped to "have better Tools to work with."[33]

Although Knowles laid no formal charges, his sentiments quickly became known in the squadron. The day after the battle Charles Powlett learned from his lieutenant that Knowles was less than happy with his conduct, and within a week he was fuming because of the rumors that were flying around the fleet. "There is a midshipman whose name is Pelham belonging to the *Oxford* on board the *Conquestadore* who has abused me in a most egregious manner," he informed Knowles, "by telling the Coxswain of one of the *Tilbury*'s boats that I was under arrest for Cowardice. I beg you will do me the justice to take notice of it to him in order to stop the mouths of People who dare assert such an untruth."[34] Predictably the accused captains demanded courts-martial to clear their names, as did Captain Holmes of the *Lenox,* who disliked the insinuation that he had deliberately fired into the *Strafford* during the general chase, when in fact he had simply made a mistake in the failing light. "My Honour, my Long Services to my King and Country & all that is dear to an Honest Man is brought into Question & put to Risk by the ill grounded & private Revenge of one Man."[35] In response, Knowles's subaltern officers went on the attack and requested that the admiral himself be court-martialed. And then, six months later and a year after the battle, Knowles retaliated by formally charging the four officers with bad conduct, breach of orders, disobeying signals, and not doing their utmost to engage the enemy.[36]

Before he sailed home in December 1748 Knowles began to prepare his case. He disparaged the notion that the battle off Havana had been fierce.

British casualties, he informed the Admiralty, had been greatly exaggerated. While it was rumored that three captains had been killed, not to mention the "incredible Slaughter amongst the common men," the reality was that the British lost no officers and had emerged from the conflict with only sixty men wounded.[37] Had his officers been more resolute, he insisted, the Spanish squadron could have been taken, noting that his opposing commander, Don Reggio, had court-martialed some of his subalterns for cowardice. Unlike some newspaper accounts, which attributed the inconclusive battle to failing light,[38] Knowles laid the blame fair and square on his officers.

At the same time Knowles took steps to safeguard his reputation. He demanded that the Admiralty deny the circulating rumors that he had pocketed the bounty of the seamen who fought at La Guira and Porto Cabello. He complained that he had "Numbers daily threatning me if I do not pay them, where by it is not safe for me to be in Town."[39] He also tried to delay the trial of Captain Robert Erskine, whom Knowles had accused of wasting government money while repairing the *Milford* in Boston.[40] Knowles had no wish to appear recriminatory, a reputation he had gained over the years in his dealings with other officers, particularly the well-connected William Montagu, brother to Lord Sandwich, whom Knowles had sent home for drunkenly and fatally shooting a slave in Antigua harbor in 1744. That particular case continued to haunt Knowles, for Montagu sued him for damages while his own trial was pending in London.[41] Further examples of his disagreements with officers might have undermined his case against the four officers at Havana.

Above all, Knowles wanted his trial to precede the others so he could clear his name. In July 1749 he wrote to the Admiralty board: "I would crave your Lordships to let me clear my own character before I am to Try others. Indeed I have neither the Strength at Present to go through the least Fateuage [Fatigue] and am advised by my Physicians to be at Iselworth for the benefit of riding Morning and Evening."[42] He could not postpone the trial of Captain Robert Erskine in November 1749 because the key witness, the former master of the *Milford*, had contracted to sail in a merchant ship.[43] Yet this particular court-martial did not really impinge upon Knowles's actions in the Caribbean, even if it could be held up as an example of his pettiness.

Knowles had accused Erskine of disobeying orders while in Boston, where he was in charge of a convoy. Knowles thought Erskine should have sailed earlier that he did in fall 1748, given that the news of the peace had arrived, and he wondered why Erskine had incurred such expense while in Boston, insinuating that the captain was soft and greedy, eager to delay sailing to oblige the merchants and to pocket the extra freight money he might obtain from late arrivals in port. Erskine protested that the main reason he delayed sailing was that many of the crew of the *Milford* had come down with fevers at Roatan and needed to convalesce. He also reported that his ship was very leaky and had to be pumped two or three times every watch to remove the two feet of water that leaked in through the rotting hull. In these circumstances, Erskine insisted, it had been important to try to dry out the vessel before it sailed. The court-martial was not unsympathetic to Erskine commissioning extra provisions to feed his men, but it did reprimand him for the delay in sailing. In the end, it decided to suspend him from the rank of captain for a year.[44]

Knowles's first court-martial of late 1749 thus proved to be a partial success, and on the trials that involved his Caribbean turn of duty, he did get the timetable that he wanted. His trial was scheduled ahead of the four officers implicated in the battle of Havana, and even before that of Captain Digby Dent, whom Knowles had court-martialed in mid-1748 for his failure to break the boom at Santiago de Cuba.

For a court-martial, Knowles's trial was fairly public; both he and his accusers were allowed shorthand recorders, which meant that the newspapers would likely pick up details of the trial and that the whole proceedings would be published in a pamphlet.[45] In his own defense Knowles admitted that he engaged the Spanish in a straggling line, but he laid the blame for this on his accusers, whom he thought could have borne down on the enemy more expeditiously. Unfortunately for the admiral, he failed to have his accusers dismissed as witnesses, and their testimony cast a shadow on Knowles's competence. They marshaled a compelling case that Knowles had organized his battle line hastily and gave confusing signals to those who straggled. The testimony of Captain Holmes was particularly damning, for Holmes had kept detailed notes of the battle, perhaps because he had been reprimanded for mishandling the *Lenox* during the battle against Port St. Louis.[46] This important evidence worked against Knowles, for Holmes could hardly be accused of being a reluctant combatant. It was his willingness to leave his convoy and alert Knowles of the Spanish squadron that had laid the groundwork for the battle.

Rear Admiral Knowles was not accused of cowardice. No one seriously doubted his personal courage and the quite reasonable claim that his flagship had been disabled during the battle. According to an account in the *Jamaica Gazette*, his flagship bore down on the Spanish for nearly half an hour without firing a gun, "though all the stern-most Spanish ships kept pelting at him." When Knowles finally did engage the enemy, the report continued, his ship "looked like H-ll, for she vomited nothing but Fire and Smoke."[47] Hyperbole or not, accounts like this suggested that Knowles showed a commendable bravery and fortitude during the battle. Yet the officers of the court-martial did think Knowles might have shifted flags during the engagement and that he had clumsily set up his battle line. Even one of his supporters, Captain Polycarpus Taylor of the *Cornwall,* admitted that the line was far from firm. Consequently, after the week's trial Knowles was found guilty of negligence and publicly reprimanded, a verdict that certainly boded ill for his reputation and judgment in the subsequent trials.

In those courts-martial Knowles's opponents mustered an impressive array of evidence of the damage and injuries sustained aboard their ships in the battle of Havana, enough to blunt the admiral's claim that they were far from valorous. Indeed, Holmes was commended for his actions before and during the battle. The insinuation that he had deliberately fired into the *Strafford* during the melee of the battle was summarily dismissed; so too were the claims that he had incompetently sailed his ship within the weather quarter of the *Cornwall* and had not borne down upon the enemy as expeditiously as he might.[48] Indeed, the fact that Knowles had given Holmes command of four vessels immediately after the battle seemed to vitiate the complaints about his performance. Certainly the court thought so, for Holmes was given an honorable discharge, a verdict that implied that Knowles's accusations were seen as groundless and mean-spirited, if not malevolent. In the other trials, however, Knowles's complaints were thought to have some substance. Powlett was acquitted of every charge save that he failed to send a boat to receive Knowles's orders. For this he received a reprimand, as did Captain Edmund Toll, who faultily placed his ship, HMS *Oxford,* to the lee rather than astern of the *Tilbury* when they engaged two of the Spanish ships. As for Captain Thomas Innes of the *Warwick,* he was found guilty of not obeying orders and suspended for three months for not pursuing another Spanish ship when the *Conquistador* had struck its sails.

Apart from Holmes, no one emerged unscathed from the courts-martial of 1749–50. Tempers ran high. Admiral Knowles believed he had been vilified by his opponents as "not only the worst officer, and rankest Coward, but the greatest Monster living." Their accusations had been aired in every tavern and coffeehouse in London, he complained, and had "wounded both my private and publick Character."[49] The fact that his conduct at Havana was faulted at his court-martial lent some substance to the malicious charges. Consequently Powlett was piqued that he had been reprimanded when he had borne the brunt of the action in the *Tilbury* and had sustained a leg injury that required four months to heal. He thought it a "calamitous situation" to serve "under discontented minds who indulge themselves in putting hard Constructions upon small events" such as failing to send a boat to receive the orders of a hotheaded commander in chief. "My reputation as an Officer, my services, & every thing valuable in this life will not be blasted by so frivolous & . . . so malicious a Charge as this now brought against me."[50] Thomas Innes was similarly angered by the charges against him, suspecting that Knowles had leveled them only because he wanted to claim the *Conquistador* as a prize. He protested that his inability to enter the battle promptly stemmed from the fact that he had the heaviest vessel in the squadron and the most leewardly. He greatly resented the accusation of cowardice. "Would not my whole Ships Company have mutinyed and shun[n]ed me as a Shameless Person," he protested. "How can such a black Crime escape so long and be reconciled to the rest of my Behaviour in the Engagement?"[51]

Matters of honor dictated further action, and that meant duels. Duels among military officers were commonplace in the eighteenth century, more so perhaps than historians have been prepared to admit. Of the well-publicized duels during the reign of George III that were cited by James Gilchrist, some 37 percent of all combatants were officers or former officers on half pay.[52] Of the fifty-four duels reported in the London newspapers for the period 1748–51, half involved military personnel, so it was perhaps not surprising that these overwrought naval officers chose to vindicate their honor through this form of ritual violence. Their choice of weapons was typical as well. By mid-century, pistols were beginning to replace swords as the weapon of choice, although only by a small margin.[53] Fifty percent of all reported duels involved pistols, 42 percent involved swords, and 8 percent involved a combination of the two. In the three duels that were known to have eventuated from the Havana affair, pistols were used. Knowles is said to have received four challenges, and it seems that he acted on two of them. Although the reports were quite cryptic, Knowles apparently fought a duel against Captain Holmes in late February, six weeks after Holmes's trial. Several shots were fired, but no one was injured.[54] Subsequently he squared off against Captain Charles Powlett, or so it was reported in the *Remembrancer*.[55] Once again no one was hurt, quite "providentially," remarked the weekly, for the rate of casualties in reported duels was very high, whether with swords or pistols.[56] In my sample of duels, 48 percent ended in a fatality. Of all combatants, 56 percent were either killed or wounded. This proportion was higher than during the Napoleonic wars, when 44 percent of all participants were recorded as killed or wounded, and substantially higher than in subsequent decades, when relatively few gentlemen were injured.[57] By contrast, in only 18 percent of all reported cases in the mid-eighteenth century did both duelists walk away without injury, sometimes because seconds insisted that the matter be settled amicably or because sentries in the major parks around London intervened before anyone was hurt.[58] Or even because the combatants were too drunk at the time of the challenge to remember where they were to meet.[59]

The third duel that sprang from the courts-martial proved a different matter. It involved Thomas Innes and Edward Clark of HMS *Warwick* and *Canterbury,* respectively. As both were commanders of the trailing ships in the British line at Havana, Innes presumably thought that Clark might be a sympathetic listener to his complaints about Knowles, who had accused him of coming tardily into battle and lethargically engaging the *Conquistador.* Innes had confided in Clark about the abuse he had suffered on Knowles's account, only to find that Clark was inclined to take the admiral's side in the dispute. Indeed, Clark seems to have alerted Knowles of Captain Innes's discontent, which Innes felt betrayed their friendship. He protested that he had written to Clark "under the protection & Tye of Friendship, which amongst Men of Honour is always held sacred."[60] Innes was very displeased that Clark had revealed his feelings and became extremely angry when Clark gave evidence against him at his court-martial to the effect that he had impeded the *Canterbury*'s progress into battle. Innes called Clark a "perjured rascal"; he thought him a "scoundrel and a coward." He vowed Clark would "sweat" under cross-examination, and if not, then "he would sweat him another way."[61] On their way back from Deptford, fellow officers James Gambier and George Davey warned Innes that he was pushing his luck, that his virulent abuse would provoke Clark to defend his honor, especially since many of the criticisms had been publicly voiced in taverns and coffeehouses. Eventually Captain Clark found the abuse too much to bear. It had intolerably tarnished his honor. And so, on 11 March 1750, about a month after Innes's trial, Clark went to Innes's lodgings in Green Street, Leicester Fields, and challenged him to a duel with sword and pistol.

The duel took place early the following morning in Hyde Park between 6:00 and 7:00 a.m. Innes's servant, William Newman, who was present at the encounter, said his vision was obscured by trees, but it appears that the two duelists stood very close to one another, no more than five or six yards apart. Clark had a pair of horse pistols with seven-inch screw barrels that he had purchased from John Frazier, a London gunsmith. Innes was armed with only a three-and-a-half-inch pocket gun; little more than a peashooter, which probably explains why they stood their ground after a few paces. Clark fired first, and according to at least one account, before Innes had cocked his pistols. His bullet entered Innes on his right side under the ribs and near the stomach and came out near his ribs on the other. Captain Innes was taken back to his lodgings where he was attended by a surgeon. He died about 11 p.m. that evening and was interred in the vault of St Margaret's Church, a stone's throw from the Houses of Parliament.[62]

Innes thought Clark was guilty of "un-officer-like" behavior at Deptford, but he did not condemn his conduct during the duel. When asked by a private from the first regiment of guards whether Clark should be detained, Innes declined the offer, insisting "he has behav'd like a man of honour." Back in his lodgings, he admitted to his landlord, Edward Welton, that Clark had fired too soon and had taken full aim. He had not observed the usual protocol of simply raising his pistol and quickly discharging it.[63] Even so, the injured Innes was quite prepared to forgive his challenger. As Welton recalled at the Old Bailey, Innes "forgave Captain Clark with all his heart, and all the world; saying, he behaved like a gentleman. . . . My wife asked him, how he could go to fight such a gentleman as Captain Clark; he said, God's will must be done, though he strove to take away my life at the Court Martial, it is done now."[64] He also told his servant, William Newman, that he was to reaffirm that Clark had acted honorably. As far as Innes was concerned the duel remained a matter of honor between gentlemen and the "rough equality of hazard," as Stephen Banks has put it, had been observed. For all its irregularities, and it is worth noting that neither seconds nor surgeons were present, Captain Innes insisted to the end that the duel was conducted honorably.[65]

Clark was arrested by the sentries who guarded the powder magazine in the park. At the coroner's jury the verdict was that Innes had been willfully murdered. Consequently Captain Clark stood trial at the Old Bailey on 26 April 1750. Mr. Beard opened for the Crown, condemning dueling as a threat to civil society, an affront to the laws of the land and quite unchristian. The Crown had no difficulty establishing Clark's culpability in killing Innes. There were enough witnesses to prove it; but the defense attempted to modify the charge to one of manslaughter on the grounds that Clark had been unconscionably provoked, a tactic that had been used before in major trials over duels. Sergeant Hayward for the Crown admitted this was the case, but he also insisted that Clark's actions were technically premeditated and malevolent and therefore the charge of murder should stand. Nonetheless Clark was able to muster an impressive array of distinguished people to testify to his good character, including lords, admirals and MPs. Admiral John Byng, who had known him for eight or nine years, thought Clark "a very well behav'd, civil, complaisant gentleman," implying that he must have been provoked beyond endurance. Admiral Fox, who had known him longer, believed him to be a "good officer of great honour."[66] After a trial that lasted four to five hours, the jury returned a verdict of guilty yet recommended mercy because of Innes's persistent defamation of Clark's character. The deference paid to Clark was such that he was brought in alone before the other malefactors to hear his sentence, a deference he should have appreciated because prisoners in Newgate were dying like flies from gaol fever.[67] In pronouncing the sentence the

Recorder of London chided Clark for upholding "that false notion of the principles of honour too prevalent in these modern times." He was sorry to see that a "gentleman who had distinguished himself many times in the service and deserved so well of his King and country, should close all with so foul a comment."[68] Clark, for his part, played up his naval record. He told the judges he hoped they would endorse the jury's plea for mercy and declared that should he receive a pardon he would spend the rest of life in the service of his country. He vowed he would prevent other gentlemen "from falling into the like Misfortune."[69]

In view of the substantial support that Clark received from the social elite, it was predictable that he would escape the gallows. His sentence was respited sine die, and a letter from the Duke of Cumberland to the king in Hanover pretty well ensured that he would be pardoned. Indeed, George II, the last British king to fight on the battlefield, tacitly endorsed dueling, as an incident in 1746 revealed. When two Scots officers fell out during the Jacobite rebellion and the offended party demanded a court-martial to clear his name, the king let it be known that he should have resolved the issue by a duel. Otherwise no officer would be prepared in future to serve with him.[70] By the end of May 1750, Clark was out of prison on bail, his sureties underwritten by Admiral Knowles. Within a month he had formally received a pardon at King's Bench.[71]

Not everyone was happy about this outcome. There were simply too many duels being fought by military officers in the aftermath of the war. "Hardly a week at this time escapes without the news of a Duel," remarked one newspaper.[72] Critics frequently mustered the argument that dueling was a serious affront to civil society; they mourned the waste of young men cut down in their prime over false notions of honor and masculinity. "He is courageous and brave who stands up for Conscience against the false but prevailing Maxims of Custom and Opinion," remarked the *General Evening Post*.[73] Opponents of duels noted that Muslim societies despised them and wondered at the presumption of so-called Christians that they should steal the "property of heaven" and defy the Ten Commandments. To these arguments were added those that touched on Britain's emerging national identity as it strove to consolidate its overseas trade routes and territories against European competition. In an age when more men were being mobilized for war and when peace treaties began to resemble temporary truces, military officers were recklessly depleting the nation's resources, forgetting that they better served Britain if they fought the French or the Spanish rather than themselves. It was time officers exercised self-restraint and a higher sense of public responsibility. "A warlike nation should learn how to kill their enemies when there is a necessity for it," remarked Jonas Hanway, "and not their countrymen when there are none."[74]

While critics strove to muster a case against the code of honor that under-girded the duel,[75] it was tacitly acknowledged that dueling was deeply embedded in upper-class British society. In the aftermath of the Forty-Five rebellion it was rumored that Parliament would bring in a bill that would make even challenges punishable by death, but there is no evidence that such legislation came before the Commons. Indeed, one writer thought that dueling had never been outlawed by Parliament because MPs were socially inhibited from doing so. Only bishops could propose such a change without incurring the stigma of cowardice.[76] This was a different argument from that advanced in the early eighteenth century, when several bills had been proposed to ban dueling and one actually reached a third reading in the Commons. In that era anti-dueling advocates proposed a court of honor to attend to demeaning insults or, perhaps skeptical that any legislation might curb the practice, sought to divorce the duel from true notions of civility and honor.[77] By the mid-century writers were more pessimistic about the prospect of eliminating dueling by such means. One pamphleteer did ponder the possibilities of having a court of honor, but he was in principle sympathetic to dueling, believing that it encouraged civility among gentlemen. Voicing an older aristocratic argument, he claimed that it allowed gentlemen the opportunity of settling points of honor without having to explain themselves before the courts. There, he asserted, a weighty purse and interest could give the moderate gentry a very hard time.[78]

Critics did reiterate the Restoration argument that the liberal use of the royal pardon endorsed dueling.[79] They claimed it sacrificed the rule of law to an outdated warrior's code, as did the tendency to attribute a lot of weight to the provocation that duelists suffered. In the Clark-Innes duel, this had worked to Clark's advantage. Unlike some duels among military men, which seem to have emanated from drunken spats in clubs and taverns, quarrels over gaming, or minor public affronts,[80] the Clark-Innes duel involved weightier matters. Even critics were prepared to admit that Clark had been intolerably abused and consistently accused of perjuring himself at the courts-martial. Along with Admiral Knowles, he had been "publicly traduced and reviled about the Town with all the rancour of abusive words such as would better become the Forecastle than the Quarter Deck," claimed one writer in *Old England*.[81] Consequently there were strong mitigating circumstances why Clark should be pardoned.

Even so, writers continued to campaign for a public crackdown on dueling and pondered which punishments might curb the gentleman's brittle sense of honor. In an age when military men had political ambitions, some thought the loss of public office might do the trick, or large fines calibrated by wealth, even disinheritance. The feeling ran high that duelists should not avail themselves of royal pardons.[82] Critics argued that officers and gentlemen should suffer for their misguided sense of honor. If this were the case, then perhaps, over time, dueling might cease to be part of their cultural repertoire. That dueling might become the cultural repertoire of men further down the social scale was not addressed, despite the fact that it could be logically deduced from Mandeville's economy of honor, and despite the brief reports of chaplains, doctors, even prize fighters, pages, and servants making or accepting challenges.[83] That issue preoccupied critics in the late eighteenth and early nineteenth century; in 1750 the concern was that dueling was an affront to Christian morality and national security. "It was a savage practice," wrote Philanthropos, "fit only to be retained among fierce, untamed Barbarians, and which ought to be banished from every Christian Country."[84]

One reason it was difficult to promote dueling as part of an outmoded code of honor in the mid-century decades was because military might, and especially naval power, was important to commercial progress. The notion of commerce as a pathway to amicable international relations had yet to be fully articulated. That would come in the wake of Adam Smith. In 1750 Britain was locked in an ongoing international struggle with imperial Spain and France in which ships and officers mattered crucially, and in which commercial success was something of a zero-sum game conducted at gunpoint.[85] No one could make much headway criticizing such deeply embedded customs as dueling in these circumstances, especially within the officer class, which probably felt, like Captain McNamara later in the century, that duels steeled officers to lead their men into "honourable danger." Although notions of politeness and civility were beginning to chip away at the code of honor, or to entangle them in a manner that made dueling superfluous, they were not that compelling. A man like the merchant-philanthropist Jonas Hanway, who proudly professed he had declined a duel over something he had written, would have been regarded by officers as an evangelical crank.[86] Dueling was considered critical to military honor and more generally was thought to deter gentlemen from throwing casual insults at one another. As Abraham Bosquett put it in the early nineteenth century, dueling was "a barrier against the encroachments of rudeness and ill-breeding."[87]

If the controversy over Knowles and his officers revealed just how difficult it was to displace dueling with an alternative mode of conflict resolution, it also revealed how recriminatory naval life could become if dreams and aspirations were frustrated by the fortunes of war. Naval careers were an important source of social mobility for gentlemen of little landed patrimony. Winning promotion and nabbing a greater share of wartime prize money were important markers of success. In 1744 the government was forced to issue a proclamation clarifying rights to prize money among flag officers because of the rancorous disputes it had generated.[88] Some of Knowles's difficulties with his officers stemmed from such issues. William Montagu, the younger brother of Lord Sandwich, was furious with Knowles for sending him home to face a court-martial because he killed a black slave in Antigua harbor. He lost his place in the naval hierarchy and his share of prize money as a consequence, and some six years later he was still trying to sue Admiral Knowles for tipping the scales against him.

Admiral Knowles, for his part, was ever eager to pick up the windfalls of war to fuel his social ambitions. In the month before his trial at Deptford, he put himself up for election against the London alderman and banker Edward Ironside in the rotten borough of Gatton in Surrey. Although there were less than twenty voters, he needed a hefty wallet to buy them off and fund a subsequent scrutiny. Some of his anxiety at the end of the war probably flowed from his hope to enter Parliament, and subsequently to strengthen his hand in his forthcoming trial. One observer certainly thought so. "The cunning admiral has got a seat in the House of Commons," he remarked, "and it is supposed he will have art enough to acquit himself at his trial."[89]

Whatever the reason, Knowles's victory at Gatton cost money, something he had acquired from the windfalls of war. As the captain of the *Diamond* he had captured two Spanish ships worth £30,000 between Florida and Cuba, one carrying 100,000 pieces of eight and clothing for the garrison of St. Augustine.[90] In the following year he picked up two more valuable Spanish prizes, with cargoes and inventory in excess of £200,000. What Knowles's share of these prizes actually was is uncertain; it could have been as much as £57,500 if he received the appropriate share of a captain under the Prize Act of 1708, a very impressive sum by eighteenth-century standards. As a commodore of the Leeward Islands station, he shored up some twenty-three prizes with Sir Peter Warren, his own share of the prize money being in excess of £3,500.[91] Among these windfalls were two large slave ships from the Guinea coast and Angola, the first with 400 blacks on board, the second with 650.[92] The latter, *Le Patriarche Abraham,* bound for Port Louis in St. Domingue, also had 163 ounces of gold and 116 elephant tusks on board. Why all this prize money and a judicious marriage to a daughter of a leading Barbadian planter did not satiate his financial ambitions remains unclear.[93] Perhaps he had simply become rapacious, perhaps he was obsessed with purchasing the social éclat that his birth had denied him. Whatever the reason, four years later he was desperately seeking the Spanish treasure fleet out of Vera Cruz, to the point of putting his crews on short allowance while they scanned the horizon. That *flota,* whose worth was estimated at 9 million Spanish dollars,[94] would have made him a Midas. He did not find it, and in the inconclusive battle that followed he lost his right to the only prize, the *Conquistador,* because it was taken after the truce.[95] These frustrations and his declining naval fortunes reverberated across London in 1749–50 as officer after officer responded to his allegations of incompetence and cowardice with courts-martial and duels. Knowles was a man who made as many enemies as friends. Francis Gashry was a master of understatement when he said the admiral had a "vivacity and impetuosity in his Temper that will carry him to great lengths."[96] Others talked of his wild temper and "unprecedented arrogance."[97] One thing is for sure. His quarrels with his fellow officers became the talk of the town in 1750, raising issues about personal honor and national responsibility that were to become the hallmark of British military culture in the mid-century decades.

2

The Sailors' Return

British sailors returned from war battered, bruised, and sometimes broken. The courts-martial of Admiral Knowles's subaltern officers in the battle of Havana explicitly exposed the perils of battle, even in an engagement where the Spanish had sustained greater casualties. On the British side 59 sailors were killed and a further 120 were wounded in the encounter with Reggio's squadron. Among those wounded were John Baker and marine sergeant Robert Middleton, both of whom lost their right legs while fighting on the *Lenox*. Richard Dungan lost his right arm and had a large contusion on his right side, and John Day sustained a fracture to his skull the size of a crown. On board the *Tilbury*, which was also in the forefront of the action, 24 seamen and 3 marines were wounded and a further 14 suffered burns from the explosion of gunpowder—to the face, hands, and in two cases to the eyes. On the *Oxford*, William Shuttuck had the bones of his right arm shattered, and his muscles were said to be "much lacerated" by grapeshot. Abraham Cochereau had the bones of his left wrist smashed to pieces, which necessitated the amputation of his arm. "He did well," noted Captain Polycarpus Taylor, which presumably meant he survived the shock and sepsis of an on-the-spot amputation. It was more than could be said for many who went under the knife.[1]

Disabled men stood little chance of making ends meet at home. The best they could hope for was a meager pension from the Chatham chest, less than

£7 per annum for the loss of a limb, £4 for an eye, and for the really sick, a bed at Haslar Hospital, which was founded in 1745. The prospects for fitter seamen were not that good either. Within a year of the peace of Aix-la-Chapelle, signed in October 1748, roughly 40,000 seamen and marines were demobilized. The merchant marine, which stood at perhaps 30,000 in the late 1740s, could not accommodate all the demobilized tars, an exodus that deeply troubled the Admiralty.[2] Others had recourse to the ropewalks, although the official yards were actually discharging men.[3] Others still labored along rivers. During a labor dispute among the Tyneside keelmen in 1750, some sailors took over the task of loading the coal barges and taking them down river. Others were recruited to suppress turnpike riots in the West Country. A few found work loading barley at King's Lynn.[4]

One of the major, and certainly the most urgent, problems confronting the returning sailor was getting paid. Although a 1728 act had legislated what it termed prompt payment, that is, at least two months' pay every six months, the navy had relaxed this regulation in wartime because it was feared it would encourage desertion. Certainly, some seamen were paid promptly when they were turned over, but as wars progressed and expenses rose, these payments were often honored in the breach. The result was that at the end of a long war sailors were often owed considerable amounts of money stretching back over years of service, not to mention any prize money they might have accrued. John Alford accrued £45 in wages and £270 in prize money from his ten years in service, mainly as an able seamen, although he became a noncommissioned officer toward the end of the war.[5] Michael Canty and Thomas Williamson were owed between £38 and £40 for their service on the *Namur* between July 1746 and April 1749. As able seamen whose net wage was 22s 6d a lunar month, they had been paid only a modest portion of their wage in almost three years of service, if at all.[6]

Many sailors had to wait around to get their wages. Once discharged from a ship, seamen were issued tickets entitling them to specified amounts of pay, but the navy was often slow in honoring them at the Pay Office in London or at the offices of the dockyard commissioners, a fact that opposition critics such as Admiral Edward Vernon routinely pointed out.[7] More critically, the Royal Navy withheld the last six months' of pay so that recent deductions for slops and tobacco, for example, could be accounted for and months of service aboard different ships confirmed.[8] On all ships some money was held back to cover claims that might be made by widows, attorneys, or by seamen who, for some reason or another, were not on board when the ship was paid off. All this took time to sort out and it was compounded by the fact that Parliament was often laggard in approving naval revenues. The crews of the *Strafford* and

Cornwall, for example, who fought their last battle off Havana in October 1748, were not actually paid off until June of 1749, for no one was paid off on a foreign station; one wonders how much longer they had to wait to redeem their net wages. Crews involved in the siege of Cartagena in 1741 were frustrated enough to wait upon the king in December 1748 to try to expedite their entitlements.[9] Other sailors were petitioning him again in January 1750.[10] The amount of money held back by the Admiralty at the end of the war was considerable. By December 1748, three months after the peace, the navy had paid out £939,000, but it still owed over £1 million in back pay. A year later, it had paid out a further £741,000, but there remained more than £500,000 due seamen and their relatives and no firm indication of when the navy might cough up.[11] Among widows the situation was intolerable; eight widows petitioned the secretary of state in July 1750, saying they had received no relief from the paymasters and were in very distressed circumstances.[12] Among able-bodied seamen, tempers could easily flare if they were kept waiting for "recalls," that is, the final balance of their pay. Commissioner Brown at Chatham remembered seamen harassing Captain John Hardy, whom they mistook for his brother, Charles, because the latter's claim had been given precedence over their own. "They fell fowl of him & beat him in a most cruel manner," he recalled, "& it was a mute [*sic*] point in them, whether they would beat me or not."[13]

Seamen not only had to wait for their pay, they also had to wait for their prize money, which sometimes amounted to as much if not more than their wage. During the war over 3,400 French and Spanish ships had been condemned as prizes for a British fleet of approximately 100 ships of the line and 70 cruisers.[14] Even allowing for the privateers who captured foreign vessels, the chances of seamen getting some prize money were high. Although prize money could be paid at foreign ports and vice admiralty courts, delays in getting prize money were legion, principally because of the contested claims it might incur. To seamen anxious to get their hands on some extra cash, this could be a frustrating experience. As a pamphleteer remarked on his visit to the Naval Office in the early years of demobilization, the rooms were filled with "the Loud Clamours of a Company of honest Tars who were bawling for their wages and prize-money."[15] In a public petition to the nobility and gentry of Britain in 1751, British seamen complained not only of the intolerable delays in securing their wages, but of the difficulties of collecting their prize money, most particularly because of "the Fraud and Artificers of our Commanders."[16]

Impatient with the delays, companies of seamen took their concerns elsewhere. In February 1748, 900 sailors waited on His Majesty to request the speedy condemnation of the prizes from the Genoese, which were said to be worth £200,000.[17] Later that year, some 1,400 sailors attended the king on his way to the Lords to solicit their return from prizes captured in the Mediterranean. Some also presented their claims to the Prince of Wales as he came through St. James's Park.[18] The reports suggest the seamen came away cheering, but there is no indication that their solicitations resolved the general issue of recovering prize money in a prompt fashion. In June 1749 seamen were still waiting on His Majesty in hopes of recovering the prize money owed to them for captures in the Mediterranean, and it was not until the following month that the Lords Commissioners issued orders to pay the seamen their Genoese prizes.[19]

Seamen were not noted for their patience or their prudence. Few sailors were imbued "with such a Power of Reflection as to philosophize their Passions into Subordination," reflected one pompous writer, "or to reason down the Impulsive Dictates of Nature into Abstinence and Obedience."[20] The fact was the majority of sailors were single men in their early twenties ready to roar through town. The prints and caricatures of Jack Tar ashore speak of reckless, carefree consumption, of sailors arm-in-arm with whores, decked out in tawdry finery, and gloriously drunk. Jack Nastyface would later recall that on the day a ship was paid off, sailors would "hurry down to their respective berths, redeem their honour with their several ladies and bomb-boat men, and then turn their thoughts to the Jew pedlars who are ranged round the decks and on the hatchway gratings, in fact, the ship is crowded with them. They are furnished with every article that will rig out a sailor, never omitting a fine large watch and appendages, all warranted, and with which many an honest tar has been taken in."[21]

Sailors on a spree could quickly blow their money. In addition to the peddlers who decked them out, there were plenty of crimping landlords and shady customers who would discount their tickets at ruinous rates, sometimes in excess of 40 percent. The rhythm of a mariner's consumption was often volatile, with high spending rapidly degenerating into penury and very occasionally even death.[22] John Alford blew over £300 in a year of easy living. John Prior, finding that he could not get some "tolerable employ" after two years as a foremastman on the *Windsor* man-of-war, splurged on "the Pleasures of the Town."[23] Such good-timers were continually vulnerable to con artists and theft. In February 1749, seamen who had just been paid at Chatham were befriended by two pseudo-gentlemen who traveled with them on the Gravesend tilt boat to London. At Tower Hill, the villains cornered one of the tars and robbed him of 58 guineas.[24] A young sailor from the *Badger* sloop picked up a "lady of pleasure" in Lock fields, only to find she had male accomplices, one of whom accused him of picking up his "wife." In the ensuing quarrel the sailor was beaten up and left for dead, robbed of 18 moidores and some silver. Another sailor, flush with prize money, was prevailed upon by a whore to get married in the Fleet, only to find when he awoke from his drunken stupor that both his new wife and most of his money had disappeared.[25] As Hogarth's moral tale of "Industry and Idleness" suggests, sailors could easily wake up in some house of ill repute to discover their valuables missing. Sailors who claimed they had had been robbed in Lemon Street, Goodman's fields, rifled the house and destroyed everything inside before a party of guards arrived to restore order.[26]

Sailors flush with money and not always sober were also targets for pickpockets, especially in places like the Pay Office in Broad Street, where early in 1750 one thief was caught attempting to finger the pocket of a tar and promptly ducked in the fountain at Copthall Court.[27] Flush tars were also the victims of more confrontational robberies. In July 1748, a seaman from the *Sea Horse* named Montgomery Creighton had been attacked by two footpads on Hounslow Heath, who robbed him of £30 in Portuguese currency as well as a gold medal. Early that year, probably during some New Year's revels, a sailor named William Courser was knocked down by two footpads as he sauntered over Tower Hill.[28] They stole 12 shillings and his shoe and knee buckles, which implied he was more than a little tipsy.

More sober seamen were likely to confront their assailants, for men who had faced death and engaged in hand-to-hand combat were not likely to back off from a hostile encounter. In November 1749 a sailor was confronted by two men near the Deptford turnpike and ordered to stand and deliver. He retorted that "they would know Sailors fought for money, and damn him if he would be robbed of it without fighting."[29] Earlier two men demanded the money of a lone sailor in Battersea fields. He protested he had none, reported one newspaper, whereupon "they began to treat him roughly, saying as he was a Sailor lately discharged, he could not be without money." The sailor drew a clasp knife on his assailants and threatened to kill the first who approached, which made them back off and fly from the scene even though they had a pistol and bludgeon in their possession. A seaman from the *Hastings* man-of-war was even more intrepid. Confronted by a highwayman as he was walking to London from Chatham, he was ordered to stand and deliver. The tar replied he had fought for his money and "he expected some Broadsides before he surrendered."[30] The highwayman promptly fired his pistol and missed, allowing the seamen time to knock him off his horse. With the help of two rural laborers, he took him to the Earl of Egmont, who committed the man to Maidstone jail.

Anecdotal as this evidence is, it does suggest that in the swell of demobilization, sailors were sometimes as much prey as predators. Yet it was in the latter capacity that tars troubled contemporaries. "The approach of peace," wrote one author in the *Gentleman's Magazine,* "has raised not only compassion, but terror in many private gentlemen, and no less, I suppose, to those in public stations, who consider well the consequences of discharging so many men from their occupations in the army, the fleet, and the yards for building and repairing the navy. As half of these poor men will not be able to get employment there is great, and just apprehension, that necessity will compel them to seize by violence what they can see no method to obtain by honest labour."[31]

Another writer, in the *London Magazine,* anticipated that the coming of the peace would result in many demobilized sailors being "turned adrift, without a visible way of livelihood, and without the least degree of thought and prudence to find any for themselves that is good and useful." A third was even more blunt. The end of the war, he predicted, would "loose upon the Nation Twenty Thousand *Sixpence-a-Day Heroes,* with perhaps a Crown in their pockets, and very little Inclination to starve for want of recruiting out of other People's Property."[32] These sentiments were reiterated by a traveler just before the peace was finally concluded: "I am just come to Town from a long Journey, and found the Roads fill'd with Shoals of common Sailors, who are now turned loose to get their Bread how they can. Some of these poor Wretches demanded my Money in the *Supplication Form.* How long it will be before they alter their Tone, Time only will determine; but undoubtedly there is too much to fear that it will be very soon."[33]

The impressionistic reports in the newspapers bear out this prediction. Sailors or men in "sailor's habits" were reported going on account, swarming people on their way to market, robbing artisans at gunpoint, stealing from shops, breaking into the houses of rich merchants in places like Devonshire Square.[34] From mid-August to mid-September 1748, as the war was winding down and demobilization grew apace, there were fourteen robberies by sailors reported in the London press, the majority in familiar seamen's haunts around Tower Hill and to the east. But there were also two robberies in the Strand, one south of the river in Kennington Lane, and several further afield, in Kentish town, Highbury, Clapham, Kew, and Richmond. The victims ranged across the social spectrum: from market women, porters, and slop-sellers, to clockmakers, watchmakers, vinegar merchants, and sugar bakers, to attorneys and gentlemen.[35]

As the corks popped and the fireworks soared and crackled, Londoners must have been aware that peace would come at a price. Roistering sailors, flush with money one day and down on their luck the next, loitering sailors waiting to get paid, these were men likely to steal to make ends meet. In June 1749 the weekly *Old England* reported that three sailors had robbed a Mr. Stavesley of 17 shillings on Bagshot Heath, telling him they had traveled from Plymouth and "having spent all their Money, were reduced to that Method to supply Necessity."[36] A somewhat different predicament beset the two sailors who confronted a ship carpenter from Shadwell as he was walking by Hanging Wood in the first week of the peace. They robbed him of 4 shillings and his handkerchief but told him they would repay him when their ship was paid off.[37]

In the immediate aftermath of the war readers of newspapers were treated to a continuous fare of violent crime, especially in the triweekly *Whitehall Evening Post,* which carried incidents of serious crime under the categories of "Robbed" and "Committed." These sheets spoke of footpads stealing watches, wigs, and purses from passersby, sometimes at gunpoint; of highwaymen haunting the heaths and roads to London and terrorizing travelers; of thieves breaking and entering houses and quayside vessels; even of gangs creating sham disturbances to commit hit-and-run robberies and sometimes having the audacity to rescue fellow thieves from prisons. Sailors rescued fellow tars as they were committed to Newgate in August 1748.[38] A few months later, twenty fellows armed with pistols and cutlasses, and very likely servicemen, rescued a man who had picked the pocket of a General Sinclair on the Prince of Wales's birthday. "Surely this instance of Daring Impudence" remarked the *General Advertiser,* "must cause every Person of Property to assemble and consult means for their own Security at least; for if Gaols can be forc'd in this manner, Private Houses can make but little Resistance against such gangs of Villains as at present infest this great Metropolis."[39]

Two themes emerged from these reports. One was the high incidence of victim-related crime as opposed to simple stealing or pilfering; the other was the impunity with which such acts were carried out. Robbers were seldom apprehended. Many went off "in triumph," beating and even wounding those who attempted to call out for help. In the aftermath of the war there was not only a significant rise in the number of robberies reported in the *Whitehall Evening Post* but a noticeable increase in robberies accompanied by violence, beginning in the months following the signing of the peace preliminaries on 30 April 1748 (see table 1). Although the pattern of highway robbery was uneven, dipping in the summer of 1749 and not rising appreciably until the summer of the following year, there was a consistently high level of street robbery, reaching a peak in the winter of 1750. Combined, the figures reveal a consistently high level of violent or threatening crime from the early days of demobilization onward.

Somewhat differently constructed figures from the *General Advertiser* tell much the same story. Compared to 1747, property crime had risen quite dramatically by 1749 and sustained itself in 1751. Violent crime, by which I

Table 1: Robberies Reported in the *Whitehall Evening Post*

	1748		1749		1750		1751	
	Winter	Summer	Winter	Summer	Winter	Summer	Winter	Summer
Crimes (N)	58	42	95	86	69	80	50	100
Highway (%)	10.3	32.5	20.0	5.8	4.3	30.0	26.0	35.0
Street (%)	48.3	46.5	54.7	53.5	73.9	47.5	48.0	40.0
"Violent" (%)	58.6	79.0	74.7	59.3	78.2	77.5	74.0	75.0

Note: The figures are derived from reports in January and February (winter) and June and July (summer) for each year. A few cases of housebreaking with violence are included in the street robberies category. Violent crimes include those where menace and actual violence is reported.

mean not only those crimes where victims were specifically said to be "put in fear" but also highway and street robbery, accounted for much of the increase. The only exception was the winter of 1751, when the *General Advertiser* seems to have zoned in on the riverside theft to the east of Tower Hill rather than street robbery in the metropolis in general (table 2).

Contemporaries were undoubtedly perturbed by the recourse to violence. "The streets of this city, and the Suburbs thereof," a writer in the *Evening Post* concluded in late 1750, "are greatly infested with a Number of Villains confederating in small companies to rob, and on the smallest Opposition, to maim and murder the passengers."[40] Although some of the violent crime was certainly anonymous, sailors or people in "sailor's habits" were often identified. It was a sailor who robbed and killed the eighteen-year-old son of a farmer for his gold and silver, and a footpad dressed like a sailor who robbed a postboy, telling him "he would have it all, or blow his Brains out."[41] Sailors attacked a vinegar merchant in Goodman's fields "in a very barbarous manner" and stole his gold watch and money; seven men "in sailor's habits" broke into Batsford's ferry at Hackney marsh, bound the master and crew, and attempted to set the float alight after they had stolen £18.[42]

If violent crime preoccupied newspaper printers and reporters, so too did the vulnerability of the wealthy. Poor men and women were certainly cited as victims of street robberies: servants, shop assistants, workmen on pay nights, and street higlers like Mary Hewitt, a seller of butter and eggs at Leadenhall Market, who was accosted by two "ruffians" on Highgate Hill as she was returning home.[43] Yet the manner in which newspapers construed property crime meant that the poor were underrepresented, even if we cast the many anonymous men and women in that category. The lower sort became less conspicuous over time in the pages of the *Whitehall Evening Post,* falling from

Table 2: Robberies Reported in the *General Advertiser*

	1747		1749		1751	
	Winter	Summer	Winter	Summer	Winter	Summer
Crimes (N)	31	28	52	83	48	72
Highway (%)	9.6	10.7	19.2	22.9	10.4	23.6
Street (%)	19.3	3.6	36.5	34.9	18.8	22.2
"Violent" (%)	29.0	14.3	55.7	57.8	29.2	45.8

Note: The figures are derived from reports in January and February (winter) and July and August (summer) of each year. Violent crimes include those where menace and actual violence are reported.

roughly 30 percent in early 1749 to less than 9 percent by the summer of the following year. By contrast, the number of middling victims remained roughly the same, allowing for some seasonal variations. On an annual basis, they rose very slightly over the two years from 38.6 percent to 41.2 percent, while the genteel victims rose more conspicuously, from 33 percent in 1749 to nearly half (49.6 percent) in 1750. Although no coffeehouse habitué would have counted, a close reader might have noticed that urban crime appeared to be more violent and more discriminatory in its targets (table 3).

The recording of these attacks was the product of eighteenth-century reporting, which from the 1720s onward had devoted more attention to sensational crime. Robberies of the rich and influential were more likely to capture the attention of the newspapers, either through information elicited from Bow Street or through client networks.[44] Yet the figures do reflect the nature of criminal activity. Robbers tended to target specific groups, preferring to steal from the propertied and well-heeled rather than the poor, out of compassion as well as expediency. When two sailors robbed a dozen passersby at Newington Butts in the summer of 1749, they returned a few farthings they took from an old woman who pleaded poverty and added another so she could get "a Pint of Beer at the next House she came to."[45] In August 1751 a highwayman robbed a lord and lady on their return home from Vauxhall Gardens but pointedly gave the footboy a guinea to drink his health.[46] Such informal generosity to the less fortunate was understood by the coachman of Dr. Cox, of Burlington Street, whose chariot was held up by two highwaymen on Parson's Green. When they discovered the coach was empty, the highwaymen robbed the coachman of 4s 9d, upon which the coachman replied that "he thought they never robbed Servants." The highwaymen retorted, "It was very low with them, and if his Money was lucky, they would return it to him again."[47]

Table 3: Victims of Robberies Reported in the *Whitehall Evening Post*

	1749		1750	
	Winter	Summer	Winter	Summer
Crimes where victims noted (N)	79	42	52	67
Women (%)	6.9	4.8	7.7	14.9
Genteel (%)	36.1	28.6	53.8	46.2
Middling sort (%)	33.1	52.4	36.5	44.8
Other (%)	30.6	19.0	9.6	8.9

Note: The figures are derived from reports for January and February (winter) and June and July (summer) for each year. I have classified as middling those artisans in the genteel trades and those who had the prefix "Mr." before their names.

In view of the risks involved, men of property were the most obvious targets, at least for the spectacular robberies that drew public attention. Among those reported in the *Whitehall Evening Post*, we find plenty of men whose cash transfers made them especially vulnerable and desirable: farmers, graziers, brewers, distillers, maltsters, hop-factors, corn dealers, and silk manufacturers. Together with the attorneys, apothecaries, surgeons, the stewards of the gentry, and respectable tradesmen, they made up a third of the victims reported by the *Post*. Equally significant were the gentlemen and -women whose conspicuous consumption marked them out as enviable prey, even from the apparent safety of their chairs and coaches. After all, gentlemen of quality were expected to bring in a good haul: a good cape, wig, watch, a pair of silver buckles, and a fat purse. On a good day robbers might even forsake the clothes and buckles. "We only take Watches and Money Tonight," declared several footpads to a gentleman in Chelsea Fields in February 1750.[48] Those who did not live up to class expectations were angrily denounced. "You ought to have your throat cut for not having a watch" two footpads told an apothecary as they robbed him in Cavendish Square. "D[am]n you," exclaimed a highwayman upon discovering a gentleman in Epping Forest with only a few shillings on his person, "what signifies shooting twenty rascals such as you, who have the Figure of Gentleman without any Money in your Pocket."[49] In popular cant, neither had been a "stanch cull," a person worth robbing.

Contemporary understandings of criminality were strongly conditioned by these images. We do not know how much incidental theft accompanied the dislocations of war or to what degree, as French historians have surmised in other contexts, this involved intraclass stealing. Seamen were not above robbing their ilk or impersonating them at the Pay Office, although those victimized would have normally been men known to have died on a voyage.[50] From the accounts of the Ordinary (chaplain) of Newgate Prison, we know that a few men became desperate enough to venture out of London and accost the first person ripe for picking. Job Savage, who admitted he had blown his prize money on "drinking and Company with Lewd Women" and was consequently reduced to casual work on the ropewalks, went on a binge with some of his mates; they rambled to Whetstone and Barnet intent on robbing whoever came their way.[51] Yet such indiscriminate theft was not of central concern to contemporaries. Rather, they were disturbed by the ubiquitous and audacious character of street and highway robbery, its accompanying violence, and the impunity with which casually formed gangs were allowed to operate. Above all, they were troubled by the threat such robbery posed to the security of property and the maintenance of the social order.

The wealthy seemed especially vulnerable to these depredations, to a point that the crime wave sometimes appeared to be a form of class retribution. The poor "starve, and freeze, and rot among themselves," commented Henry Fielding, "but they beg, and steal and rob among their betters."[52] These anxieties were not viewed in the abstract. They were personally experienced by men and women of wealth and influence, fueling fears in the highest circles. Henry Pelham's eldest daughter was so troubled by reports of street robberies that she hid her diamond earrings under the seat of her hackney chair "for fear of being attacked" on her way to Court.[53] Among those confronted by footpads and highwaymen during these years were the Reverend Dr. Terrick, the prebend of Windsor, soon to be promoted to an Episcopal see, and such members of the nobility as the Earl of Leicester, the Countess of Albemarle, and her son and daughter-in-law, Lord and Lady Bury. John Clevland, the MP for Sandwich and the secretary to the Admiralty, was held up by a highwayman on Barnes Common. Prominent bankers such as Sir Thomas Hankey, were not left out of the account, either; he and his lady were told to stand and deliver on Clapham Common.[54] So, too, was Horace Walpole. In November 1749 he recalled: "As I was returning from Holland House by moonlight, about ten at night, I was attacked by two highwaymen in Hyde Park, and the pistol of one of them going off accidentally, razed the skin under my eye, left some marks of shot on my face, and stunned me. The ball went through the top of the chariot, and if I had sat an inch nearer to the left side, must have gone through my head." A year later he was bemoaning the fact that "robbing is the only thing that goes on with any vivacity," and reported that dining out was as dangerous as a military sortie "owing to the profusion of housebreakers, highwaymen and footpads — and especially because of the savage barbarity of the two latter, who commit the most wanton cruelties."[55]

Was Walpole exaggerating? Was fear of crime the product of media hype? Certainly, as I have already suggested, newspapers kept the issue of crime, and especially violent crime by armed men, before the public eye. In fact, the number of newspaper references to "robbery" rose in the aftermath of the war, reaching a high point in 1751.[56] Yet there is compelling evidence that these referents registered real changes in the crime rate in London. The number of offenses tried at the Old Bailey, London's central criminal court, rose conspicuously in 1748, peaked in 1749, and remained high until 1754. The number of defendants tried for those offenses rose similarly, with over 600 tried annually in the years 1748–54. In the broad category of theft, the trajectory is much the same. The number of defendants charged with theft of all kinds rose from 374 in 1747 to 491 in 1748 to 567 in 1749, a 31 percent increase over one year and a 52 percent increase over two (see graph 1). Committals for theft also remained high until the mid-1750s, hovering between 59 and 67 percent of all offenses. Moreover, most theft was committed by males, rising from 43 percent in 1746 to roughly two-thirds of all theft offenses in the years after 1748 (graph 2). Instructively, the rise in male crime was also recorded at the quarter sessions, for there is a significant rise in the number of males on bail for assault as demobilization unfolded. In June 1747 male assault ran at 49 percent of all assault cases brought before the Middlesex quarter sessions; in 1749 and 1750 it was 60 percent or more.[57] If we zone in on violent theft recorded at the Old Bailey, upon emphatically male crimes such as street or highway robbery, there is a startling increase in the years 1749–51: 350 percent higher than in the previous three years. A similar pattern can be found in burglary. By the early 1750s burglary offenses were 300 percent higher than their prewar years.[58] In sum, demobilization increased male violence on the street and prompted a spectacular spike in violent robbery and burglary.

How did the courts respond to this veritable crime wave that accompanied the aftermath of war? There does not seem to have been a dramatic change in the proportion of people found guilty for theft. With the exception of 1747, that proportion hovered around 60–65 percent for the years 1746 to 1755. Most of those found guilty were transported to the American colonies. Indeed, there was a slight increase in the number sent to Virginia and other American colonies, rising from 65–67 percent in the years 1747–48 to 71–78 percent in the years 1749–1752. Much of this increase was taken up by men, perhaps understandably given the public concern with both random and gang-related theft by young males in the postwar context. Starting in 1750 there was also a noteworthy increase in the proportion of those found guilty who were sentenced to be executed, rising from 4.5 percent in 1749 to 8.1 percent in 1750 and only once falling below 7 percent in the next five years. In the category of

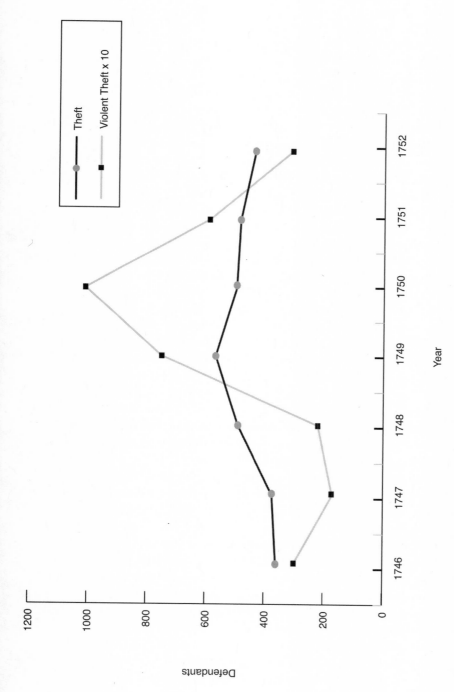

Graph 1: Number of defendants charged with theft and violent theft in London, 1746–1752. *Source:* Old Bailey Proceedings Online, 1746–52.

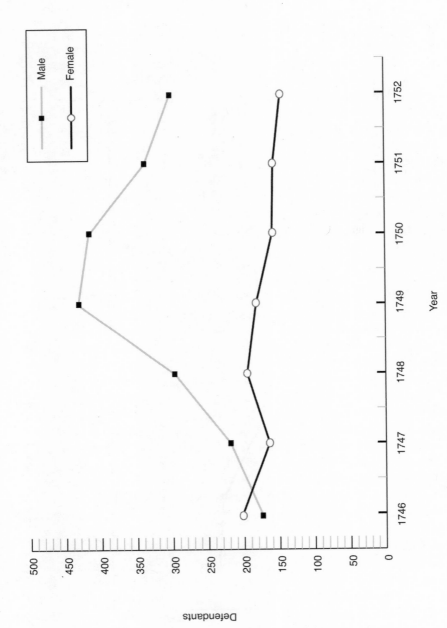

Graph 2: Defendants by gender charged with theft in London, 1746–1752. *Source*: Old Bailey Proceedings Online, 1746–52

violent theft there was again no discernable pattern in the proportion of people found guilty over the years 1746–55, but there was a noticeable rise in the proportion sentenced to hang, rising from 63 percent in 1749 to over 80 percent annually in the years 1750–54. Confronted with the crime wave, the courts were increasingly prepared to make the most dramatic judicial examples.

Among those who met their death at Tyburn were seafarers, or more accurately people who at some point in their early lives had been to sea. The majority was not "bred to the sea," as the Ordinary put it; that is, they were not deliberately apprenticed to a master mariner, or sent off as a cabin boy by their parents, or even, as was the case of Thomas Atkins, sent to sea for fear he would fall into "bad company."[59] More often they were youngsters who had defied their parents' choice of occupation for them, or who simply could not settle down in their assigned apprenticeship, men like Dominic White, from Limerick, who served four and half years of his indenture before he entered a man-of-war.[60] Several drifted into seafaring when their father died or because seafaring seemed a freer, if uncertain, prospect to the jobs they had taken up. Edward Busby of Fulham was taken out of school early because his parents were of "indifferent circumstances"; he didn't like the menial task of brick making and "without recommendation or interest" entered the Royal Navy at the first opportunity.[61] Similarly, John Prior from Clerkenwell was initially apprenticed to a calico printer in West Ham. His master died after six months, a death that sent Prior to the workhouse and to a pauper apprenticeship as a gardener's assistant. He struggled with that job for three years, likely at the behest of his uncle, but eventually he enlisted in the Windsor man-of-war.[62] Declining family fortunes, poverty, poor prospects — all propelled young men to the sea.

About a third of all the men executed at Tyburn in the years 1748–51 had sea experience, which was appreciably higher than the usual roster of "sailors" who met their fate at the Triple Tree.[63] Some had done substantial service in the Royal Navy. Thomas Wallis, who was convicted of robbing a servant of the Reverend Mr. Stephen Rowe of his master's portmanteau and clothes, had spent ten years with Admiral Boscawen in the East Indies. Thomas Applegarth, who was impressed on a man-of-war after two years in the merchant marine, served seven years in the Mediterranean. John Frimley, who began life as a papermaker, spent over nine years in the navy, largely with Haddock's fleet in the Mediterranean. Edward Smith, whose apprenticeship to a saddler was curtailed by bankruptcy, spent four to five years in the navy in Gibraltar and the West Indies. William Brown, who was better educated than most and might well have gone to university, joined the *Hampshire* man-of-war in 1741 and followed his patron, Captain George Mackenzie, on several ships before becoming a midshipman.[64]

None of this service to king and country seems to have mattered much to judge and jury, not even in the case of Brown, who was convicted of forging a letter of attorney to retrieve the prize money of a master's mate.[65] Wallis, whose theft was attributed to "necessity and bad Company," was reprieved, yet this had little to do with his naval record. It had a lot more that had to do with the dubious character of the main prosecuting witness, who was discovered with some of the stolen goods on his person, and to the fact that the Reverend Stephen Roe seems to have confused Wallis with another offender when he visited Newgate.[66] The same also seems to have been true of William Watson. He was found guilty of robbing John Loveless (or Lovelace) on Ratcliff Highway, and although the petition launched in his favor did mention his war service on a bomb-ketch and the *Exeter* man-of-war, the decisive factors in his conditional pardon were twofold. First, the prosecutor admitted he had difficulty detecting Watson in the darkness of the night. Second, Watson was able to marshal substantial local support for a merciful judgment. Church wardens, overseers, the local minister, and even a JP from Tower Liberty, all vouched for his good character.[67]

Naval service was also of little help to John Newcome, who was accused of robbing an attorney at Featherstone Buildings in Holborn. He had crewed on the *Non-such*, the *Princesss Louisa*, and the *Carcase* Bomb and, according to his petition, had "always behaved with the strictest honour and Honesty." His attack upon Mr. Clayton, "an attorney of merit," was nonetheless violent. In grabbing Clayton's hat and wig, Newcome had cut him with a hanger, and when he cried out, Newcome fired two balls at him, one of which grazed his cheek. These actions conformed to the stereotypical violence that was the staple fare of newspaper accounts and hardly put Newcome's theft in a favorable light with judge or jury. Nor did the fact that Newcome was regarded as a "harden'd desperate fellow" who had regular dealings with the criminal fraternity. These actions and impressions compromised his petition for mercy. In the end, his eleven years service in the navy, which began at age ten when his father died, counted for nothing.[68] He may not have killed a man, as did Captain Edward Clark, but he was regarded as a public menace who deserved to die for an outrageous robbery on a man of standing.

Rather like Newcome, seamen were typified as reckless adventurers by the Ordinary of Newgate, John Taylor. In his moral narratives their roving disposition and refusal to take a settled position on land marked them from the beginning as incipient criminals, especially when they had defied their parents' wishes. Once these twenty-year-olds had spent their wages and prize money on drink and whores, they fell prey to London's low life, took up or were duped by more seasoned criminals, and finished their young lives on the gallows. That is how their tales were typically constructed, although it is sometimes possible to discover more complexities to their crimes, to read them against the grain.

John Perry, who was impressed three times in his teenage years and emerged from the navy with only £13 in his pocket, found it difficult to settle back with his parents in London. He had been deep in his cups when he robbed one Terence Walden of his waistcoat and handkerchief, enough to take him to the gallows at age twenty-one. Thomas Perry, an illiterate seaman who served in the navy and aboard privateers throughout the war, squandered his money on drink. Driven to desperation, he seems to have become enmeshed in the business of forging seamen's tickets, in which he was clearly a novice and quite possibly an unwary accomplice. Edward Busby was driven to crime as he awaited his wages and racked up debts that put him in jail. Once released from prison, he tried but failed to get another berth before resorting to robbing in the Islington area with an ex-coachman nicknamed Captain Flash. Thomas Holly entered the *Success* man-of-war at age thirteen and spent some time in New England before returning to the navy. Upon his discharge after the war, he struggled to support his parents and partner and eventually robbed two females in Limehouse to pay for his own woman's lying-in expenses.

None of these stories conform to the formulaic narratives of youthful defiance, roving, and moral decline that informed the Ordinary's *Account*. Or even to Tom Idle's tale in William Hogarth's *Industry and Idleness*. They are complicated by the difficulties of returning to civilian life in an age when pay was withheld from seamen for intolerable lengths of time and according to rules that were not well understood. They are also compounded by demographic misfortune, of parents dying before their children were securely placed in society, setting them adrift in a world where interest, influence, and extended kin provided the only real safety nets. Thomas Hazard, whose father died when he was nine and whose mother more or less abandoned him thereafter, was apprenticed into the merchant marine where he was badly mistreated and ran away. He eventually gravitated to the Royal Navy, where he spent more than a decade. Marked as a deserter from the *Mercury,* he had difficulty recovering his pay, and while attending the Pay Office he fell in with some hardened thieves. They included William Cavanagh, a twenty-five-year-old seaman from Dublin, who believed that thieving "was a better trade than others and that at the end there would be a 'scragging' and that would be the end of it."[69] Recruited to their gang, partly because he owed money to Cavanagh's landlord, young Tom Hazard robbed several gentlemen along the waterfront on both sides of the Thames before being taken up and hanged with other members of the gang. Ned Ward of Waterford, whose soldier-father brought him to London when his mother died, served over four years to a cutler on Tower Hill before joining the navy and serving on three ships of the line. Upon discharge he tried to recover a job in the cutlery business but was able to do so only intermittently, finally committing several burglaries in the east end of London to make ends meet. John Newton was an orphan who had managed to carve out a reasonable career in the Royal Navy, serving twelve years as a common sailor before becoming a boatswain's mate. Unfortunately he quarreled with the ship's mate, who resented the fact that he "looked upon himself in the Capacity of an Officer, tho' of inferior degree." Newton received some "rough treatment" at the hands of the mate in Milford Haven, at which point that he decided to quit the service and return to London, where he discovered he had missed his chance to recover his prize money, which had been sent on to the Chatham Chest. Reduced to unloading coals on the docks, he fell in with the wrong crowd and was inveigled by a local criminal, one Symonds, alias Spanish Jack, to embark on a series of thefts in the area. This proved his undoing.

How, then, did these seamen respond to the awful judgment of the courts? In view of the difficulties they encountered in recovering their wages for service to king and country, did they rail at authority for the harsh punishments they received, or at the very least gesture their defiance of the law's legitimacy? Some certainly did. Like the "active, daring spirit" Billy Cavanagh, who proudly confessed he had been thieving since the age of fifteen, some seamen were resolved to die hard. Patrick Demsey, a thirty-two-year-old seamen from Ireland who was hanged alongside his brother for robbing a merchant in Lombard Street, refused to remove his hat at the Old Bailey "in Defiance of all Law and Justice." To reiterate the point, he was "insolent" and "audacious" at Tyburn and showed no signs of penitence.[70] Similarly, Ely Smith, a twenty-one-year-old from Smithfield who had done a spell in Bridewell and had endured five hard years in the navy, appeared undaunted at the gallows, as did his fellow gang members.[71] So, too, did Joseph Peacock, a Westminster lad who began life as a cabin boy and moved in and out of the navy for the rest of his life, sometimes pilfering from his mates and always spending his money faster than he made it. According to the Ordinary, he behaved at the gallows in a "very surly manner," an unrepentant pilferer and thief who showed no remorse for his actions.

Bringing malefactors to a true repentance was part of the Ordinary's job as the chaplain of Newgate prison. Within the ritual of an execution it was of some importance that the criminal repent, ask God for forgiveness, and, it was hoped, tell the congregated audience of the perils of pursuing a life of crime. This was not simply for the criminal's own sake; it was because criminals were "public examples." As one writer in 1754 stated, "The use and intent of punishment is not to gratify the person injured, but to procure, by exemplary correction, a benefit to the public."[72] Criminals who appeared undaunted at the gallows, or in some manner denied their guilt, compromised the spectacle of punishment. At the very least they blunted its official message. In the mid-century decade this did not happen often. Even malefactors who joked with others in the press yard seem to have become more contemplative as they approached the gallows at the end of Oxford Road. As the Ordinary put it, they "quietly resigned their breath to the Satisfaction of the Law."[73] John Robertson, who was sentenced to hang for burglary in October 1751, troubled the Ordinary a great deal. Although he attended chapel, he seemed a "harden'd" criminal. "No Admonitions could perswade, nor any Threats affright him; he was invincibly bent upon Wickedness, and, as far as he could, he pursued it to the last." On his final day he kicked off his shoes with disdain as the cart moved out of Newgate, not wanting to fulfill the proverb of dying in his shoes; that is, dying a violent death. In the cart he seemed "as little unconcerned as if he had only been going to a whipping," observed the Ordinary, but "when he came to the fatal Place, he grew pale and stood aghast, and great Horrors indeed he seemed to be affected with."[74]

The Ordinary, John Taylor, seems to have recalled this with some relief. On this occasion four tough smugglers accompanied Robertson to the gallows, not to mention one seaman with an "intractable temper" and another who was basically framed by a thief-taker. With this company Tyburn could easily have become a site of defiant insolence rather than exemplary justice, something that a raucous irreverent crowd might well have enjoyed. Fortunately, Taylor concluded, "The whole melancholy Scene was conducted with the utmost Peace and good Order."[75]

Taylor was not alone in his anxieties. Over the decades there had been a mounting criticism of the Tyburn procession and execution. "All the way, from Newgate to Tyburn," wrote Bernard de Mandeville in 1725, "is one continued fair for Whores and Rogues of the meaner sort." Idle apprentices and old offenders made the procession a sort of "Jubilee," he complained, to which "young Rakes of Fortune" joined after a "Night's Debauch." Their behavior subverted the purposes for which public hangings were designed; namely, to deter the public from crime and to heed the spectacle of the condemned. The criminals themselves were also diverted from seriously pondering their fate by the number of gin cordials they received as the procession wound its way to the Triple Tree. Drunk, insensate, the most notorious of them also received boisterous accolades of support from sympathetic onlookers.[76] The press of the crowd, the often brutal efforts of the sheriff's men to drive a line through it, and "the want of order among the Attendants" made the processions "very void of that decent Solemnity that would be required to make them awful."[77] Or so Mandeville thought. The reluctance of the sheriffs and under-sheriffs to attend executions did not help either; petty officers struggled difficulty to contain rambunctious crowds along the route and were often quite overwhelmed by the throng that greeted them at the gallows.[78] As the penultimate scene in Hogarth's *Industry and Idleness* depicted (figure 3), the admonitions of the Methodist preacher to Tom Idle are totally drowned out and overwhelmed by the cacophony of the jostling crowd, with its hawkers, peddlers, pickpockets, and bemused onlookers.

Whether the Tyburn procession was quite the carnival of misrule that Hogarth and Mandeville depicted has been much debated by historians. There are those that emphasize its countercultural features, its Brechtian irreverence in the face of official homilies. The canting language of the day, so the argument goes, saw a hanging very differently from that of officialdom. The words uttered by the judge at the sentencing were "cramp words"; the execution became a "collar day," the Sheriff's Ball," or "Paddington Fair."[79] To be hanged was to swing, to morris or dance, to be jammed, collared, nubbed, or tucked up. A public hanging was not a pretty affair. Since the malefactor was simply turned off the cart to dangle from the Triple Tree at the end of a rope, it normally took fifteen minutes or so to die by asphyxiation. Lighter folk were sometimes weighed down so their death agonies would be reduced. Hoods or, the in case of women, handkerchiefs concealed the bloated face and lolling tongue, although nothing could hide a pissen pair of pants. Popular cant jested with the majesty of the law and the dreadful nature of the execution, without detracting from its physical effects. Its mock jollity was supplemented by the gay clothes and bouquets that the condemned sometimes wore. The preferred color was white, as if the victims were going to their wedding rather than their death, or perhaps, assuming they were religious and believed they could be saved, as if they were going to meet their Maker.

Some historians have argued that the Tyburn fair was cathartic rather than countercultural, that it really was about inversion rather than subversion.[80] But contemporaries did not see it this way. It seemed to mock death not prompt awful examples. One writer thought public executions did not inspire "pity and terror" and made no "visible impression on the minds of spectators." Executions were "not only useless," he declared, "but dangerous, as they accustom the populace to look on violent death with indifference, and instead of rendering the punishment terrible, insensibly render it familiar."[81] Henry Fielding, a justice of the peace for Westminster and Middlesex, was troubled in much the same manner. He was appalled by the intrepidity of the condemned, by men who joked with the executioner rather than confronting

Fig 3: William Hogarth, the scene at Tyburn, plate 11 of *Industry and Idleness*, 1747. © British Museum.

death with the appropriate piety and penance. Commenting on the executions of March 1752, he observed that "the Criminals themselves behaved with the wonted Affectation of Mock-Heroism, and instead of endeavouring to give any marks of true Contrition and Repentance, seemed to vie with each other in displaying a Contempt of their shameful Death, and a total Indifference as to what might befall them after it." Their friends "seemed to have exerted their utmost skill, by all manner of Sports and Pastimes, to keep up the Spirits of the present Sufferers." The consequence was that "instead of making the Gallows an Object of Terror, our Executions contribute to make it an Object of Contempt in the Eye of the Malefactor; and we sacrifice the Lives of men, not for "the Reformation, but for the Diversion of the Populace."[82] He was beginning to think that it would be better to dispense with the procession to Tyburn altogether and to execute people in private. "A murder behind the scenes, if the poet knows how to manage it, will affect the audience with greater terror than if it was acted before their eyes." The following year he noted approvingly that the rumor that three men were hanged at Newgate had struck horror among the "lower People."[83]

One of the issues that compounded the problem of disorder at Tyburn concerned the bodies of the condemned. Under grants given by Henry VIII and Charles II, surgeons were allowed each year six corpses of those executed at Tyburn for the purposes of dissection. This practice did not endear surgeons to the general populace, for in popular belief dismemberment of the body meant that the soul could never rest. As Ruth Richardson has sensitively shown, there was a long-standing conviction in Christian thought that the soul should remain close to the body until the Last Judgment, and because it did not immediately depart the body upon death it had to be protected from evil spirits.[84] Moreover, in the liminal period between death and burial the body itself was neither alive nor dead, and if not properly attended, it could return to haunt the living. Viewed in this light, the disposing of a corpse was not taken lightly. It was a matter of grave concern to kin and friends to buy a coffin and arrange a funeral rather than allow the hangman to hand over a body to the surgeons.[85] No concession was made to science. The appropriation of a body for dissection was a violation, a travesty to the soul, a monstrous act that no amount of scientific pleading could dispel.

Consequently there was a continuing struggle for the bodies of the condemned at Tyburn, something that amused Mandeville. After the "Tragedy" of the hanging, he sardonically reported, "the next Entertainment is the Squabble between the Surgeons and the Mob about the dead bodies of the Malefactors that are not to be hang'd in Chains. They have suffer'd the Law (cries the Rabble) and shall have no other Barbarities put upon them. We know what you are, and will not leave them until we see them buried."[86] In Mandeville's eyes, the "superstitious Reverence of the Vulgar for a Corpse, even of a Malefactor, and the strong Aversion they have against dissecting them," was "prejudicial to the Publick" for all improvements in the science of surgery were to be encouraged.

This was not how the Tyburn crowd saw it. As the College of Physicians explained to Parliament in 1720, the condemned went to their deaths in such dread of dissection that they often prevailed upon "their Confederates & other disorderly people to take & carry away the executed bodys in defiance of all legal authority in a forceful and violent manner."[87] The Company of Barber Surgeons made the same complaint. It noted that the soldiers on duty at the gallows sometimes sympathized with the crowd and facilitated the rescue of bodies from the clutches of the surgeons. The surgeons asked for further reinforcements, although this request seems only to have intensified the struggle at the gallows. At various points in the next two decades the surgeons complained to the aldermen of London that "great Numbers of loose and disorderly persons" had congregated at Tyburn and had impeded their efforts to secure corpses. Among these were sailors. In 1738 a "great many Sailors" rescued the body of James Buchanan from Execution Dock at Wapping. The next year, after a struggle over bodies at Tyburn, "the Rabble was so outrageous that they tore away one of the Bodies from a private Surgeon in Featherstone Buildings after he had got it to his house, and carry'd it off in Triumph."[88] A decade later, around the time of the proclamation of the peace, eight sailors armed with truncheons snatched the body of John Lancaster, a velvet weaver who had robbed his master, from the surgeons' men who were carrying it to the company hall. The sailors carried the body in state through Islington and Houndsditch before delivering it to Lancaster's mother.[89]

The intervention of the seamen in October 1748 spelt trouble for the authorities at Tyburn. Normally the sheriffs would have chosen unclaimed bodies for dissection, and the hangman was keen to sell them to Surgeons' Hall. The bodies of seamen were prime candidates for the surgeon's slab because the majority of them had no kin in London, probably not even extended kin, and unless mess mates were present, their bodies were unlikely to have been recovered from the gallows. But the many seamen who congregated in London for pay and prize money after the war were determined not to let this happen. They were tetchy enough about the fact that many of their fellow tars were turned off to begin with. In February 1749 a gentleman in a Spring Garden coffeehouse flippantly remarked on a seaman who had recently been hanged at Tyburn. He was promptly hauled out of the tavern by some sailors who took exception to his tone, forced to his knees in the street kennel, and ordered to ask their pardon.[90] As tempers rose over the number of tars hanged at

Tyburn, seamen congregated at the gallows to ensure that they were at least given a decent burial. In February 1749 they took away the corpse of John Frimley, a sailor convicted of highway robbery. At the following "hanging match," sailors rescued the bodies of Thomas Holley and John Burk, two young seamen from Dublin and York, both of whom had fought in the war and had come to grief in the postwar demobilization.[91] Thereafter seamen mustered to demand the bodies of any tars vulnerable to dissection. The most critical confrontation occurred in October 1749, when nine of the sixteen hanged were seafarers, and few were likely to have friends in London to reclaim their bodies. None of the maritime malefactors was born in London. Only one was born in England, the others coming predominantly from Ireland, but also from as far afield as Denmark, Virginia, and the Guinea coast.

On this occasion hundreds of seamen assembled at the gallows armed with cutlasses and bludgeons, an assembly made more ominous by the controversial hanging of a wigmaker involved in some sailor-dominated bawdy house riots on the Strand. That episode I shall discuss in the next chapter. The sheriff at the time, Stephen Theodore Janssen, was offered military aid, but he chose to face the music without military support. He sought to reassert civil authority at Tyburn and insisted on a full turnout of his officers. Janssen mustered a substantial posse of constables, as many as 300 it was reported, some of them on horseback. From this position of strength, he parleyed with the sailors. The sheriff offered them the bodies in return for their good behavior. One newspaper reported that Janssen promised to "do them all the Service in his Power on every Occasion," although he also reminded them that if there was any trouble, he would read the Riot Act.[92] This informal agreement was accepted: indeed, some papers were relieved that the seamen appeared to treat Janssen "with every imaginable respect."[93] In the melee that followed there were some irregularities, although these occurred offstage. In the rush to retrieve the bodies from the clutches of the surgeons, four of the corpses were left in the fields near Tyburn until a gentlemen paid for their burial. The following day body snatchers dug them up and sold them to private surgeons. Whether all of them reached the medical men is unclear, for one paper reported that people in the neighborhood of Paddington prevented two getting to the surgeons.[94]

The executions of October 1749 established a rough-and-ready understanding between the local authorities and the seamen: essentially the pact meant bodies for a modicum of decorum. Sailors would continue to muster in force to recover their fellow tars, but they were persuaded to preserve the peace once promises were made to keep the corpses from the surgeons. The local authorities, for their part, were able to maintain a reasonable flow of corpses to the surgeons because the solidarity of the seamen tended to be occupational rather than class-based. The tars were not interested in protecting every plebeian body from dissection, only those of their ilk. The sheriffs had little difficulty sending murderers to the surgeons, for conventionally murderers drew little sympathy from a scaffold crowd. By late 1752 this practice was facilitated by the Murder Act, which gave judges the statutory right to order a dissection. But the sheriffs sent others to the surgeons before the Murder Act came into effect. Two malefactors without friends were handed over to the surgeons in June 1750, for example, and in October of that year, at the crowded Tyburn which saw the highwayman-celebrity James Maclean die, one John Griffiths, a young merchant seaman, was made available for dissection, even though he was born in Bishopsgate Street and must have had kin in the city.[95] Very occasionally the authorities alerted the public that they would hand malefactors to the surgeons. These included two Irishmen, Richard Broughton and James Hayes, who were well-known thieves in Covent Garden and who had badly cut up one of the turnkeys in Newgate when endeavoring to escape. No one came to claim their bodies, which were cut down "without the least stir or worry." The same happened to that of Henry Grover, a former laborer from Hertfordshire accused of horse theft.[96]

Although the newspapers seemed relieved that some solemnity and decorum had been reestablished at Tyburn, particularly over the disposition of the bodies, not everyone agreed that it was sufficient to sustain the majesty of the law. Henry Fielding, for one, continued to rail at the mock-heroism of the gallows, singling out another former seamen, Robert Lake, for his jests to the executioner in April 1752. Indeed, he remarked of the five sentenced to hang that day, "No Heroes within the Memory of Man ever met their Fate with more Boldness and Intrepidity, and consequently with more felonious Glory."[97] This was hyperbole, but the fact remained that not every criminal approached the gallows with a becoming penitence. There were enough examples of gallows bravado, of criminals insisting on their innocence, to unsettle the official link between justice and law and destabilize the purpose of public execution as a deterrent and signifier of royal justice.

On balance, however, contemporaries came through the crime wave of 1748–53 without any strong sense that public capital punishment was seriously compromised. The notion that the respectable classes were becoming increasingly disenchanted with the spectacle of Tyburn on grounds of humanity and propriety does not appear to hold up. Very few voices were heard on that score. More seem to have responded to the crime wave by demanding that the number and severity of executions be increased.[98] "Plain Truth" in the *London Magazine* wrote that all bodies should be given to the surgeons precisely because "the generality of mankind have a very great aversion to be anatomized."[99] Henry Fielding hoped to curb the bacchanalia of executions by having private executions, thereby eliminating the procession to Tyburn, which sometimes took two hours to complete. In an open letter to the Commons committee on crime in 1751, another person suggested that the introduction of galleys and the enslavement of some offenders not only would make better use of the young men who were cut down in their prime but would render Tyburn a more solemn and select affair.[100]

Yet some believed that such radical surgery was unnecessary. In the eyes of the one pamphleteer, the reaffirmation of civil authority at Tyburn by the London sheriffs had revealed that the conventional system was not beyond repair. "Our laws are just, merciful and perfectly agreeable to the genius of this nation," wrote Philonomos. Public executions could remain "the true language of the law."[101] Sheriff Janssen's spirited conduct had confirmed this. "The Order, Decency, and Solemnity, visible in the melancholy Processions," remarked the *London Evening Post,* "shew our Constitution in its most distinguish'd light; and manifestly prove that a small Military force is sufficient to procure and protest us from intestine Feuds and Commotions."[102] All that was required was more care in ensuring that malefactors were sober at the gallows, for a drunken offender might not be awed by the gravity of the occasion or be appropriately contrite. Furthermore, the custom of allowing richer offenders to travel to the gallows in hackney coaches should be discontinued. It was an "injustice to the Publick . . . to suffer one Malefactor to be distinguished from another," thought one author, "for as all Executions are, and ought to be an Example to the Living to deter them from the like End, so surely, the Ignominy and Shame attending thereon cannot be too much and too openly exposed."[103]

All that was needed was more selectivity in choosing who should face the full spectacle of punishment and with what choreography of fear. Certainly the demobilization crisis had dictated that this choreography should be fearsome. In the four years 1748–52, no less than forty malefactors were hanged in chains in the southern counties of England, twice as many as had been gibbeted in the previous four years.[104] These included irresolute smugglers in the southeast, whose audacity, as we shall see in chapter 5, was deeply troubling to the authorities. In fact, at least one in every four smugglers hanged during these years were suspended in chains to rot in the wind, sometimes from prominent sites such as Selsey Bill in Sussex in full view of the coast, as well as at the scene of their crimes.[105] Others included highwaymen, such as Gabriel Tomkyns, who had killed someone while robbing the Chester Mail and was condemned to hang in chains outside of Bedford, where the incident occurred;[106] James Cooper, who had robbed and killed the park keeper of Sir Kendrick Clayton, near Croyden in Surrey; and, most controversially, Thomas

Colley, who was sentenced to death at the Hertfordshire assizes for the murder of Ruth Osborne, a reputed witch. Osborne had been subjected to a "swimming" at Marlston Mere, in the parish of Tring, at which Colley presided, and although he won local sympathy for his actions, the judges were determined to make an example of him. In fact, they delayed his execution and gibbeting until a large detachment of Horse Guards could be mobilized to ensure order at the gallows and beyond.[107]

The years after Aix-la-Chapelle saw no relaxation of the doctrine of "maximum severity" as Sir Leon Radzinowicz suggested. Quite the contrary. From the Fens to Portsmouth, gibbets groaned with the bodies of smugglers, highwayman, and outrageous murderers. In London and Middlesex, the proportion of malefactors who were capitally convicted *and* executed was higher in 1748–53 than after the Seven Years' War (1763–68) and the War of American Independence (1783–88).[108] The balance of terror and mercy swung perceptibly toward to former after 1748, and the logical extension of this trend was the Murder Act of 1752. It asserted that judicial terror would work if it was properly applied to the right cases and in the right manner; that is, by marking out murderers for public dissection or by hanging their corpses in chains, punishments that quite deliberately dismembered and scattered the body in ways that touched deep anxieties in the plebeian public. Framed as property crime was peaking in the metropolitan area, it registered the ruling-class fear of robbery with violence, among smuggling gangs and demobilized servicemen, in particular, and the threat this posed to life and social order.[109] This explains why penalties were introduced in the act against anyone who attempted to rescue culprits, something that would seem incongruous if the crime had simply been domestic murder.

What the language of the statute did not disclose was that the Murder Act was also a face-saving measure to the current predicament at Tyburn. By legislating that murderers could and should be dissected, the statute took some of the heat off the sheriffs who had been besieged by angry sailors demanding the bodies of their fellows. It was the demobilization crisis of 1749–52 and the collective action of the sailors wanting to save their fellow tars from the ignominy of dissection that had tested the integrity of public executions.

In the panic over the crime wave and the renewed debate about what forms of punishment might best address it, the sociological dimensions of the crisis tended to get lost. At first sight this seems surprising. The idea that demobilization might be a tonic to crime was understood. It was reinforced by the conspicuous number of seamen who were hanged at Tyburn and by their crew mates who thronged to collect their bodies. When Janssen confronted the sailors in October 1749 one observer remarked: "It were indeed greatly to be wish'd some effectual Means were fallen upon to employ so useful a Body of Men in the Time of Peace, the want of which is one of the principal Causes of the many Robberies and other Mischiefs committed in this Metropolis." This observation was not a casual one. In January 1751 the *London Evening Post* featured a petition from the "British Mariners" to the "Nobility, Gentry and Commonalty." It pointed out that while the navy was touted as the bulwark of England and one of the sources of its commercial success, the common seamen and their families suffered the consequences of long delays in the payment of wages and prize money. "We are grieved to the Heart for the ignominious Deaths of many of our Fellow-Sufferers," the petition stated, "who, driven into Despair through mere Necessity, have run headlong into Male-Practice, purely to keep themselves from starving, and made their exits on the Gallows."[110]

Public petitions like this very explicitly linked demobilization to the upsurge in crime. Yet such an observation does not seem to have dislodged or seriously undermined the persistent and prevailing notion that criminality was at root a failure of the moral order, an individual failing, and within the laboring class aggravated by deficient schooling or parenting and a plebeian predilection to luxury and idleness.[111] Necessity was sometimes offered as an excuse for crime, but it was treated with skepticism and all too frequently wrapped in moral censure by people like the Ordinary of Newgate, who wondered whether needs were not really generated by debauchery and drink. Consequently the plausible connection between demobilization and crime remained unstable and in the end marginal. Jolly tars were, after all, stereotypically reckless young men whose wanderlust propelled them to low company, adversity, and all too frequently, to crime.

Certainly the relation of demobilization to scarcity and crimes of need scarcely touched the conscience of the political elite. When Parliament debated the manning of the navy, comments about de-mobbed tars ending up on Tyburn were virtually absent. Only Robert Nugent referred to unemployed seamen rotting in debtors' prison or hanging on the gallows.[112] Rather, MPs were absorbed with issues of national security and fiscal retrenchment when discussing how many sailors should be retained or discharged at the peace, turning a blind eye to the social repercussions of demobilization.

To be sure, the government did support some proposals to reintegrate seamen into society. It offered them the opportunity of taking up trades without the usual apprenticeships; it exempted certified seamen from the vagrant laws so they might search for work without harassment, although it did not exempt them from the debtors' laws.[113] When philanthropists and merchants promoted a British herring industry in the aftermath of the war, the problem of addressing the ill effects of demobilization was also recognized. One of the principal promoters of this scheme, John Lockman, urged that seamen, "so valuable a Part of the Commonwealth," should be gainfully employed so that they would not slip into a life of crime or join foreign fleets. He wanted a ready-made naval reserve that could be redeployed quickly in war conditions. Yet Lockman, who recognized that society had a Janus-faced attitude toward seamen, revering them in time of war and discarding them in peace, was something of an exception.[114] As we shall see in subsequent chapters, the conventional links between crime and luxury, or crime and idleness, were profound. Too often the causal connection between theft and demobilization was scattered in the winds of anxiety about violent crime and immorality.

The Sailors' Revenge

On 1 July 1749, three sailors from the *Grafton* man-of-war visited a brothel, the Crown tavern near St. Mary le Strand. We know nothing of their sexual encounters, but we do know that they lost their watches and a lot of money; according to contemporary accounts, 30 guineas, 4 moidores, and a bank note worth £20. In total about £60, probably a good deal of their wartime earnings. The sailors complained to the landlord that they had been robbed by the women. When they demanded restitution, the landlord had his bouncers toss them into the street. Promising vengeance, the seamen returned with a great many of their fellow tars and proceeded to gut the house. They "entirely demolish'd all the Goods," the *Bath Journal* reported, "cut all the Feather-Beds to Pieces, and strew'd the Feathers in the Street." They made a bonfire of the household effects, including all the "Wearing Apparel," and turned the women they found in the house "naked" into the street; that is to say, clothed in little more than their shifts or petticoats.[1] The sailors then proceeded to break all the windows and inflicted some damage to the adjoining house. By the time a guard of soldiers arrived from Somerset House and the Tilt Yard to quell the riot, the tavern was a wreck. All that was achieved was the arrest of two rioters found in the house and the prevention of an attack on a brothel a few doors to the east (see figure 4).

The tars were not intimidated by this military intervention. On the follow-

Fig 4: Charles Mosley, *The Tar's Triumph, or Bawdy House Battery*, 1749. © British Museum.

ing evening they returned to wreak havoc on their second target, the Bunch of Grapes run by one Joseph Stanhope. In roughly three hours they gutted the house and burnt furniture, beds, and clothes on a bonfire, taking care, so John Cleland later reported, to discourage looting.[2] They then moved farther east, almost to Temple Bar, where they began to attack the Star Tavern opposite Devereux Court. The keeper of the Star, Peter Wood, managed to alert Saunders Welsh, the high constable of Holborn. Unable to prevail on the mob to disperse, Welsh applied to the Tilt Yard for a military force to disperse the crowd.[3] This time the troops arrested six rioters, including Bosavern Penlez, a journeyman wigmaker, who was picked up in Carey Street.

None of the men examined before Henry Fielding at Bow Street on the morning of 3 July were sailors. The tars had been quick to defend their comrades from arrest and had even broken into the watch-house to rescue the two taken up on the first of July. Even so, Fielding was fearful of further rescue attempts. He wrote to the Duke of Bedford, his patron and the secretary of state, claiming that 3,000 sailors were assembling in Wapping and threatening to march to Westminster to pull down more bawdy houses.[4] In Fielding's mind, the gravity of the situation was underscored by the terms on which he committed the rioters to Newgate. All save one were charged under the Riot Act with attempting to pull down dwelling houses and "levying war against the king."[5]

These were very serious charges. Not all contemporaries would agree with the newly appointed Bow Street magistrate that attacks upon brothels were inherently treasonable acts. As the *Remembrancer* remarked, "the *occasional* Chastisement of such Houses by the Hands of the Populace has been formerly connived at by our Magistrates, if not by our Laws, in the same Manner as the Chastisement of Covent Garden pickpockets is connived at now."[6] Attacks on brothels and prostitutes had in the not-too-distant past been a Shrovetide revel, part of the rough justice of the street. In view of the difficulties of prosecuting bawdy houses through local presentments, many were probably pleased to see brothel keepers getting their comeuppance at the hands of hearty tars, especially Peter Wood, who had been prosecuted and fined for keeping a house of ill repute, and would be again.[7] John Cleland certainly thought so. Although he used the brothel as a site of sensual pleasure and pornographic voyeurism in his novel *Fanny Hill,* he was far more censorious about its immoral contaminations in his reflections on the Strand riots. Brothel keepers like Wood were in a state of war with mankind, he asserted, preying on one sex and exploiting the other. They virtually enslaved their whores in a vortex of debt, forcing them to wear flimsy, gaudy dresses and to affect a "nauseous gaiety" to ensnare their prey. "Any man who encountered such a whore and was "not entirely swallow'd up by Passion," he reflected, "might easily read through this outward Shew in her wild distracted Looks, how little she is affected with the Man she hugs, kisses, and embraces, while his Money is her only Aim."[8] All too frequently these women ended up as "infected gangreen'd" members of society, destroyed by "the Rottenness of Diseases, or the intrail-burning Fire of Spirits in a Gin-Shop."[9] They were so corrupted that they missed their potential vocation as the virtuous wives and daughters of a healthy commonwealth. Cleland spurned the idea that the sailors' attack on the brothels was seditious. It was disciplined, focused, and largely sanctioned by the public, he asserted, even by the troops who could have intervened earlier than they did.

Fielding clearly had other ideas about the nature of the attacks, and doubtless his experiences as a magistrate influenced his outlook. Earlier in the year he had been involved in bringing to trial the Hawkhurst gang, a band of notorious smugglers operating on the south coast that had openly defied the authorities for several years, to the point of flogging, torturing, and killing customs officers and informers who had attempted to bring them to justice. Like the attorney general, Fielding doubtless interpreted their behavior as a war against the government, threatening to bring the system of law and order into disrepute. In London the reverberations of this outlawry were felt in the extra security measures required when conveying smugglers to Newgate and the condemned to Tyburn, not to mention and the daring and successful rescue of at least two of the smugglers, William Gray and Thomas Kemp, from this prison.[10] In the context of the postwar crime wave and the glaring robberies in the heart of London, Fielding felt social relations had reached a crisis of confidence in which plebeian rebellion and licentiousness threatened to overwhelm the system of government.[11] In his efforts to take informations against the Strand rioters he had been forced to request military support. When the rioters were eventually conveyed to Newgate, further rescue attempts were made. Confronted with this disdain for the law, Fielding was disposed to take a hard line against sailors and others who attacked property, even if that property was an unwholesome as the brothels he had condemned in his charge to the Westminster grand jury a few days earlier. There he had described the bawdy houses as seminaries of vice that corrupted city youth and tainted British posterity.[12]

The Duke of Bedford, the secretary of state and Fielding's patron, agreed with his client's assessment of the situation. He consented to a public prosecution of the six men, but only three went forward to trial. One, James Hetherington, died in prison. The bills of indictment of two others were found ignoramus, including that of Edward Wrench, the only gentleman among the group, who was said to have egged on the rioters with shouts of "My boys, haul away."[13]

That left three: Benjamin Launder, Bosavern Penlez and John Wilson. Launder had an alibi. He had been drinking at the Globe in Brydges Street between midnight and 1:00 a.m., when the attack on the Star was in motion, and although he was later apprehended coming down the stairs there, it was by the very soldier, James Ives, with whom he had earlier shared a pint. This made him look like an innocent or curious bystander, or at least was constructed as such. As a result of Ives's testimony and a tough cross-examination of Peter Wood by his counsel, he was acquitted, both for the indictment under the Riot Act and also on a charge of stealing a poker from Joseph Stanhope, the keeper of the Bunch of Grapes. That left Penlez and Wilson. Both of these journeymen were seen sometime after midnight breaking down the partitions in the parlor and threatening Peter Wood on the stairs. Wood said that when he pleaded for his life, they exclaimed, "You dog, are you not dead yet?"[14] On this evidence these two young men were found guilty and sentenced to hang.

Many were upset with this verdict. To begin with, convictions under the Riot Act were controversial. Some thought the act little more than a ministerial ploy for suppressing legitimate protest. A writer in *Old England* suggested that it was a "M——st——l Law obtained in the times of Party Violence, when the Rage of the Whigs carried them even beyond the Excesses they had imputed to the Tories."[15] Whether one concurred with this view or not, people would have remembered that when it first came into force in 1715, the act was used to penalize rioters who attacked chapels and partisan alehouses, not brothels. Moreover, both Penlez and Wilson had good reputations in the neighborhood and were able to summon character witnesses, including past employers. The only testimony against them came from a pimp, his wife, and a servant, hardly trustworthy people. At the trial it was disclosed that Wood used others as the nominal tenants of his brothel, evidently in an attempt to shield himself from further prosecutions for keeping a house of ill repute. Wood also admitted that he had been fined for keeping a house without a liquor license. His and his wife's reputation was so low that the collector of the local scavenger rate said "he would not hang a cat or dog on their evidence." It seemed patently unjust that two young men should be cut off in the prime of youth on the evidence of such rogues. Even the jury at the Old Bailey appeared to subscribe to these sentiments, for while it acknowledged the culpability of Penlez and Wilson, it also recommended them for a royal pardon.

Three weeks later, eighty-seven of the principal inhabitants of St. Clement Danes petitioned the Duke of Newcastle for the reprieve of the two men, and more petitions followed from genteel circles to the Privy Council and to the king at Kensington.[16] Neither these petitions nor the jury's recommendation were entirely successful. Although it was reported that the king was sympathetic, the presiding judge, John Willes, Chief Justice of the Court of Common Pleas, insisted that some example be made.[17] Wilson, the journeymen shoemaker, seems to have had deeper roots in the neighborhood and was alleged by one employer to have "followed his business as hard as any I know in the trade."[18] He was thus reprieved at the eleventh hour. Bosavern Penlez, the son of a native of Jersey and an Exeter clergyman, had been apprenticed as a wigmaker by the Sons of the Clergy. He had been in London only two years working as a journeymen. Although one contemporary commentator thought wig-making journeymen were "pretty constantly employed," the constant changes in style made it a precarious business, in one day and out of fashion the next.[19] Fully employed journeymen were likely to get £12–15 a year plus room and board, but many appear to have led a hand-to-mouth existence. As one journeymen remarked, "The greatest part of us, after Working all our lives, must, at last, die Beggars."[20] Judging by Penlez's testimony he was somewhat down on his luck when the riots occurred, having changed his residence on the very day he drank with his pals. His indiscretions and his relative obscurity took him to the gallows.

Penlez bore Wilson no grudge for his good luck; he wished him well. He seemed reconciled to his fate. In fact he urged his friends to discourage the Tyburn crowd from making any rescue attempt.[21] Such an event was quite possible, for previous executions had seen battles over the bodies of the condemned to prevent their dissection at the hands of the surgeons. The executions of some notorious smugglers had necessitated an armed guard for fear they would be rescued. There was some fear that the sailors who mustered at the gallows might rescue Penlez, or at the very least, given the sympathy that had swelled around his sentence, prevent his body ending up on the dissection table of Surgeons' Hall.[22]

Extra guards were sent to Holborn bar to accompany the sheriffs and his officers in their procession to Tyburn. But the sheriff, Stephen Theodore Janssen, dismissed them and proceeded up Oxford Road to the Fatal Tree with the high constables and their men. In the tumbrels with Penlez were several sailors in the royal and merchant marine, found guilty of highway robbery,[23] as well as a woman, Mary Dymar, found guilty of robbing a captain of his silver watch and his wig on the highway. There was also a former corn chandler, transportee, and slave overseer, James Arnold, whose addiction to gin had gotten the better of him. Thousands of sailors armed with bludgeons and cutlasses assembled at the gallows, but no serious disturbances accompanied the hangings. Surrounded by hundreds of petty constables and horsemen, Janssen placated the tars by pledging that none of the bodies would be handed over to the surgeons, provided they did not incite disorder.[24] As for Penlez, his body was taken to an undertaker in Wych Street and then to the church of St. Clement Danes where it was buried by private subscription. "The Corpse was attended by an infinite number of Persons," remarked the *Worcester Journal,* "much lamenting the unhappy Fate of the Sufferer."[25]

One would think that Janssen's ability to defuse the situation at Tyburn might have put paid to the Penlez affair, but it did not. In the interval between Penlez's sentence and his execution, Viscount Trentham, one of the incumbent MPs for Westminster had also been approached to support his reprieve.[26] Trentham was the son of Lord Gower, a former Tory but now a supporter of the ministry. He was also the brother-in-law of the Duke of Bedford, one of the secretaries of state and a principal landowner in London. His family connections, it was presumed, would work wonders for the reckless wigmaker. But Trentham declined to intervene on behalf of the unfortunate Penlez, to the dismay of many inhabitants in the eastern parishes of the Strand. This would not have mattered had not Trentham been obliged to put himself up for re-election in this populous borough a month after the execution, on account of his acceptance of a position on the Admiralty Board. As a result Penlez's ghost spilled onto the hustings. In the opening shots of the election campaign, Opposition canvassers circulated a mock advertisement in which the brothel keeper Peter Wood was put up for nomination as MP, having "distinguished himself for the Services and Pleasures of the Public in General and of this City in particular."[27] At the hustings before Covent Garden, an open coffin was carried about attended by a number of lights, in which a man in a shroud, a mock Penlez, harangued the crowd about his fate.[28]

The indications that Penlez's execution might become an electoral issue were evident in the run-up to the election in November. In a pamphlet issued in the second week in November, John Cleland portrayed the bawdy-house riots as a rightful exercise of rough justice and deplored the conviction of Wilson and Penlez on the evidence of such a notorious cock bawd as Peter Wood. He claimed the neighborhood was sympathetic to the attacks on these houses of ill repute and that the discipline of the rioters themselves was remarkable, with very little evidence of looting. Poor Penlez was simply swept up by the moment, he asserted. He became involved in "the Heat of Young Blood, as a pleasant Frolick."[29] In Cleland's estimation he did not deserve to die for such recklessness. Indeed, Cleland emphasized that he was not alone in this view, suggesting that around 900 signatures had been collected to petition for his pardon. Cleland not only thought Penlez had been unlawfully committed under the Riot Act, but his execution was an example of class justice. Why, he asked, did this young, twenty-three-year-old journeymen die at the hangman's noose for being part of a bawdy-house riot when the young gentlemen who had recently pillaged the Haymarket theater in protest to a theatrical hoax had not been prosecuted at all?[30]

Four days before the Westminster election, Henry Fielding published his own pamphlet about the case. It was not a direct reply to Cleland, for Fielding had been working on it since September, but it was certainly designed to take the sting out of the Opposition's case that Trentham and his ministerial accomplices had been guilty of a miscarriage of justice. Of course at a more obvious level it was a personal vindication of his part in the criminal process. In his account Fielding suggested that the indictments under the Riot Act were necessary because property had to be defended in these turbulent times. Indeed, there was a reasonable fear that the riot would escalate into an attack on nearby banking establishments. This was alarmist; all the evidence suggests that the riots against bawdy houses, which continued for a few days beyond the events in the Strand, remained on target and showed no disposition to turn into some sort of jacquerie. This was also true of the attack on a brothel in the Old Bailey and at Goodman's fields, where sailors broke the windows of several "Houses of ill Repute."[31] Fielding was conjuring up specters of discontent that did not exist.

On the culpability of Penlez, Fielding was not much better. Having stressed the need to take a hard line against insurgent sailors and their allies, Fielding then justified the hanging of Penlez by noting that he might well have been indicted for burglary, which also carried the death sentence. In his pamphlet he mustered a deposition from the watch and from one of the constables indicating that Penlez had the linen of Jane Wood in his possession, and that not only had he attempted to hide it but he had also manufactured two lame excuses as to why the bundle was on his person. This evidence was produced by Fielding to counter the rumor that the linen had been planted on the inebriate Penlez while he slumbered in Carey Street. The deposition was not dated, however, and the passing reference to Penlez's execution revealed that it must have been taken in late October, at least two and a half months after the incident. Indeed, it would appear to have been inserted into the pamphlet at a relatively late stage, for the first draft of it was ready for publication by the end of September.[32] In other words, Fielding was rebuilding a narrative of Penlez's culpability well after the event, presumably in an attempt to take some of the sting out of the accusations of Trentham's indifference to the journeyman's fate. What makes this hypothesis more compelling is that fact that Fielding failed to mention that John Wilson was indicted (but not tried) for stealing a silk petticoat worth 40 shillings from the house of Peter Wood.[33] This was a hanging offense, and had it been widely known, it would have undermined Fielding's argument for making an example of Bosavern Penlez, one that he had apparently pressed upon members of the Privy Council when they were considering whom to hang.[34]

Fielding's pamphlet was written not only to defend his own role in the Penlez affair; it was timed to offset any adversarial consequences the event might have for Trentham. That Trentham should have needed help seems, at first sight, remarkable. His family connections assured him of many deferential votes and the hefty weight of one of the biggest landowners in the city was at his disposal. Moreover, Trentham had been easily returned in the general election of 1747, when the Opposition forces in Westminster collapsed in a wake of an upsurge of loyalist sentiment and anti-Jacobitism. Then he was considered by the Duke of Newcastle "as popular . . . as ever Man was."[35]

But 1749 was not 1747. In the aftermath of the war there was a deep unease at the fragility of the peace settlement of Aix-la-Chapelle. As a writer in the *London Evening Post* noted, there were many who predicted the peace would be little more than a hiatus from war, and in some disputed territories, not even that.[36] Moreover, there was a mounting chorus of complaint that the seemingly victorious British had conceded too much. The settlement in Nova Scotia was precarious in the light of the return of Louisbourg to the French and the continuing disputes over the boundaries between Acadia and British territory; the French were dragging their feet over the evacuation of Tobago, one of the neutral islands; merchants trading to America and the Caribbean were disappointed at the reparations they received from the Spanish; and Britain's allies in Europe seemingly prospered while she bore the burden of war. As one rhymester put it: "Tho' the *Germans* and *Dutch* had enjoy'd all the Gains, / Still the *Honour* was Ours and th' Expence and the Pains."[37]

Some of this anxiety was visited upon Trentham, although in a seemingly trivial and indirect way. In mid-November 1749 there were protests against a troupe of French actors at the Little Theatre, Haymarket, who were performing an Italian comedy entitled *Les amants reuinis*. This outburst of Francophobia built on a billowing cultural nationalism and spiraled with the peace. It drew on a growing unease about the patronage of foreigners at a time when Britain needed to settle its demobilized servicemen and stem the tide of artisans leaving the country to work for Britain's competitors. Before the protest, in fact, a writer in the *London Evening Post* had declared that the licensing of such French "vagabonds" was "an insult to the Nation" and wondered whether Britain would soon be overrun by other foreigners, or whether the admission of the French comedians was not part of some secret deal with Britain's erstwhile enemies.[38]

However trivial these complaints might seem, they played upon the anxieties of the moment. At the Haymarket, Viscount Trentham drew his sword against the demonstrators in the gallery, and the following evening, when the comedians staged Molière's *L'École des femmes,* he reputedly hired a group of bouncers to keep the rowdies under control. Whether Trentham did either of these things is unclear.[39] He vigorously denied both charges and had the purported leader of the bouncers swear an affidavit that the viscount was in no way implicated in the Haymarket demonstrations. But the charges stuck, perhaps because it was well known that Trentham had helped sponsor the visit of the French comedians to London.[40] In the public mind he came to represent the typical aristocratic Francophile, whose taste and mannerisms were unfitting a representative of libertarian Westminster. In the doggerel of the street Trentham was Gallic at heart, a man who could hardly be trusted to do his patriotic duty at the Admiralty Board.[41] When Opposition voters paraded at Covent Garden with a white banner inscribed "United for our Country, No French Strollers," they were expressing their dissatisfaction with a man who so evidently preferred foreign over British theater and, by extension, with one who flouted the sacrifices of those who had put their lives on the line for their country. How, asked one broadside, could people like Trentham support such a troupe when Britain had just fought a war "at an infinite Expense to keep the French out, not to bring 'em in?"[42]

Viscount Trentham's opponent in the by-election was Sir George Vandeput, a baronet of little consequence whose only claim to fame was that he was good-looking and had a solid libertarian pedigree. His family hailed from Protestant refugees who fled the Spanish Netherlands during the reign of Elizabeth. His grandfather, Sir Peter, was one of the sheriffs of London who defied James II during his brief, infamous reign. Beyond that ancestral connection, Sir George was a nobody, a baronet who lived on a mercantile inheritance in Grosvenor Street. In fact, he was not the Opposition's first choice. He was a late substitute for George Cooke, a local justice of the peace who decided to stand in the nearby constituency of Middlesex, where a by-election had been called upon the promotion of Sir Hugh Smithson to the earldom of Northumberland.[43] In fact, Sir George's Dutch origins, remote as they were, proved something of a handicap in an electorate fueled by xenophobia, with Court hacks denigrating his reputation with some anti-Dutch doggerel.

These handicaps were not irrevocably damaging, for the strength of the Opposition lay with the Independent Electors of Westminster, a caucus of professional men, surgeons, lawyers, and large dealers who had orchestrated the victory of Admiral Edward Vernon and Charles Edwin in 1741. It was still around in 1749 despite some embarrassing links to Jacobite cells of disaffection during the Forty-Five. These Jacobite associations lingered in 1749, and Trentham's supporters tried to make the most of them. One observer highlighted the Independents' indiscreet, if not downright seditious, oaths at local dinners and their refusal to subscribe to the loyalist counteroffensive during the Forty-Five.[44] Others pointed to the continuing Jacobite affiliations of some of their leaders. Alexander Murray, for example, one of the electoral managers, was the brother of the Jacobite Lord Elibank.[45] Samuel Johns, an attorney of Lyons Inn and reputedly their "Commander in chief," was thought by one of Newcastle's spies to be "intimate with the principal Jacobites all over the kingdom." Years later, he would impudently strike up the old pro-Stuart song "When the King shall enjoy his own again" before Kew House when the royal family was walking on the river bank.[46]

Yet the Westminster Independents were able to draw on a broad swathe of political support beyond the Jacobite constituency. Edward Vernon, the hero of Porto Bello and the admiral in charge of the Channel fleet during the Forty-Five, remained an enthusiast, to a point that he was invited to join the Opposition's committee to investigate the electoral proceedings. Frederick, Prince of Wales, and his Leicester House coterie offered financial aid, as did a raft of Tory MPs, Independents, and leading aldermen from the Opposition-dominated City of London. In fact, eight London aldermen, including the Lord Mayor Sir Samuel Pennant, contributed to Vandeput's scrutiny of the vote.[47] London's intimate connection with the Independents would also eventuate in the election of Matthew Blackiston, a Strand grocer, tea importer, and active member of the Westminster caucus, to the aldermanic court in June 1750.

The Westminster opposition was broadly based. It was also fired by the politics of resentment. In the halcyon days of 1741–42, the coalition of Country Whigs and Tories had managed to oust Sir Robert Walpole from power, only to suffer disappointment after disappointment. Important politicians from both camps had defected to the government, including Lord Gower, Trentham's father, a critical patron in the West Midlands where Toryism had hitherto been strong and resilient. From 1746 onward, the government was firmly in the hands of the Pelham brothers and their allies, with Opposition support in the large urban constituencies slipping badly in 1747.[48] The Westminster by-election of 1749, in which the political nation at large would likely take a keen interest, was seen by many Opposition politicians as a chance to get back on track.

Trentham himself certainly offered that opportunity. Quite apart from his miscalculations over Penlez and the Comèdie Française, he had the reputation of being an arrogant irascible aristocrat, a veritable "Lord Tantrum," propelled to a position of power at the Admiralty by his brother-in-law's influence. One writer sarcastically remarked that the viscount was distinguished by "juvenile judgment, Family Independence, and unutterable Elocution."[49] He seems to have spent more time gambling than troubling himself with politics. The French ambassador thought he was "un jeune homme sans aucune sort de consideration,"[50] hardly a compliment. Trentham riled voters by failing to observe the customary courtesy of offering himself for re-election before a general meeting of the voters, which was certainly expected from this large, diverse, rate-paying householder constituency, whose electors reached into the thousands. One handbill wondered whether his refusal to present himself to the voters "did not imply a sovereign Sufficiency in himself as well as Contempt of his Electors" and, in the light of his promotion, pondered whether "the *Admiral* can *command* what the *Lord* formerly condescended to *solicit.*"[51] It went on to question "whether a Place is such an Ingredient in a Member of Parliament as is likely to render him of more constitutional service to his Country or Constituents." In other words, Trentham not only ignored the conventional proprieties of the electoral process, he represented the sort of politician, an officeholder no less, whose allegiance to his paymasters would likely prevail over his constituents. In Westminster, a riding where political independence was cherished and where there had recently been a series of instructions to MPs demanding the exclusion of placemen from Parliament, this rhetoric would likely strike a responsive chord.

Nonetheless, Trentham could count on a lot of support by virtue of his connections to the big houses and to the powerful political patrons of the day. Although there were a number of well-known parliamentarians and magistrates who gave their votes to Vandeput, the bulk of the "quality" rallied to Trentham. Parliamentarians resident in Westminster voted strongly in his favor. Only a handful of country Tories like the Dashwoods, the Leicester House set, and Independents like James Peachey, who was described as "naturally a republican Whig of levelling and wild notions of Government," gave their votes and interest for Sir George. The same was true on the Westminster Commission of the Peace. Here seventy-six of the eighty-three men who voted rallied to Trentham. This pattern continued among the wealthy and well-to-do. In the parishes of St. Margaret Westminster, St. George Hanover Square, and St. James Piccadilly, the allegiance of the esquire and gentleman was overwhelmingly in favor of the viscount: as high as five-to-one in the first, if we include military officers in the calculations, and three-to-one in the others. Even in St. Anne Soho and St. Martin's, where Trentham failed to secure a majority, 79 and 75 percent of the gentry resident there voted in his favor. Only in St. Clement Danes and St. Mary le Strand was this trend reversed. Here the lawyers of the Inns of Court showed a marked preference for Sir George rather than

Trentham, with the result that two in three of the so-called gentlemen and esquires voting in these parishes opted for the Opposition candidate.

With the "quality" vote behind him, Trentham should have had the election sewn up. In many other constituencies in the country this would have been the case, for whom you knew and whom you could squeeze mattered in eighteenth-century contests, especially when one's electoral choice was visible to all. But Westminster was a large diverse constituency of somewhat imponderable size, around 9,000 in 1750. All rate-paying male householders had the vote, save for foreigners, that is, and this meant that every nook and cranny in this crowded constituency potentially brought forth a modest tradesman or artisan. Lord Perceval, who represented Westminster from 1742 to 1747, calculated that the "dead weight" of the Court amounted to 2,000 votes while the die-hard opposition of Jacobites and general malcontents could count on less than 1,000.[52] In his view the bulk of the voters were really "Moderate and Independent," tradesmen and artisans who could be swayed by the issues and personalities of the candidates. If the Opposition was to win Westminster, he surmised, it had to make headway among this broad band of voters.

Essentially this is what happened. On the first real day of polling on 24 November, Trentham surged ahead by almost 200 votes, but his opponents mounted a successful counteroffensive and within three days Vandeput was leading by about a hundred votes. Sir George's strongest support came from the eastern parishes of Westminster along the Strand not from the fashionable squares of the West End and the precincts around Parliament and Westminster Abbey. His showing was particularly strong in St. Clement Danes and St. Mary le Strand, the area where Bosavern Penlez had lived and where his hanging remained a smoldering grievance. As Sir Thomas Robinson remarked to the Duke of Richmond, "Penley's Ghost (wch they have carried about in Triumph & surely a high insult on Governmt) has rais'd more People to vote for St Clems [Clement Danes] than there are Houses in the Parish."[53]

What was also instructive about Vandeput's support was his strong showing among the tradesmen, artisans, and shopkeepers, whether tailors, shoemakers, peruke makers, or innkeepers and provision merchants. The preponderance of votes for the Independent candidate increased, moreover, as one moved down the social scale. Of the nine wards in St. Martin-in-the-Fields, only the wealthiest, Charing Cross, emerged with a majority for Trentham. Of the others, Vandeput's support was most convincing in the poorer wards, such as New Street and Bedfordbury, and along Long Acre, Drury Lane, and the Strand. Even in the parishes where the vote between the Court and Independent candidates was more evenly spread, a similar pattern is evident. In St. Anne, Soho, for example, the richer ward, King Square, sided with Trentham, the poorer, Leicester Fields, with Vandeput. In St. James, where the Court party emerged victorious with a total of 1,113 votes to Vandeput's 991, the less fashionable wards of Golden Square and Marlborough Street each gave Vandeput a small majority.[54]

So it was the lower to middling tradesmen of Westminster who were the backbone of Opposition support, and a rough correlation can be made between the genteel character of the Court vote and the petit bourgeois character of their opponents. To some extent, contemporaries recognized this. One electoral broadside had a fictional Viscount Trentham decry his opponents in sociological terms. "Do you think these *jambefouttres* of Tradesmen, Shopkeepers, Tories, Jacobites can defeat us in an Election!" he is said to have complained to his cronies. "The Impudence of these Bourgeois! To set themselves in Opposition to such a Number of Quality and Distinction."[55] Yet this is clearly what happened. Indeed, Trentham was forced to mobilize all the channels of patronage at his disposal in order to fend off the challenge of "trade and independency."

Precisely how this was done is worth considering. To begin with, an arrangement was made between Trentham's father, Lord Gower, and his brother-in-law, the Duke of Bedford, about the viscount's electoral expenses. Bedford was to foot the bill for the contest, with Gower financing the scrutiny, should one transpire.[56] Bedford's bill came to more than £6,400, a formidable sum, and more than double what he had paid in association with Sir Peter Warren in 1747. The bulk of these expenses were for the 222 taverns that Bedford opened on Trentham's behalf, and for the disbursements of the managers who supervised the entertainment of the voters. "Treating" was a well-established custom of eighteenth-century elections; until the end of the century it was considered a virtual right of the voters to be wined and dined at the candidate's expense. In Westminster, treating even occurred when there was no contest, as in 1754. At the same time, managers recognized that they were obligated to deliver voters to the poll, and their tavern bills frequently included a list of the voters whom they herded to the hustings. To be sure, there were a few voters who secured a free lunch. On Otman Muller's list for the King's Head in Downing Street there were a few voters who do not appear to have polled. There were also four foreigners whom the manager hoped might sway legitimate voters or perhaps vote illegally themselves.[57] But on the whole the managers seem to have been fairly assiduous in bringing in their men. A letter from one manager, a timber merchant in Berwick Street, illustrates the calculating and punctilious spirit in which treating was conducted. He informed Bedford's steward that he had informed the landlord at the Ham in Wardour Street that he might "open his house to treat those in the interest of Lord Trentham that had not poll'd and that wou'd poll for Lord Trentham, and that he treated no others by my express orders. And for all such as he got, I gave him this liberty, that he might treat them to 3, 4, or not exceeding 5/-a piece, and I would see him paid."

Bedford's managers and inspectors were drawn from a broad swathe of the Westminster population, although they were always powerful men in their own locality. They included gentlemen, a saddler, an ironmonger, a coal merchant, a wheelwright, and quite a few contractors who had worked for the duke on his Bloomsbury and Covent Garden estate. They included Henry Cheere, the well-known sculptor, who had produced several statues for Oxford colleges and had consolidated his position in polite circles as the official carver of Westminster Abbey. He was a prominent landlord in the area of the Abbey, in St. Margaret's Westminster, leasing properties from the dean and chapter and renting them to gentry who wanted to be within a few minutes' walk of Parliament.[58] As a prominent vestryman, he was an important manager of Trentham in his parish, one who would prove critical to his patron's success.

Henry Fielding, the Bow Street magistrate and novelist, was also enlisted to do some ground work for Viscount Trentham. He was indebted to the Duke of Bedford for his property qualification as a Middlesex justice of the peace, having leased from his lordship several properties in the vicinity of Great Wild Street and Drury Lane.[59] As we have seen, he had defended the government's hanging of Penlez and had also sworn the affidavit of John Haines, who denied any involvement in the defense of the French comedians. During the election he hosted the entertainment for Trentham at two local taverns, the Old George and Punch Bowl in Drury Lane and the White Bear in Bow Street. Yet his main contribution continued to be journalistic. Among other things, he penned a broadside, *Ten Queries submitted to every Sober, Honest, and Disinterested Elector,* in which he reiterated Trentham's innocence in the Haymarket disturbance, pressed his claims as a "truly English" aristocrat, and poured scorn on Vandeput's foreign lineage. He also launched an attack on Paul Whitehead, one of the literary lions of the Independents, in a mock broadside, *The Covent Garden Journal.*[60] Whitehead had been savaging Trentham in several biting broadsides, but he also had been active at the hustings. On the first day of the election Bedford's bruisers under the leadership of Benjamin Boswell had attempted to obstruct the path of the Independent voters to the poll on the grounds that they were trespassing on his lordship's property in Covent Garden. Alexander Murray, one of the Opposition managers, had two sympathetic JPs, Sir Thomas Clarges and John Upton, commit them to the roundhouse. According to Bedford's sources, Whitehead was among those who helped jostle Boswell into the lockup, telling Boswell he would personally ensure he was "sent to Gaol or he would be Damn'd Else."[61] Fielding must have known about this incident because he was the JP who bailed Bedford's bruisers, earning himself the epithet of a "Bruiser of Justice" working to protect "Bruisers of Bodies."[62]

Bailing out Trentham's rowdies was probably the most unsavory activity Fielding was called upon to fulfill in the Westminster election; at least it was the one that brought him closest to the insipient violence and flagrant coercion of popular elections. It is doubtful that Fielding had to marshal voters to the polls in quite the way that attorney Michael Mulwainey was obliged to. Mulwainey had protested to Bedford's steward that his business had "suffered prodigally" during the election when he "had been up several Nights . . . in order to keep the People together & prepare them for the ensuing Day."[63] Fielding's gout and social standing likely precluded this kind of work, and in any case Fielding was neither an inspector nor manager in the strict sense of the term.

Those that were employed in this capacity certainly used persuasion and bribes to hurry voters to the polls. In the aftermath of the election it was revealed that a Dutchman from The Hague he been persuaded to vote by the sculptor Henry Cheere. He confessed "he was sorry he poll'd" but "Mr Chear told him there wod be no Scrutiny." Similarly, a Knightsbridge agent deluded a local laborer into believing that all lodgers paying £2 rent a year "had a Right to Poll."[64] Such delusions, fuelled, no doubt, with a little money, victuals, or drink, were enough to get other poor men to the hustings. Among the voters objected to by Vandeput's counsel was a Knightsbridge chandler who lived "under a Hay loft of part of Swann Inn." Another was a smith from Queen's Square lodging in a tenement "worse than Newgate." In counsel's opinion he was little more than "a beggar."[65]

Where gentle persuasion failed, veiled or more open threats of coercion were used. William Joyce, a painter in New Broad Court, confessed that he thought he had no right to poll but was solicited to do it. At first he refused, but then the Duke of Bedford's steward came "& say'd he insisted upon it."[66] The same happened to a Welsh tailor who lodged in an inn in Kensington. He rightly thought he could not vote but was forced to do so by his landlord. Similarly William Scott, a haberdasher at the King's Arms, Round Court, facing the New Exchange, was told by one of Trentham's agents that his lordship "would be glad to know that I might not give him nor his Friends much trouble." Otherwise he would be subject to legal action for failing to pay the rates.[67] John Reddesford, a shoemaker and pensions who lodged in a garret above the Three Tuns, in Green Alley, St. Martin's, for which he paid a mere 10½d a week, was handled more directly. He was taken away to poll by three or four gentlemen in a hackney coach, who told him, "If he would not Poll for Lord Trentham . . . he should be turned out of his Pension." Similar treatment was given to a wigmaker from Duke's Court, who was threatened with incarceration in the roundhouse if he did not vote for Trentham and so was brought to the hustings "Nolens Volens." And to a cow keeper and former Chelsea pensioner in Pye Street, who was threatened with garrison duty if he did not poll for his lordship.[68] Such heavy-handed treatment by the managers and their marshals was sometimes complimented by special services. The regular contractors on the Covent Garden estate — Edward Ives, plumber; John and William Spinnage, painters; William Perrit carpenter; and Richard Norris, bricklayer — transformed their workforce into an electoral militia in 1749. Their bills in the Bedford papers reveal that during the eleven days of the poll they provided the Court party with at least 150 bruisers to carry on the battle at the foot of the hustings.[69]

Bedford could clearly mobilize a powerful electoral machine in his own right, but he was also able to complement and fortify this in various ways. The presence of the main government departments and the royal household within Westminster gave the Court party a ready-made source of electoral influence. The streets and alleys around Whitehall, the Royal Mews, and the stable yard at St. James were emphatically pro-ministerial precincts. The inhabitants of Scotland Yard, for example, were described in 1749 as "all Gentlemen that belong to the Court, to the Board of Works . . . all the three yards were Inhabited by people that had places." It was customary to admit all householders from this area to the poll, in spite of the fact that they were technically non-rate-paying householders. Vandeput's scrutineers contested this right without success and had to resign themselves to the disqualification of a few minor Court dependents. They took exception to John Tucker, the admiralty gardener, and to Thomas Lawrence, who organized His Majesty's coal and timber supply. They also objected to a number of Whitehall "gentlemen" who turned out to be livery servants, petty clerks, a laborer's foreman connected to the Board of Works, and the king's glazier.

Men such as these could be expected to vote for the Court without prior solicitation, but in 1749 a close watch was kept on potential backsliders. On 29 November Lord Trentham wrote to the Duke of Richmond, the Master of Horse, requesting his services in mobilizing the Royal Mews vote, "it being infinitely material to us to get a head of the Poll today if possible." Two days later he begged "the favour of yr grace's influence over Greening the King's Corn Chandler in St James market who refused to vote." While this was happening, his brother-in-law the Duke of Bedford was mobilizing his friends and associates to ensure that others supported the Court candidate. One list contained the following entries.

Revd Mr Butler Jnr North St Westmr by ye Bishop of Norwich

Mr Hartley King's Messenger, Jermyn St to be influenced by Coll Pelham

Mr Cornwall who shows ye Tombs at Westr Abbey — the Bishop of Rochester

William Goodwin butcher St James's Market by Lady Georgina Spenser and Lord Granvillle

Charles Light Butcher St James Market to be influenced by Lord London (polled)

Mr Blundell a carpenter in the Pav'd Alley by St James Market to be influenced by his Honr Vane & the Duke of Cleveland

Mr Hancock, shoemaker Tothill St by Coll Russell of 1st Regiment.[70]

As this list suggests, the patronage that Trentham could mobilize was complex and ramified. From Bedford House and the great government departments it spanned out to encompass members of the great Whig circle and their dependents, parliamentarians and their local clients, tradesmen of the Court and their contacts. The tradesmen associated with the royal stables secured 250 votes in their interest alone. The more prominent retainers included Galfridus Mann, a draper on the Strand and a local vestryman; Richard Buckner, the official purveyor of the royal stables and a Page of the Back Stairs; and Henry Godde, the royal sadler. The Duke of Bedford thought Godde was a little "cold in ye cause," but with a little goading from Richmond, the Master of Horse, he ultimately proved faithful to his masters and brought in some forty electors for the Court. A list of his supporters reveals he could command votes in Clare Market, Covent Garden, and Soho, as well as in the area around Charing Cross. They were drawn from a fairly representative sample of local trades: food retailers, carpenters, bricklayers, as well as watchmakers and high-class saddlers. The web of Court patronage went well beyond genteel clients. It penetrated the lower and middle strata of Westminster society.

Even so, the Court party was hard pressed to win this election. The revolt of the trades ran deep. There was a strong surge of electoral independence in 1749, a deep reluctance to kowtow to the great. One electoral ballad talked of Westminster voters daring "to be Free/Tho' Busy Corruption dealt round the vile Fee" and applauded those who ennobled themselves with virtue and honesty and refused to defer to the "dignify'd dregs of Britain's fallen race." Early in the campaign, voters were urged to assert their liberty by "shaking off all Dependence on those who call themselves their Superiors."[71] This adage seems to have been heeded. Despite the fact that the Court rallied its battalions, Vandeput remained ahead in the polls into December. The clearest evidence of Vandeput's strong support among the trades comes from the luxury sector, which would have normally sided with the Court and its quality clientele. For in this Mecca of conspicuous consumption, the pull of the genteel customer was formidable. Fashionable tradesmen were wary of offending their large customers and in this election sometimes abstained from voting. Yet in the end, the Court could not mobilize the fashionable trades in a decisive manner. Although Trentham scored well among the saddlers and linen drapers, he did not break even among the silversmiths and failed to secure a majority among goldsmiths, mercers, cutlers, upholsterers, and jewelers. Among these seven trades, Trentham secured 98 votes to Vandeput's 129. Within the medical profession, Trentham did marginally better, winning conspicuously among the surgeons but falling behind a little among the apothecaries. Yet the failure of Trentham to obtain the vote of all trades and professions that serviced the quality signaled the deep reservations that many of the middling sort had with his candidature.

Ultimately the Court party did not win the election by twisting the arms of existing voters. It did so by creating new ones. When the poll closed on 8 December, the number polled was 9,465, 2,000 more than had voted on any previous occasion and certainly more than the number of eligible household-ers.[72] As the newspapers recognized, Trentham began to make inroads into Vandeput's majority only when he swamped the poll with voters from St. Margaret and St. John the Evangelist. These two parishes had more than 400 empty houses in 1749 and over a thousand tenants who did not pay the rates.[73] Many soldiers and ex-soldiers lodged in this area, and many trades-men had links to the Royal Mews and Horse Guards. It was homemade terri-tory for creating new voters, as the Opposition realized, for it had reminded the High Bailiff that if every "kind of house" had a right to vote "it would be bringing in all the Refuse of the City to subvert & overturn the whole Libertys of the City."[74] Nonetheless, the pro-Court vestry in St. Margaret went about its business of finding Trentham many new voters. On 4 December Sir Thomas Robinson informed Richmond that it was "difficult to say when Germination will stop, as an instance 600 more on the Close of Saturday's poll had voted for St Margaret's and St John alone than ever polled before." A week later he confessed he "wished some Supernatural power (for nothing else can) could against the time of the scrutiny conjure up houses for the Nos who have polled without." Among those rounded up were poor beggarly soldiers who lived in haylofts, Chelsea pensioners, street sellers, and hackney coachmen who lived above their stables.[75] With the help of the overseers of the parish, the Court party strove to find good reasons for their votes. In early January, when the scrutiny for the election was under way in the neighboring parish of St. George Hanover Square, Robinson was able to report there were only 142 Court supporters not on the parish books of St. Margaret. "Before the scrutineers get to the Vestry," he chirped, "I believe we shall find good reasons to support their votes."[76]

Had the parishes of St. Margaret and St. John been taken out of the equation, Sir George Vandeput would have won the election by just over 600 votes. Once these parishes are included, Sir George lost by just over 150. The Independent Electors of Westminster hoped that the scrutiny would expose Trentham's flagrant abuses and highlight his swamping of the electorate with bogus voters. But one crucial ruling by the High Bailiff, Peter Leigh, frustrated this hope. Leigh determined that the franchise in Westminster fell on the inhabitant householders who were *liable to pay* scot and lot, that is, the basic parish taxes and their associated responsibilities; not simply that who had actually paid. On balance this prejudiced Vandeput, for while he certainly mustered some false votes in St. Clement Danes, he lacked the vestry support that might have enabled him to disguise them.[77] In fact Sir George's scrutineers were only able to requalify 13 percent of the votes objected to by the other party in this parish, the lowest percentage of any requalification.[78] To further complicate matters, the High Bailiff appears to have allowed compound householders to vote, another decision that redounded to Trentham's advantage.[79] In the scrutiny that dragged on into May 1750, the viscount was predictably returned as the MP for Westminster.

The Opposition did not take kindly to this decision. It had invested a lot of time and energy in this election. At a general meeting of the Independent Electors on 9 January 1750, the chairman had declared his hope that the election would establish a "universal Pattern of Freedom and Independency throughout the whole Nation."[80] When Leigh declared Trentham the winner, he was accused of accepting bribes. His house was threatened; Court sympathizers were insulted. "The mob were outrageous," recalled Horace Walpole, "and pelted Colonel Waldegrave whom they took for Mr Leveson [Trentham] from Covent Garden to the Park, and knocked down Mr Offley who was with him."[81] Two petitions were drawn up in protest to the result, both alluding to the returning officer's partiality toward the Court, but neither won a hearing before a hostile Commons. Instead, the Lower House elected to hear the High Bailiff's complaints of intimidation by the Independents and effectively frustrated an inquiry into his conduct.

In the ensuing investigation, Richard Crowle, one of Vandeput's counsel, was found guilty of prolonging the scrutiny, and John Gibson, an upholsterer from Covent Garden, was found guilty of accusing the High Bailiff with accepting bribes. In addition, Alexander Murray was charged with using threatening language toward the High Bailiff and of rallying a mob to assault him in Covent Garden.[82] Murray refused to acknowledge his guilt. His only offense, if it could be called one, he said, was to remark to a chimneysweep that Lord Trentham was a rogue.[83] When the Commons moved to place Murray in close confinement in Newgate, he resisted the Commons' censure. He refused to hear his sentence on his knees in the appropriately contrite manner. The House was outraged. Only the redoubtable Admiral Vernon swam against the tide, caustically suggesting that the Magna Carta should be referred to the committee. "The Speaker stormed," Walpole recalled, "and the House and its honour grew outrageous at the dilemma they were got into." "If he gets the better" of the House, he continued in his letter to Horace Mann, "he will indeed be a meritorious martyr for the cause." And that is what he became. Remanded to Newgate Prison for "his dangerous and seditious practices," he was released by the London sheriffs during the parliamentary recess to shouts of "Murray and Liberty."[84] One MP bridled at the way he "made a sort of cavalcade along the streets in a triumphant manner, as if he had been suffering for the cause of liberty" (figure 5).[85]

When the Commons returned in autumn 1751, it hounded Murray out of British political society by stamping a £500 reward for his recapture. But like Penlez's ghost, Murray continued to haunt the halls of Westminster. While Murray was in Newgate, a pamphlet appeared in his defense, written anonymously by Paul Whitehead. It claimed that Murray had reasonably protested to the High Bailiff about the difficulties of getting voters to the polls on the first day of the election, given the interference of Bedford's bruisers, and that in the legal battle that followed, his actions had been exonerated at King's Bench. As for the threatening remarks that Murray allegedly made to the High Bailiff, there were plenty of reputable witnesses to swear to the contrary. Whitehead insinuated that Murray was prosecuted only because he was prepared to blow the whistle on the High Bailiff's partiality toward the Court party. The government-dominated Commons went along with this strategy, to a point of putting Murray's life at risk while he was in Newgate suffering from gaol fever. This was an audacious argument to make in the light of the Commons' censure of Murray, and it was hardly surprising that the Commons condemned the pamphlet as a "false, scandalous and seditious libel." Henry Fielding committed Anne Jenkins to one month's hard labor for hawking it about the streets and had the offending libel publicly burnt before his door.[86]

Within less than a week from its publication, the printer and publisher of the tract were detained in custody. The government, led by two of its stars — Attorney General Sir Dudley Ryder and Solicitor General William Murray (later Lord Mansfield) — led the prosecution against William Owen, the printer, of Homer's Head, Temple Bar. The case against Owen seemed straightforward. "If the FACT is proved," Murray reminded the jury, "the LIBEL proves itself." The jury were simply "Judges of the FACT, the Judge determines the LAW." The government produced plenty of evidence that Owen had sold the pamphlet on

Fig 5: The demonstrations on Alexander Murray's release from the Tower, anonymous print entitled *The British Patriot's Procession*, 1751. © British Museum.

the first few days of its publication, but to press the point home, Murray advised the jury not to be influenced by the "artful and false insinuations" of the Opposition press that it should stray from its mandate. "These sort of Libels can lead to nothing but Sedition" he declared, "for how can the Mob or People redress but by Tumult and Rebellion and thereby subvert the Constitution?"

The leading defense counsel, Mr. Ford, did not challenge the fact of publication at all. He offered some palliating remarks about Owen's loyalism during the Forty-Five, backed this up with a few character witnesses, and suggested that on this occasion Owen had not maliciously or seditiously impugned the dignity of the Commons. Only the second counsel, Mr. Pratt, insinuated that the current laws of libel impeded freedom of speech. "Will it be right to tell a free People," he asked, "happen what will, you shall never complain?" The judge, Lord Chief Justice William Lee, was not impressed by this libertarian flourish. In his summing up to the jury, he advised them to bring in a verdict of guilty, since he considered the fact of publication proven.

But the jury, which included several common councilmen from the Opposition-dominated City of London, thought otherwise. When it brought in a verdict of not guilty, huzzahs rang through Guildhall. At the request of the attorney general, one witness reported:

> They were called into Court again, and asked this leading Question, viz. "Gentlemen of the Jury, do you think the Evidence laid before you, Of Owen's *publishing* the Book by selling it, is not sufficient to convince You that the said Owen did sell this Book?" At which the Foreman appeared a good deal flustered; and the Judge repeated the Question; upon which the Foreman, without answering the Question, said 'Not Guilty, Not Guilty,' and several of the Jurymen said 'That is our Verdict, my Lord, and We abide by it,' Upon which the Court broke up; and there was a prodigious Shout in the Hall. The Attorney General desired more Questions might be asked, But the Judge would not, neither would the Noise permit it.[87]

So the Westminster election did end on a libertarian flourish, even if the forces of oligarchy ultimately prevailed. The very temper and tone of the election, in fact, illustrated one of the paradoxes and contradictions of early eighteenth-century British political society: the coexistence of a well-entrenched system of clientage with a vibrant political nation. Both aspects of politics were on display in 1749. On the one hand, the by-election revealed the sinews of aristocratic patronage in operation; on the other, it revealed a contentious political culture that sought to expose and challenge the rule of the great. Throughout the six months of electioneering and scrutiny, newspapers, both metropolitan and provincial, routinely ran articles and squibs on this controversial event. Vandeput and Trentham became household names among the politically literate, which by the mid-century probably constituted 50 percent of the adult male population and a good many women besides. Within the metropolis, the Court party alone employed six printers to produce tens of thousands of electoral broadsides.[88] Not only were they distributed to the major taverns and coffeehouses of Westminster, they were circulated door-to-door. Some were disseminated in the City of London and Middlesex. Ten thousand handbills, for example, were printed for the inhabitants of St. Martin le Grand, a liberty attached to the dean and chapter of Westminster, whose householders had the right to vote in Westminster elections despite the fact they resided within the City of London. Others found a wider audience. Three anthologies of electoral propaganda streamed from the London press for the provinces. William Grove sent one collection to his friend Thomas Grimston in Yorkshire, and even Lord Trentham gave orders to send the *Covent Garden Journal* "into different parts of England as it will have a very good effect."[89] A hotly contested Westminster election proved to be a national event. As a synecdoche of English popular politics, the whole political nation took a keen interest in its outcome.

If the by-election was a triumph for oligarchy, the manner in which it was conducted also sowed the seeds of its demise. Writing to the Duke of Richmond at the conclusion of the poll, Sir Thomas Robinson expressed his satisfaction at the way in which the Court had rallied and cajoled the lesser inhabitants of St. Margaret's in its favor. Yet he wondered whether the Court had stirred forced beyond its control. "I think in all future elections," he declared, "the power of the Court is weakened & the lower Class of voters will determine Victory whichever side they take — my reason is, that you have now opened a door to about 1500 of a lower class of the People than ever Voted before, & who will be influenced from popular Cryes or Caprice or Money. For when we see what a *French Play* and *Penley's Ghost* has done at this Juncture, can any Juncture be without Scarecrows of such base materials."[90]

Sir Thomas rightly sensed that the expansion of the electorate would confront the forces of oligarchy with real problems in the future. Indeed, within thirty years the popular voice would resonate more decisively in this bastion of aristocratic privilege. He also recognized that the election had stirred up emotions that had unpredictable political consequences, ones that were not easily contained. To be sure, Robinson misunderstood the signifying power of the issues that plagued the election. Bosavern Penlez's execution had raised the matter of justice and fair play in a criminal code where mercy conventionally mediated judicial terror. The fracas over the French players spoke to issues of British national identity and patriotism in an age of bellicose mercantilism and empire, to powerful populist sentiments that future politicians would have to take into account. Sir Thomas gave no hint that he really understood this, but he did acknowledge the volatility of such issues and the way in which they might erode or highjack the conventions of clientage. In the next six years, over the Jew Bill and the fall of Minorca to the French, the Pelham brothers would be forced to recognize the same thing.

4

Fire from Heaven:
The London Earthquakes of 1750

During a particularly stormy, turbulent spring, full of northern lights and gale force winds, London experienced two earth tremors, the first in February, the second exactly a month later. These tremors toppled a few teacups and dislodged a few chimneys, but no fatalities or serious injuries were reported. Even so, some forty pamphlets and poems recorded the event and sought to make sense of it, some offering naturalistic explanations of the quakes, others providential. As Horace Walpole remarked, Londoners were "swarmed with sermons, essays . . . poems and exhortations" on the subject.[1] The fear of a third, more devastating, earthquake prompted hundreds to flee the capital in late March and April, to the amusement of some skeptics. How were these events understood in the context of demobilization and the crime wave? What does the public response tell us about the timbre of public discourse at the mid-century and the status of the clergy within it? These are the questions I plan to address in this chapter.

The first earthquake occurred around 12:30 p.m. on 8 February. The shock "was felt very much on both Sides of the River Thames, from Greenwich almost to Richmond," the *Whitehall Evening Post* reported: "In all the Places the Inhabitants were struck with so great a Pannick that they left their Houses, and ran into the streets."[2] The tremor was strongest along the river, where boats tossed at their moorings and a few chimneys tumbled down. Yet the only real damage within the six-mile radius of the epicenter of the quake was the collapse of an old slaughterhouse in Southwark.[3]

Exactly one month later, London shook again. Around 5:30 on the morning of 8 March, Charles Wesley was preaching to his congregation when he felt the tremors. As he recorded in his journal:

> We had another shock of an earthquake, far more violent than that of February 8th. I was just repeating my text, when it shook the Foundery so violently that we all expected it to fall in upon our heads. A great cry followed from the women and children. I immediately cried out, "Therefore will we not fear, though the earth be moved, and the hills be carried into the midst of the sea: for the Lord of hosts is with us; the God of Jacob is our refuge."[4]

Unlike Wesley's zealots, most Londoners were asleep when this earthquake struck. Horace Walpole thought someone was "getting from under my bed, but soon found it was a strong earthquake, that lasted near half a minute, with a violent vibration and great roaring."[5] Others treated the shock with less equanimity. According to the newspapers, some "ran from their Houses and Beds almost naked," as the ground waves rumbled from west to east, "being in a great Consternation at this unusual Visitation."[6] Predictably a few more chimneys collapsed, pewter mugs topped from shelves, and this time some bricks fell from the spire of Westminster Abbey. But again the damage was slight and no deaths were reported. Many Londoners did, however, report flashes of lightning prior to the shock, and some talked of a ball of fire in the sky reminiscent of a blazing sun. Was this really a second warning from God?

Certainly some contemporaries thought so. "Britain, attend the warning Voice," ran a poem in the *Whitehall Evening Post,*

> And dare be deaf no more;
> The God that makes *Still Sounds* his Choice
> Can bid his Thunders roar . . .
>
> But Earthquakes now speak louder yet,
> And shake a guilty Shore:
> Ye Fools who slumber near the Pit,
> Wake now, or wake no more.[7]

This poem circulated rapidly throughout the provincial press. The fact that it did registers something of the curiosity or alarm that the earthquakes evoked and the fear that God's judgment was imminent. Within weeks the voices of the clergy were added to the admonitory chorus. On 16 March, Thomas Sherlock, the bishop of London, published his letter to the "clergy and people" of London and Westminster urging them to shrug off their moral torpor and heed God's warning. First printed on fine paper for a shilling, this short pamphlet was soon sold in bulk orders of 100 for four shillings, and a subscription was opened to subsidize 20,000 cheap, accessible copies.[8] In the wake of this letter, printed sermons on the meaning of the earthquakes flowed from the press. Philip Doddridge, one of the most respected Dissenting ministers of his generation, took time off from his *Family Expositor* to publish a sermon he had given at Salters' Hall seven months earlier. "Is not the Voice of this Earthquake," he asked, "like that of the Angel of the Apocalypse . . . saying with a loud Voice, Fear GOD, and give Glory to him."[9] He went on to compare London to biblical Capernaum for its ostentation, frivolity, and vice and warned of divine judgment on Britain's imperial city for its abandonment of religion and obsession with pleasure.

This line of argument, that the earthquakes were a providential sign to Britons to repent their ways and recapture the true spirit of religion before God delivered a harsher punishment, typified the sermons that hit the press in the aftermath of the shocks. As Horace Walpole rather sardonically noted, even those who sought to cover the earthquakes in a more comprehensive manner ended up by insisting that "it was nothing less than a judgment."[10] To the Reverend John Allen, earthquakes were God's "solemn warnings to the guilty world"; to John Milner, they were "tokens of his displeasure"; to Thomas Newman, they were the "effects of perfect wisdom as power"; and to Charles Wesley, nothing less than "God's proper judicial act."[11] None of these men imbued their providentialism with apocalyptic predictions, as had been the case in the previous century.[12] The only one who came close was John Wesley, who talked of "the kingdom being near" in one of his hymns devoted to the earthquake.[13] At the same time most divines had plenty of biblical texts to reinforce their warnings, nearly all of them drawn from the Old Testament. Some cited Numbers 16:32, "And the earth opened her mouth, and swallowed them up," or Isaiah 29:6, "Thou shalt be visited of the Lord of Hosts with Thunder, and with Earthquake." Or even the more obscure Joel 3:16, "The Lord shall roar out of Zion, and utter his voice from Jerusalem; and the heavens and earth shall shake." Interestingly, all avoided the Muggletonian choice of Revelation 11:13, "And the same hour was there a great earthquake, and the tenth part of the city fell, and in the earthquake were slain of men seven thousand: and the remnant were affrighted, and gave glory to the God of heaven."[14]

Citing biblical authority was not essential, for the mid-century divines knew they were capitalizing on a panic. Philip Doddridge was very explicit on this point. "Considering the Lethargick State of so many Souls," he declared, "I have long thought it the Prudence of Christian Ministers, to improve those *publick Alarms,* which remarkable Providences may excite in the Minds of considerable Numbers, by renewing those plain and earnest Remonstrances, which in calmer Life Men are so ready to neglect."[15] The sense of anxiety was visible after the first shock. As Elizabeth Montagu wittily remarked on 20 February, "The madness of the multitude was prodigious, near 50 of the people I had sent to, to play cards here the Saturday following, went out of town to avoid being swallowed."[16] After the second tremor, a veritable panic set in, fanned by the prophecies of a field preacher and delirious soldier, who both foretold a third and final earthquake in early April. The field preacher was arrested in Carnaby Market and committed to jail for false prophecy; the soldier, a Swiss lifeguardsman, was considered too deranged to cause much mischief. He bragged he had been responsible for the earthquakes, that he had a ball of fire in his body and a sword that could cut devils in two. Yet his madness did prompt an exodus from the capital, as did the rumor that a hen in Edmonton had laid an egg inscribed "Beware of the third Shock" (see figure 6).[17]

Some writers disparaged this popular credulity: "Low stupid Pannicks speak a *Pigmy* Race" ran one couplet, "Let such, no more, our learned Isle disgrace."[18] "Rise from your lurking Holes, each dastard Fool," ran another, "Creep back to Town and go to *Wisdom*'s School."[19] This did not stop "great numbers of people" flocking to the fields on the anticipated judgment day to wait out the catastrophe. "This frantic terror prevails so much that within these three days 730 coaches have been counted passing Hyde Park Corner," reported a bemused Horace Walpole on 2 April.[20] For this richer set, prices for beds at Windsor, generally considered to be good place of refuge since it was well beyond the previous danger zone, reached one guinea each. The "concourse of people" there, it was reported, was as great as at a royal installation.[21]

The London earthquakes of 1750, then, were conspicuous for their panic and their providentialism. In a way this was hardly surprising. Despite the growth of Newtonianism, providentialists had a strategic advantage in explaining extraordinary events, such as earthquakes, because of the underdeveloped theory of disasters in the natural science of the time, known more often as natural philosophy. Sir Isaac Newton had posited God as a sort of cosmic watchmaker who created the universe but whose laws of nature could be rationally explored and understood. Newton's vision of the solar system as a stable system of forces was readily applied to the terrestrial sphere, creating the notion of a passive earth formed of hard, inert, and impenetrable matter. Within this paradigm, natural philosophers had great difficulty accommodating dramatic changes in the earth's crust without invoking God's clear intervention, what was often termed "special" or "particular providences." Some progress toward establishing a natural history of earthquakes was made through the empirical investigation of fossils, for it was thought that the exis-

Fig 6: Louis Philippe Boitard, *The Military Prophet: or A Flight from Providence*, 1750. © British Museum.

tence of petrified matter could only have been caused by the eruptions of subterranean earthquakes and volcanoes. Robert Hooke argued this in a series of lectures before the Royal Society in the late seventeenth century, speculating that earthquakes and volcanic eruptions were responsible for the uneven surface of the earth and the often dramatic appearance of islands. Hooke was careful to say that his speculations were "not an Argument against the Omnipotence, Providence and Wisdom of the Creator, who though fit to create them,"[22] but he did go a long way toward integrating quakes into a primitive geology of the planet.

Still, the natural causes of earthquakes eluded Hooke, as they did the next few generations of natural philosophers. No one had discovered tectonic plates, which were not part of the scientific agenda for another century. All explanations were dependent on ancient histories, travelers' tales, and eyewitness accounts of earthly "concussions," as they were sometimes called. These accounts veered to the descriptive, focusing more on effects than probable causes. By mid-century, there was no consensus about what caused an earthquake. In seeking some explanation for its readers in the aftermath of the first shock, the *London Evening Post* prefaced its remarks by observing "that the Earth every-where abounds in huge subterraneous Caverns, Veins and Canals; some of which are full of Water, others of Exhalations, and some replete with Nitre, Sulphur, Bitumen, Vitriol, and the like igneous Substances."[23] It was the chemical reaction of three elements — air, fire, and water — upon the fourth, the earth, that produced the tremors, an explanation that clearly had a genealogy in the four elements of ancient lore. The only alternative explanation was electrical, the "fashionable cause" of the mid-century according to Horace Walpole.[24] In the immediate aftermath of the London earthquakes, William Stukeley and Stephen Hales both hazarded that it was the interaction of airborn "coruscations" with subterranean "vapors" that set off the shocks. Stukeley, in his contribution to the Royal Society in April 1750, explicitly repudiated the view that the earth was extensively cavernous and refused to "enter into the common notion of struggles between subterraneous winds, or fire, vapours or water, that heav'd up the ground, like animal convulsions."[25]

In view of these different and rather hazy speculations, it was not difficult for divines to dismiss natural explanations. Bishop Sherlock referred to their advocates as "little philosophers, who see a little, and but very little into natural causes."[26] Another referred to them disparagingly as "dealers in second causes."[27] Yet not all were so condescending. The dissenting minister Samuel Chandler thought natural explanations of the world important but not sufficient. He admitted that it was difficult to determine when God acted by "immediate Interpositions," although he thought that in the case of earthquakes, in particular, God displayed the "lively Awes of his sovereign Power"[28] The same argument was maintained by Stephen Hales and William Stukeley, both of who were active naturalists as well as theologians. Instructively, they both recognized the potential tensions between religious and scientific explanations of natural phenomena, and in 1750 they compartmentalized their providential and naturalist explanations of London's tremors to avoid controversy.[29]

For all the disclaimers that earthquakes merited "the first title to the name of warnings and judgments,"[30] Hales and Stukeley were really enthusiasts of material causes. Not everyone was able to deal with the problem of first and second causes with quite their equanimity. Many feared that natural philosophy undermined God's plan and subverted the true course of religion. These anxieties were voiced after an earlier London earthquake, in 1692, but they were stronger in the mid-century commentaries. In an essay published in both the London and provincial newspapers, "Philanthropos" berated those who flew "in the face of Providence" by attributing the tremors simply "to the common operations of Nature." The "minute Philosopher," he continued, "ignorantly pretends to expound the Law of Nature, ascribing to ethereal and subterraneous cases those scenes of Desolation that involved *Sodom* in Fire, and sunk *Lima* to the Center."[31] Similarly, a Londoner pleaded with his fellow citizens not to be deceived "by the empty Vanity of mortal Wisdom — we might delight in the ingenuity of natural explanations but there remains the various unfathomable Train of Wonders thrown everywhere around us."[32] Within this climate of anxiety, one widely circulated pamphlet took the *London Evening Post* to task for presuming to explain the first London earthquake in naturalistic terms without "a Word of the Moral and Judicial Causes."[33] This attack on naturalistic explanations continued in a front page of the *Derby Mercury*. "There is not any Thing that has help'd more to the secluding of Providence" than natural philosophy, its author claimed, "or, by taking away that awful Impression and Inspection, to encourage and promote irreligion and vice. Shall we content ourselves with being told that the late terrible shocks are occasioned by Air pent up, by sulphureous Exhalations, or the Ruin of some Mountain in the abyss of Waters, without recollecting that not one Atom of Matter can change . . . but by the immediate Agency of God's Will?"[34]

In delivering this pitch the providentialists were protesting too much, and it is debatable whether their readers found their protests utterly compelling. Certainly readers had some liberty of choice. Naturalistic causes vied with providential in virtually every newspaper, whether metropolitan and provincial. In the monthlies, where travel narratives and natural histories had been a standard fare from their inception, the naturalistic explanations predominated.[35] While naturalistic formulations of earthquakes were often crude, the scientific endeavors of many naturalists had generated a welter of information about the effects and frequency of earth tremors that potentially curbed the discursive power of providential judgments. This source material was necessarily incomplete, particularly for the Far East, where large earthquakes and tsunamis were underreported.[36] Yet the compilers, whose scholarly pretensions were generally modest and who recognized the difficulties of constructing a comprehensive list of earthquakes from the Gutenberg era onward, were beginning to find some patterns in the geographical distribution of severe earthquakes, at least for Western Europe and the New World. The most devastating earthquakes seemed to cluster in the Andean region and along the Sicilian littoral: so said John Michel, one of the most perceptive scientists of his generation, who also surmised that earthquakes were more likely to run along clefts, what we would call fault lines, in the earth.[37]

What became clear from this empirical research was that Britain had not within recorded history experienced an earthquake of the devastating proportions of Jamaica in 1692, Sicily in 1693, or Lima in 1746, all of which were well known to eighteenth-century readers. Natural historians had identified about thirty earthquakes in Britain since the eleventh century, and some fifteen from 1650, when the empirical data became richer, thanks largely to the efforts of the Royal Society. None of the reported tremors was as devastating as those in Italy and the Andes, a fact noted in the press; as the *London Evening Post* remarked, earthquakes "are not attended here with the terrible Appearances that they have in hotter climes."[38]

Some commentators tried to ignore this fact, particularly with respect to the London earthquake of 1692, which was preceded by the devastating tsunami that destroyed Port Royal, Jamaica, and then followed by an equally destructive earthquake in Sicily. None of the 1750 sermons mentioned the previous London quake at all, although it must have been within public memory.[39] This was because dramatically destructive earthquakes were more powerful mobilizers of fear. Some pamphleteers admitted that Britain's earthquakes were typically minor tremors, but they then tried to back away from the implications of their statement, recognizing that it undermined the admonitory potential of the earthquakes, if not the whole doctrine of judgments. We should not presume, argued one, that Britain was providentially blessed compared to those "nations where the affliction was greater."[40] This argument became even more urgent in 1755–56, when the Lisbon earthquake destroyed much of the city but left some British factories there standing and Britain unscathed. Charles Bulkley confronted this dilemma in his sermon at the Old Jewry by insisting that although some countries were less vulnerable to earthquakes "by the very nature of their climate," that did not lessen our obligations to "a divine presiding presence."[41] One wonders whether his audience found this casuistry particularly compelling. Similarly in 1750, when preachers berated their congregations with stories of biblical chasms and warned that London could be the next Lima, some rational hearers must have treated their remarks with skepticism.[42]

Skeptics were not afraid, moreover, of challenging the presumptions of the clergy to expiate on God's judgments. Joseph Besse, a Quaker who originally wrote under the nom de plume of "Aminadab," openly questioned whether the bishop of London had the power or authority to cast the earthquakes as "effects of a special providence threatening vengeance upon a wicked and profligate generation."[43] This "supernatural" as opposed the "natural" explanation of the quakes not only presumed that the bishop had the power of revelation, Besse asserted, it drove people to despair rather than repentance. It would have been better if Sherlock had offered a rational explanation of the quakes and led people to repentance by noting that they would have no forewarning of such disasters in the future.

This argument proved popular, for Besse's pamphlet ran through five editions in as many months. It was accompanied by others who believed the clergy had been fear-mongering. Thomas Gordon, a libertarian Whig best known for his *Cato's Letters,* thought Sherlock had inflicted more "terror" on the inhabitants of London than had the earthquakes, both of which were perfectly explicable within a naturalist idiom and had in fact inflicted less damage than some spring storms. In his *Seasonal Expostulations* Gordon compared Sherlock unfavorably to Thomas Sprat, a cleric and fellow of the Royal Society who later became bishop of Rochester. In his sermons on the devastating London plague and fire of 1665–66, Gordon reminded his readers, Sprat refused to construe a "mere Account of Nature into a Judgment of Heaven" and resisted the temptation to raise fears or fan the "visions of Enthusiasts."[44] Not so Sherlock, Gordon insisted. People of his ilk were fanning the fires of popular incredulity and giving ground to quacks and mock prophets, to visionaries, judgment-mongers, and "Sharpers in Theology."[45] A writer in the *Remembrancer* was of the same opinion. Fear was a "painful passion" but "not always a useful one," the author concluded. "We may grow giddy in hearkening to the phrensies of enthusiasts" and mistake "occasional incidents ... familiar to nature tho' new and strange to us, for prodigies and portents."[46]

Certainly the clergy was vulnerable on this score. Although many wished to uphold the doctrine of revealed religion and defend the power of prophecy, there was an unsavory legacy of pseudo-messiahs, astrologers, and crazed millenarians from the civil war era that most wished to forget. In the years prior to the earthquakes there had been attempts to redraw the boundaries of just who had the power of prophecy. The Sussex clergyman John Bristed, one of the participants in the earthquake debate, had striven to redraw the boundaries of legitimate prophecy to include "calm heads" and "honest minds," in effect authoritative, respectable clergymen who delivered their messages in a rational, unaffected manner.[47] William Warburton, who also penned a pamphlet on the biblical story concerning earthquakes, believed that natural philosophy itself was a good tool to eliminate the "the rank air of inventive prodigy" from a proper understanding of God's miracles.[48] In other words, natural philosophy could be a useful filter to ponder God's power and bring some reasonableness to revealed religion. This was an argument that Thomas Sprat had propounded during the Great Fire of London in 1666, as Gordon pointedly reminded his readers. "This wild amusing Men's Minds with Prodigies and Conceits of Providence," warned Sprat, "has been one of those Spiritual Distractions of which our Country has long been the Theatre."[49] Only through a proper application of reason and revelation could God's warnings be distinguished from the ravings of conjurers, mock prophets and unscrupulous astrologers who might prey on people's credulity.[50]

Mock prophets were less conspicuous in the mid-eighteenth century than they had been in the era of English civil war and Restoration. Even so, the distinction between rightful revelation and false prophecy was undermined, at least in the eyes of moderate churchmen, by the swarm of mechanic preachers who rose to prominence with Methodism, a few of whom proved to be wild prophets. These included a former journeyman carpenter called Charingtone, aka Dr. Whimwham, who in May 1750 foretold an earthquake in Amersham, Buckinghamshire. He reputedly told people to go to Weedon Hill as a place of refuge, where he would preach to them, assuring his hearers that if they followed his advice they would live until seventy.[51] Unfortunately for Charingtone, the thunder and lightening storm that burst forth electrified one of his hearers and so terrified one pregnant woman that she miscarried, leaving the preacher to face the hazards of a plebeian skimmington. Charingtone was not the only itinerant Methodist to run into trouble. Another was arrested in Frome, Somerset, for acting as if he was a messiah, reputedly restoring the sight of a blind woman and, in the manner of Jesus, "converting his Oatmeal into Cake and transforming his Water into Wine."[52]

Prophecy and revelation could potentially enhance the reputation of the clergy as guides to natural disasters, but it could also stoke the embers of religious enthusiasm in damaging ways. In 1750 the stigma of enthusiasm was damaging because it reminded the public of the bitter internal struggles within the church about the status of Methodism, whose preachers were being routinely mobbed at the behest or connivance of angry squires and parsons. In the

same year as the earthquakes, the pews and benches of the Methodist Mr.
Perronet were burnt in the palace yard at Canterbury by an angry mob, egged
on by the vergers of the Cathedral church.[53] This was a telling reminder of
how the bitterly divisive issue of enthusiasm had penetrated the highest quar-
ters, to the discredit of the established church.

The difficulties of policing the social boundaries of prophecy were, of course,
patently manifest in the earthquake scenario, this time in the shape of a field
preacher and a demobilized soldier. Their antics had the unfortunate effect of
subjecting the clergy to ridicule. Although the clergy disparaged the false prophets and warned people of the folly of fleeing London, for God's hand was everywhere and he could strike at will,[54] the migrations damaged the credibility of
the clergy. To begin with, many people simply did not heed the clergy's advice to
stay in London. Others mischievously suggested that it took "one crack-brain'd
ignorant soldier" to accomplish more "in a few days than all the whole order
could do in some Years." Bishop Sherlock, predictably, was singled out for
scorn. "From the Harangues of Coffeehouse Libertines and Grubean Pamphlets," one commentator remarked, his lordship had become "the public Butt
of abusive Ridicule."[55] As one poet playfully put it to Sherlock:

> You tax the Age with Unbelief
> But where has your Attention been?
> The Scene is chang'd-dispel your Grief
> *Credulity's* the reigning Sin
>
> Britons attend! From Folly's Bed
> A *Dreamer* starts, and tells his Tale,
> And by his Brain-sick Dreams are led,
> Both the *Great* Vulgar, and the *Small*
>
> See SHERLOCK! A believing Age
> *The Word of Prophecy* reject;
> But when a *Dreamer* mounts the Stage,
> Him they receive with *all* Respect.[56]

Determined to illustrate the ineffectual influence of the clergy on public
opinion, anticlerical critics traded stories, some fictional, some not, about the
country's incapacity to reform. Horace Walpole reported to Mann that men
were actually gambling on the causes of the earthquakes at White's. These
wagers so enraged one parson that he declared "such an impious set of people"
would bet a "puppet-show against judgment" if "the last trumpet was to
sound."[57] In a pamphlet that rapidly ran into seven editions, the waggish
dilettante Richard Bentley mimicked prophecy by imagining that the third
earthquake had actually happened. He cast Bishop Sherlock as its first victim

for zealously selling his pamphlet thirteen to a dozen and depicted the fussy Duke of Newcastle, the leading patron in the country, buried in a mass of paper and red tape. Among his other witty scenarios, Bentley had Sir John Barnard, one of the leading financial voices in the City, propose a parliamentary tax on fear and folly, to be levied on all who "transported themselves out of the Reach of the Earthquake." In a topical reference to the recent Westminster by-election, which blazoned across the newspapers, metropolitan and provincial, Bentley had the Opposition caucus, the Independent Electors of Westminster, wishing that the courtiers and their allies were buried in the rubble.

Bentley mischievously imagined inveterate gamblers buried with their cards still in their hands, and lascivious ladies confusing earth tremors with their sexual orgasms.[58] This sort of ribald humor marked several essays on the elite response to the earthquake, satirizing the beau monde's taste for extravagant luxury and libertinism. In one reprinted in the *Newcastle Courant,* for example, the two earthquakes prompt fops to down drops and cordials, ladies to repent their sexual indiscretions, unfaithful husbands to forsake their mistresses, and lawyers to venture to church for the first time in forty years. This genteel company was so panic-stricken by the prospect of a third tremor that they purchased pills against earthquakes from a quack, although sooner or later, the author surmised, they would all revert to the "same state of wickedness" as before.[59]

This appears to have been a parable of what actually happened. After the initial panic, London reverted to form. Bishop Sherlock had called for an end to the London masquerades whose nocturnal revelries and deceits, so he believed, promoted vice and lasciviousness. As one previous pamphleteer put it: masquerading meant "entering into a League with the World, the Flesh, and the Devil."[60] Yet the Venetian-styled Jubilee Ball scheduled at Ranelagh Gardens was allowed to take place, despite protests to the contrary. The single concession that the magistrates made to reformist pressure was to ban faro tables.[61] Cock fights at the south end of St. James's Park continued to be advertised, and the eagerly awaited prize fight between Broughton and Slack, in which thousands of pounds were won or lost, was extensively reported.[62] Even John Cleland's *Fanny Hill* made a reappearance after the second quake, although this time without the homosexual encounter that Fanny watched through a peephole.[63] This was the pornographic novel of the decade, one that Bishop Sherlock had striven to suppress on its first appearance in 1748. In his diocesan letter on earthquakes he had obliquely referred to it as "displaying the most execrable scenes of lewdness" and feared it would inflame "the corrupt passions of the youth of the nation."[64] In the circumstances, he must have been especially peeved to find it thrust under his nose as he renewed the campaign for moral reform in the wake of the tremors.

The fact is that the clergy's call for moral reform fell largely on deaf ears. "The Receptacles of Pleasures and Provocatives in Iniquity are so numerous," remarked *Old England* in May 1750, that "they encrease yearly in this town. Every Season produces new scenes of Dalliance. . . . The Clergy may preach, but they preach in vain. Admonitions have no effect upon us." The authority of the clergy as the arbiters of social reform was openly called into question. Several authors, including Gordon, were troubled by the clergy's campaign against pornography, believing it curbed the freedom of the press. "Spiritual tyranny" had no place in a land of freedom. In any case, making a Mandevillean move, Gordon thought some vice and luxury was the inevitable by-product of a thriving consumer economy and typical of metropolitan centers.[65] The implication was that the clergy were out of touch with the realities of urban life and lacked both the moral authority and political acumen to promote a viable program of social reform. In the context of the aftermath of the War of Austrian Succession, which threw thousands of demobilized soldiers and sailors on the streets on London and generated a veritable crime wave, the tough issues of law, order, and social regulation were best left to local government and Parliament.

Gordon's comments are illuminating, especially when they are set in a larger historical context. In the wake of the London earthquake of 1692 there had also been calls for moral reform. In this instance the clergy helped launch the Reformation of Manners movement whose goal was to crack down on Sabbath-breaking, swearing, public lewdness, and prostitution. By 1701 there were twenty such societies. Their work was supported by Country MPs and a few bishops and for a time was publicized by the Society for the Propagation of Christian Knowledge (SPCK). Although the clergy sounded the tocsin of moral reform, much of the real business of the societies was performed by laymen — merchants, prominent tradesmen, lawyers — who rather controversially used informers to prosecute Sunday tipplers, traders, and blasphemers. Over time the clergy became increasingly distanced from these policing operations, and indeed some divines, such as the bishops of York and Exeter, proved hostile from the beginning, suspecting that these voluntary societies, whose members included Dissenters as well as Churchmen, would undermine the authority of the established church.[66]

The aspirations of the clergy to become the leaders of a moral revolution after 1688 proved to be in vain. The Reformation of Manners movement reached its zenith early, between 1689 and 1701, and thereafter was riven by denominational rivalry. In London it sustained itself rather longer, but after

1725 it was in terminal decline.[67] By then Convocation had collapsed, the Anglican monopoly over schooling had died with the repeal of the Schism Act, and the church's monopoly over moral offenses had declined. Outside of a few dioceses in the north, the business of the church courts shrank. In London the decline was especially marked. In the case of defamation suits, the principal business before the courts, the number of prosecutions dropped from two hundred a year in the 1620s, to forty cases in the early eighteenth century, to a mere twenty by mid-century.[68] By that time more defamation suits in London were being handled by the quarter sessions than by the church courts, a sure sign of the growth of secular power over religious.

The decline in the moral machinery of the church meant that its role in social reform issues was largely exhortatory and educational. Yet at the parish level the presence of the Anglican clergy in eighteenth-century London was declining. Pluralism was on the increase, weekday services had virtually disappeared, and by mid-century more than half the churches offered only one service on Sunday rather than the prescribed two.[69] The decline in services was matched by the decline in strict religious observance. In the interrogatories of the church courts, witnesses were sometimes asked how often they took the sacrament. In my limited sample, a third of all respondents said they had never taken communion, and a further 22 percent said they had not partaken of it within the last five years. These figures indicate a lack of zealotry among the London servants and poor, the principal witnesses in church court cases. It is quite possible, of course, that these witnesses attended sermons even if they did not take the sacrament on a regular basis. Such was the case of Rosa Jones of St. Clement Danes, who claimed she had heard one hundred sermons in seven years, though she could recite only the Creed and the Lord's Prayer but not the Ten Commandments.[70]

None of this suggests a particularly vital church in London during the first half of the eighteenth century, nor one, judging from Rosa Jones, that effectively transmitted its moral message. Certainly the church did help to launch a charity school movement in the 1730s and continued to expiate on the moral benefits of reclaiming the poor through workhouses and hospitals. Through its more evangelical wing, the church also had a hand in the transatlantic awakening and the reclamation of aboriginals, although denominationally these were competitive fields of activity. Even so, the clergy's role in promoting social reform at home became increasingly formulaic and marginal.

In the light of the seemingly intractable social problems confronting London in the eighteenth century, the initiative for social policing and reform fell to a loosely connected group of lay reformers, MPs, JPs, and philanthropic businessmen who launched new enterprises, such as the Foundling and Magdalen hospitals, on an already established base of civic charity. The technical problems of framing new legislation, policing the streets, and funding new philanthropic ventures made the clerical role secondary, more a matter of moral exhortation than the real business of reform. To some clergy this may not have been a problem. Whereas a third of the clergy of the diocese of London were clerical born and bred and thus likely anxious to maintain the integrity and autonomy of their order, an increasing number hailed from the mercantile and professional classes of the metropolis and from bourgeois families who aspired to gentility.[71] As sons and younger brothers of the very class assigned the job of policing London and promoting its philanthropy, they probably accepted their diminishing role in the business of moral reform.

The interweaving of lay and clerical reform is perhaps best illustrated by looking at the one social problem that transfixed the nation in the middle years of the century, the gin craze. The popularity of cheap gin cordials as the drink of choice gave rise to serious misgivings about the "luxury" of the poor, its propensity for vice and crime, its neglect of labor, and its poor reproductive capacities. In the efforts to regulate the sale of gin and curb the addiction of the poor tofor this often adulterated product, the clergy certainly played their part. Thomas Wilson, for example, an active member of the SPCK, wrote a highly influential pamphlet that helped promote the Gin Act of 1736, the act that raised the taxes on spirits and the licensing fees for publicans in an effort to drive the street-sellers out of the market.[72] Yet in the legislative revisions that strove to curb gin drinking as well as provide some revenue for the government, the wishes of the upper clergy were not always respected. In 1743, when the government introduced a bill that increased the excise on gin yet reduced licensing fees in an effort to suppress the black market in cheap, unlicensed gin, the bishops found themselves unable to persuade the government that this was simply a tonic to vice. Thomas Sherlock was so outraged by the proposal that he described it as "the most unchristian Bill that was thought of by any government."[73]

The reservations of the bishops were swept aside. In a time of war, the government was too interested in the revenue-raising potential of the new act to pay much attention to the opinion of their principal prelates. Seen in this context, the flurry of epistles and sermons that followed the earthquakes of 1750 may aptly be seen as a renewed attempt by the clergy to regain the high ground of moral reform, this time in a period of peace when the government's immediate revenue requirements declined, despite calls for further revisions of the rate of interest to contain the national debt. Indeed, the admonitory chorus of 1750, calling upon the nation to heed the warnings of God and repent its ways, was in many respects a reprise of 1692. Its targets were often the same: blasphemy, irreligion, lewdness, and debauchery.

Very occasionally clerics singled out specific issues for redress. Stephen

Hales, long horrified by the gin craze, predictably focused on this issue. William Stukeley emphasized Sabbath-breaking, seeing it as the source of all evils in luxury-ridden cities. Samuel Hull, who delivered a sermon at Loriners' Hall three days after the second earthquake, zoned in on the escalating crime rate. He painted a picture of the capital as a site of ostentatious wealth and desperate misery, where poor men were tempted to commit capital crimes out of necessity and thus "oblig'd to breathe out Life at the Gibbet, and swing into the unknown World in the Cord of Infamy and Scandal."[74] Yet despite these clearly topical themes, most of the messages from the pulpit were framed in general terms. The earthquakes were a wake-up call from God, a providential sign for reformation, and that took in just about everything: from swearing to sodomy, from prostitution to crime, from gambling to masquerades, from moral complacency to preparing oneself for the final summons and receiving it with "transporting Joy." It was an omnibus of social and moral failings, delivered in a tone that was virtually ex cathedra.

Some of the non-clerical pamphleteers were more pointed in their criticisms. One citizen self-consciously amended Bishop Sherlock's charge to lambaste the rich. In his view they rioted "in Excess of Luxury and Debauchery, without Controul or Consideration," and were in danger of dwindling into "a Race of flimsy, foppish, affected, apish beings." Another zoned in on the scandal of Fleet Prison marriages where dissolute clergymen married off the most incongruous of couples or connived at opportunistic marriages solely designed to allow women to cheat their creditors. He was also appalled at the ways that patronage and cronyism had undermined the charitable goals of the Chelsea and Greenwich hospitals.[75] On these specific issues, the clerical voice was ominously silent. What was said about luxury and corruption tended to come from the Dissenting sects rather than the Anglican. Only people like Samuel Chandler and Joseph Besse openly condemned the venality of the age, believing that the "inordinate love of money" was the "reigning sin."[76] Anglicans were more evasive about the sins that beset the rich and well-to-do. They tended to produce a catalogue of do-nots. They called for abstinence and virtue but without addressing the concepts of socially useful appetites or national utility, which is why it was momentarily heeded and then ignored.[77]

Amid this burr of clerical admonition, one clergyman did point the way forward. He was Isaac Maddox, the bishop of Worcester, who on Easter Monday 1750 preached a sermon before the Lord Mayor and Common Council of London and the various governors of the London hospitals. Maddox made no mention of the London earthquakes and certainly did not pitch his sermon in a style of high providentialism. He was preoccupied with two issues: the need to bring the poor, particularly the youthful poor, to labor and to inculcate good work habits; and the need to stamp out the addiction for gin. On the first issue Maddox had relatively little to say beyond commending the use of bridewells to discipline the poor, but he did expatiate on what he saw as the burning social problem of the day, gin. Maddox did not simply denigrate gin-drinking as a moral evil; he sought to show how costly it was to the country in terms of drug-induced crime, lost labor, lost consumerism, and a generation of infants neglected by addictive mothers and callous wet nurses who used gin as a pacifier. In Maddox's view, the gin craze was a "pestilence, the most pernicious that ever befell this kingdom."[78] Unless it was brought under control, civil society and Britain's future as a great commercial and maritime power was threatened.

Maddox did not argue from biblical injunction; he assured his audience that he spoke from "evidence."[79] To show the deleterious effects of gin on the birth and death rate he cited figures from the London Bills of Mortality. In a subsequent pamphlet on the same theme, he cited Henry Fielding's well-known tract *An Enquiry into the late Increase of Robbers* to reveal how gin encouraged crime. Beside Thomas Wilson's well-known missive of 1736, he cited new anti-gin tracts by Stephen Hales and Josiah Tucker, and one by a Dr. Hoffman on the medical effects of drinking cheap liquors.[80]

Throughout Maddox revealed an easy familiarity with neo-mercantilist arguments about the gin problem; that is to say, he calculated the cost benefits of reducing the popular dependence on gin, balancing revenues gained through gin consumption against revenues lost. Maddox recognized that jeremiads against luxury and idleness were not enough to combat the sale of gin or the powerful distilleries that had a stake in the commodity. The argument for regulating gin drinking had to be framed in terms of national utility. Evoking the contemporary unease with the breakdown of law and order in the aftermath of the War of Austrian Succession, Maddox saw the resolution of the gin craze as part of the larger task of repairing civil society, from which Britain could spring more easily to "a military and maritime superiority."[81]

What is important in Maddox's sermon and epistle is the role he assigned the City of London authorities. He saw their participation as crucial to the success of any social reform in the metropolis. In his words, they were the "effectual instruments in the Hand of Providence, for stopping those many, pernicious growing Evils." Not only did the City fathers and merchants have a long legacy of helping the poor through their own charitable institutions, and more recently through new philanthropic institutions like the Foundling Hospital, they also had the capacity, as City magistrates, to "police"; in eighteenth-century parlance, to supervise and regulate social reform. In his *Epistle* Maddox elaborated on the potential forces making for reform. Working from the bottom up, he began with family governance, then he stressed the supervision of "servants" by masters, then the clergy who through door-to-door admonitions and public preaching could alert their flock to new social evils. Next Maddox moved to the magistrates responsible for the implementation of social policies, and finally to the parliamentarians for their legislative enactments.[82] There was nothing particularly novel about this conceptualization of how social reform might be promoted. A former bishop of London, Edmund Gibson, had said much the same in one of his sermons to the Society for the Reformation of Manners.[83] It was the sort of strategy that made zealots of social hierarchy very comfortable. Yet Maddox had a surer sense of how social reform worked in mid-eighteenth-century practice and of the clergy's place within it. He was not averse to deferring to rich merchants and bankers like the lord mayor and aldermen of London when social problems so dictated.

Maddox was a clergymen attuned to a desacralizing age, familiar with all the contemporary arguments that surrounded so critical a social issue as gin drinking. It is through his exhortations that the City of London, and subsequently other large cities, petitioned for a new Gin Act in 1751, which raised the excise and licensing fees on British spirits and prevented distillers from retailing their products.[84] Through his efforts he did more than all the earthquake sermons and admonitions had done, notwithstanding their willingness to address social and moral issues. This is because Maddox understood the public sphere of discourse and discussion, how social issues might be successfully promoted, in ways that some of his clerical colleagues did not.

Maddox was a successful promoter of social reform whose arguments served to highlight the poverty of others. In the hubbub of clerical admonition that accompanied the quakes, his voice was heard. What the earthquake episode of 1750 underscored was not the hegemonic role of religion in British society, let alone providentialism, so much as clerical opportunism, an attempt to seize a moment of panic and uncertainty to reinvigorate the role of the clergy as the moral guardians of the age. It would take more than two tremors to do it. By the mid-eighteenth century coffeehouses and clubs mattered as much as pulpits, and in the field of print, religious tracts were losing out to newspapers, novels, travel literature, and natural history. Sermons continued to be an important mode of communication, to be sure, but they had to meet the challenge of newspapers and the public's disposition for different and varied genres of reading, a tendency that worked against the intensive reading of a few books of piety that had marked the previous century.[85] Circulating libraries in London reveal that by the mid-century religious books routinely comprised less than 10 percent of the published catalogue, and if the Bristol library is indicative of the trend, fewer of those books were actually borrowed.[86] Clergymen needed to negotiate the more secular discourses of print if they were to have the power to persuade; they increasingly discovered they could exert more influence if they actually joined the bench rather than preach to it at some national anniversary. At the very least they had to collaborate with laymen in some form of reform association if they were to win over powerful audiences.

The providential language of the mid-century was increasingly what Charles Taylor would call "immanent" rather than "transcendent." God was not overridingly present so much as simply there, as the divine creator. In the space that was opened up between divine agency and materialism there was room for what Taylor calls the "buffered self," a mental state that fostered a spirit of individual inquiry and a new confidence in moral ordering.[87] Even in the context of catastrophes, where one would expect the clergy to have a captive audience, one finds them frequently on the defensive, carping against natural science, religious indifference, and witty skepticism and blowing up their sermons with the admonitions of divine judgment. This is hardly a hegemonic stance. The discourse of catastrophe was an embattled terrain in which the clergy struggled to make a compelling case for their doctrine of judgments: that natural disasters were retributions for sin, and near-disasters providential warnings. We see this is the earthquake episode of 1750, where admonitions from the clergy were sometimes met with wit and ridicule, and where the providential languages of the pulpit were never able to subdue those of natural science nor to advance, at a time of virtual moral panic about the state of lawlessness in the country, a viable agenda of social reform. As we shall see, that agenda was framed by parliamentarians and by public-minded magistrates like Henry Fielding. It was not framed by the clergy, who, in the early months of 1750 had sought to mobilize their conventional status as the arbiters of manners and morals to reflect on the parlous state of London.

5

Riots, Revels, and Reprisals

One of the great puzzles of the mid-century crime wave is why it engendered such a panic relative to the dimensions of demobilization. The number of servicemen who were actually demobilized was not especially large, in the region of 80,000 as opposed to 157,000 after the Treaty of Utrecht, 35 years earlier. In real terms, around 4 percent of the adult male population was discharged at the mid-century, less than half the number prior to the Hanoverian succession.

Part of the reason for the public anxiety in 1748–53 was the conspicuous reporting of crime in the press. At the time of the Utrecht treaty, robberies around London were reported in a few lines in a two-page paper, and sometimes newsmen satiated the public's appetite for crime stories by simply highlighting the publication of the forthcoming *Criminal Lives*.[1] By the mid-century, crime was routinely reported in larger publications, and occasionally triweeklies and weeklies would indulge the public's fascination with the topic by offering open letters on its wider ramifications for governance and the law. In the expanded public sphere of the mid-eighteenth century, when there were more than 500 coffeehouses in London where clients could read the newspapers, the rising crime rate became a matter of social commentary and debate among a broader audience. Pamphlets like Henry Fielding's *Enquiry into the Causes of the late Increase of Robbers,* which was first published in mid-January 1751, were well advertised, reviewed, debated, and even excerpted in the monthlies. Despite its price of half a crown, the tract sold swiftly: some 1,500 copies in the first run and a second edition of 2,000 within a month. It even inspired a poem in blank verse, "The Morning Walk, or, City Encompassed," in which the author self-consciously linked hands with Fielding and other spokesmen, such as Isaac Maddox, to expose and check the "reigning Evil" of gin tippling and crime that threatened to overwhelm the metropolis.[2]

Another reason why the aftermath of the war generated deep anxieties about social order was that the ruling class was beset by various forms of plebeian recalcitrance. It might be argued that there was nothing particularly unusual about this. In the years 1738–40, for example, as the War of Jenkins' Ear was beginning, disputes over wages, work conditions, and the distribution of food cut deep into the social fabric. The disturbances that coincided with the Peace of Aix-la-Chapelle, however, were noteworthy for their legal intransigence. It was difficult for the Crown to secure prosecutions without over-bearing legislation and considerable political pressure. The opposition to the Gin Acts, which we will discuss in the next chapter, was an object lesson in the cumbrous nature of law enforcement. Legislators could not contain the illegal traffic in gin, nor could they effectively deploy informers to weed out the small fry who serviced the working poor from their stalls, cellars, and street carts. Henry Fielding referred to this resistance in one of his diatribes against the "Fourth Estate." Although this "estate" had not yet demanded a legislative veto as had its counterpart in ancient Rome, he averred, it had "exercised this Power" in the actual execution of laws, "particularly in the Case of the Gin-Act some years ago." In a similar vein he cited the opposition to turnpike trusts, which had been "erected against the Good-will and Pleasure of the Mob," as another troubling sign of plebeian truculence.[3] Once again the Crown had difficulties prosecuting protesters in local jurisdictions.

On a more personal front, Fielding's work as a London magistrate brought him into contact with what he perceived as disturbing signs of collective bargaining by city journeymen, disturbing in that the conventional reciprocities between masters and journeymen had been subverted and the role of JPs as mediators undermined. Fielding's involvement with the prosecution of smuggling gangs drew his attention to the alarming state of affairs in southeast England, where customs officers, troops, and naval cutters proved unable to control the contraband trade in tea and brandy and where the state had recourse to increasingly repressive legislation. Fielding was certainly not alone in viewing the situation in the southeast with alarm. Smugglers rode around the country in large armed companies daring customs officers to arrest them. Their behavior had come "to such a Head," remarked one observer, "that it may not be improperly call'd a Kind of Rebellion."[4] One prominent Whig, Charles Sackville, Lord Middlesex, suggested that the smugglers could only be subdued by mobilizing a propertied militia to supplement to existing forces of law and order.[5] Cumulatively, these symptoms of plebeian discontent gnawed away at the confidence of the patrician class to exercise its authority in what should have been a hierarchical, deferential social order.

The problem of order also surfaced over popular Jacobitism. The military defeat of the rebels in 1746 at Culloden Moor had by no means extinguished the last vestiges of Jacobite sympathy. Well into the peace the government agonized over whether France might fund another rebellion. Through its spies, it was constantly on the lookout for any signs of French-Jacobite preparations for another uprising. In the immediate aftermath of the Forty-Five, the government's policy was one of repression and military policing. Highlanders were harassed and sometimes put to the sword if incriminating evidence of their participation in the rebellion could be found. The Highland forts and garrisons were reinforced with new roads and bridges, and seven foot regiments and three from the dragoons patrolled the disaffected areas, including the islands of the northwest.[6] Every effort was made to eliminate the clan culture and informal economy that might sustain the military presence of the disloyal Highlander. There was consequently a crackdown on smuggling and cattle theft. Ward tenures, by which tenants could be recruited for military service, were abolished. So, too, was the wearing of Highland dress. Beyond this, the government tried to develop commercial farming on the forfeited estates, which were not put up for purchase as before but remained the property of the Crown. A Scottish herring fishery was launched to wean the Highlander from those pastoral habits that many felt encouraged thievery. And somewhat later, in 1756, an act was passed to simplify the laws pertaining to the curing of fish and to suppress the imposts levied on fishermen by local landlords. In this way the government hoped that all feudal obstructions to industry and commerce might be removed, so that a "civilized" Highlands could be better assimilated into the Union.

The Jacobite threat had always been most formidable in Episcopalian Scotland, especially the Highlands, but there were other areas of the country where the embers of disaffection still burned. During the 1745 rebellion, most parts of England and Wales had remained loyal to the Hanoverian dynasty. But in the march south, and it should be remembered that Prince Charles's army reached Derby, the Jacobites picked up supporters. This was especially the case in Lancashire. In Manchester, Stuart supporters raised a regiment to fight King George's armies, a reckless adventure that resulted in some grisly executions. Francis Townley, the man responsible for raising the Manchester regiment and very briefly the governor of Carlisle, was sentenced to be hanged, drawn, and quartered, a particularly gruesome punishment reserved for those found guilty of treason. So, too, were some other Manchester notables, included Thomas Deacon junior, the son of a non-juror minister, and Thomas Syddall, a prominent wigmaker whose father had been executed for his role in the meetinghouse riots of 1715. In July 1746 these three men were taken from New Gaol Southwark to Kennington Common, where they were briefly hanged, beheaded, and had their entrails burnt in the executioner's fire. From the accounts in the newspapers, it does not appear that they were subjected to an evisceration while alive, as many a Tudor treason-maker had been.[7] Even so, these executions, watched in the rain by thousands of spectators, were brutal enough. Townley's head was piked at Temple Bar. The heads of the others were pickled and carried back to Manchester and Carlisle, where they were exhibited to remind people of their "foul" crimes.

Eleven officers of the Manchester regiment were executed in 1746; two were banished; three were transported to Antigua. Apart from those who gave king's evidence, only one was pardoned. The soldiers in the regiment suffered similarly, especially the sergeants, although a higher percentage was sent to Antigua rather than face the noose.[8] In meting out these punishments, the government hoped to close a troubling chapter in northern Jacobitism. These expectations proved premature. In one circulating ballad, Townley's ghost returned to remind the Duke of Cumberland of his brutal suppression of the Highlands. The heads paraded at the Exchange in Manchester disappeared. And although the tide of political sentiment ran very much in favour of the Hanoverians after 1745, white roses were defiantly worn on Stuart anniversaries.[9] In the few closed boroughs where the power of Tory-Jacobite patrons was still unassailable, some gentlemen went even further. In November 1748, for instance, Peter Legh and his Tory cronies regaled themselves at a dinner of the Newton Hunt and flamboyantly declared the Pretender at the Market Cross. They had the audacity to offer money to "any likely Fellow" who would enlist for Prince Charles. For these serious transgressions, which were technically treasonable acts, they drew the ire of a Whig mob from Wigan. The mob smashed the windows of their inn and reappropriated public space by proclaiming King George.[10]

The geography of disaffection at the mid-century was different than it had been earlier, in the first years of the Hanoverian succession. In 1750 it was concentrated in areas of the country where Whig-Tory rivalry was still intense and sectarian animosity sharp. It was particularly resilient in those regions of the North and Midlands where there had been a rash of attacks upon Dissenting meetinghouses in 1715, a phenomenon that prompted the passing of the Riot Act. The government had a taste of this during the Staffordshire elections of 1747, when the defection of the Leveson Gowers to the government side provoked accusations of perfidy from Tory ranks and raised the stakes of party conflict. At the Lichfield races on Whittington Health, two Tory knights appeared at the head of the Burton mob, "most of 'em in Plaid Waistcoats, Plaid Ribbons round their Hatts, and some with White Cockades." Those from Birmingham were similarly attired, and many drank the Pretender's health in the streets. One loyal soldier who had the audacity to shout "God Bless King George, Down with the Plaids," had his arm broken, and at the races themselves, the Duke of Bedford, the cousin of Lord Gower, was roughed up. Among the rabble-rousers were tailors and leatherworkers from Lichfield, a butcher, a shoemaker, a maltster and innholder from Sutton Coldfield, the son of the current mayor of Lichfield, and two laborers who worked for Samuel Hill, Esquire, and Lord Uxbridge.[11] We know this because the attorney general, Sir Dudley Ryder, was bent on prosecuting them.

The flurry of disaffection that broke out in Lancashire and the West Midlands in the aftermath of the Forty-Five did not end with the Lichfield and Newton hunts. In 1750 the government encountered other instances of Jacobite revelry that it felt compelled to investigate. In Walsall a trooper witnessed a ritual burning of the Hanoverian monarch at the Hill Top just outside of town on Restoration Day. According to his account, an effigy of King George I or II was hoisted on a pole to the amusement of hundreds of spectators.[12] Dressed in a brown paper coat, decked out with hose, shoes, gloves, and wig, along with horns affixed to the barber's block of a head and a bunch of turnips in one hand and an orange in the other, the effigy was ritually abused like a cockshy and even fired upon. Later that evening, the effigy was taken down and dragged around the market cross. It was then taken to the churchyard, where it was burnt "with great rejoicing." According to the testimony of the soldier, the mob paraded the streets until nine o'clock crying out, "Down with the Rumps and Down with the Hanover Line."[13]

Initially the officers stationed at Walsall wrote the episode off as a frivolous affair, an act of sheer juvenilia. But as rumors began to circulate about this revel, higher authorities pressed for an inquiry. The mayor of Walsall had conveniently been out of town on business on 29 May, the day of the revel. Initially he seemed willing to cooperate. "The Hill Top was a bad place to live in," he assured Captain Hamilton. "There were thereabouts several disaffected poor low-lived Fellows of bad characters."[14] Yet when he was pressed for further information, he simply made "lite of the matter." His prevarications might not have mattered had not a buckle maker strolled down the streets of Walsall singing treasonable tunes in anticipation of the Pretender's birthday on 10 June.[15] At this point the government sent the king's messenger, Nathaniel Carrington, to investigate. The local leatherworkers clearly resented the intrusion. They were no doubt doubly irritated that Carrington conducted his inquiry with the help of Sir Richard Wrottesley, JP, Lord Gower's son-in-law, who had run in the controversial Staffordshire election of 1747 in the Gower interest. Some of the angry defiance exhibited at the Lichfield races stemmed from Wrottesley's efforts to unseat the popular Tory Sir Walter Bagot.

Not surprisingly, Carrington had considerable trouble collecting evidence about the effigy burning, especially on the question of whether the effigy itself represented the reigning monarch. Eventually he felt confident enough to arrest six of the rioters and commit them to Stafford gaol. To do so he had to confront a mob of five to six hundred people, but no violence was offered.[16] Still, Carrington feared there might well be an attempt to rescue the rioters, especially when it was rumored that the local colliers would join the buckle makers in some sort of showdown. He called for more troops, thus escalating the already tense situation. Six troops of cavalry were called in to deal with "the Confusion" that had now spread to Birmingham and Wednesbury. Dragoons from Sir Philip Honeywood's regiment clashed with rioters, and several soldiers were killed.[17] Once order was restored, the Restoration Day rioters were prosecuted at the local assizes in August 1750. Charged with shooting at an image of his present majesty and "other treasonable practices," the rioters were admitted to bail on condition that they appear at King's Bench at the beginning of the next term. Eight were charged at the next Staffordshire assizes, March 1751, most for firing at the effigy. Six were found guilty and ordered to appear at King's Bench to receive their judgment. There, the four male offenders were ordered to stand in the pillory, at the Royal Exchange, at Charing Cross and at Temple Bar, where spectators could also gape at the heads of traitors. They were then subjected to two years' hard labor in Bridewell. Their female companions fared a little better. They did not have to face the humiliation of rotten eggs and filth upon their person but were given a year's hard labor in the House of Correction.[18]

The government was clearly troubled by the Walsall revels, enough to order an official inquiry and pack the culprits off to King's Bench, away from courts where they might win sympathy. What frayed the government's nerves was the knowledge that trouble was also brewing at Shrewsbury. Like Walsall, this Shropshire town had a strong legacy of sectarian rivalry, one that in 1715 had manifested itself in the destruction of the Dissenting meetinghouse. During the 1720s the Whigs had captured the town's political representation only by drastically reducing its electorate. Tories responded to this situation with a festive politics that was anti-Whig and anti-Hanoverian. In 1749 on the Pretender's birthday inhabitants paraded around town a white flag bearing the words "Long Live Prince Charles."[19] To prevent a similar occurrence in 1750 the local commander ordered troops to police the street on the eve of the tenth. On their rounds they encountered a master bricklayer and his laborers singing "Charley O," a Scottish ditty commemorating Bonnie Prince Charlie's march to Derby in 1745.[20] The patrol confronted the revellers but was humiliatingly driven down the street for its pains. The troops returned with reinforcements, and a full-scale brawl ensued in which several soldiers and laborers were wounded. The town blamed the soldiers for the disturbance and began a prosecution against them at King's Bench. A paper discovered in the marketplace urged the "Honest Lads of Shrewsbury" to take to arms and act "as Englishmen, as Men of Courage."[21] The commanding officer, for his part, urged the government to defend the soldiers. If the Tories won this legal suit through the testimony of "a parcell of Jacobite Witnesses," he told the secretary of state, "there will be no room for any of His Majesty's Troops to live in this Town, nor any one about us."[22] As it was, his soldiers had been subjected to humiliating taunts to drink the Pretender's health and continually had to stomach the singing of Jacobite songs in the streets.

The Walsall and Shrewsbury episodes illustrated a residual Tory resistance to Whig rule, aggravated by the intrusive presence of troops and commanders who saw "traitorous" riots at every turn.[23] Walsall and Shrewsbury Tories used Jacobite symbolism to tease the Whigs, to reaffirm their own political traditions, and to demarcate their territory. However droll these mischievous revels might appear, they troubled the Whigs, who were determined to erase the memory of the Stuarts from the political lexicon.

The government also faced opposition farther south, in Bristol. West-Country Jacobitism was waning at the mid-century and not causing the local authorities much concern.[24] But trouble was brewing on another front, one associated with turnpikes. Turnpikes were designed to improve the communication networks necessary for Britain's booming capitalism, moving materials across the country more efficiently and cheaply. Higher transportation costs nonetheless cut into the incomes of petty producers who resented the extra tax imposed on carrying their goods to local markets. In the Bristol area turnpike trusts represented one potential site of the new political consensus forged by Whigs and Tories in the mid-century decades, for members of both political factions were actively involved in the enterprise, which was organized under the umbrella of the local common council. The turnpike trusts smacked of commercial oppor-

tunism, for the early investment in roads was not accompanied by any percep-
tible improvement for the producers who had to use them. Consequently the
new trusts met with protests. In 1727, the local muscle in the Bristol area, the
Kingswood colliers, resented the idea of having to pay extra tolls on their coal
and the expropriation of furze from the commons to repair the roads. Seeing
the turnpikes as an assault on their customary economy by a confederacy of
"jobbers," the colliers destroyed the turnpikes that ran through their forest
and threatened that "if any more are erected, they will serve them in the same
manner."[25] They were as good as their word: when the trustees attempted to
re-erect the gates, they immediately destroyed them and marched through the
center of Bristol "with clubs and staves in a noisy manner" to let the authorities know they meant business. The following year Parliament passed an act by
which anyone convicted of destroying a turnpike or river work was liable to a
public whipping and three months' imprisonment for the first offense, seven
years' transportation for the second. Yet in 1731, when new roads were developed by the Bristol turnpike trust, the colliers rose again and burnt all the
turnpike houses in the vicinity. The local JPs attempted to wrestle with this
rash of protests, which had now spread north into Gloucester and Hereford-
shire. They did so ineffectually, despite troops, the transportation of ringleaders, and a new act in 1735 that made the destruction of turnpikes a capital
offense. In 1739 the Bristol Trust was still inoperable because "the colliers
have pulled down, and do constantly pull down, the turnpikes."[26] As late as
1749, a parliamentary petition revealed, no turnpike gates had survived popular destruction.

In 1749 members of the Bristol gentry petitioned Parliament to renew their
trust and to extend their control of the roads to the south and west of the city
as well as to Bath and Gloucester. They broadened their proprietary base
beyond Bristol by adding new names to the board of trustees. They also offered a strategic concession to the colliers in an effort to forestall any serious
opposition. Under the terms of the new act, carts of coal were allowed to travel
toll-free, whereas under the previous act only coals carried on horseback were
given a concession, and then a half toll.[27] This change did a little to placate the
colliers, but it certainly did not deter others from destroying turnpikes. In late
July some "country people" from Somerset descended on the turnpike at the
Ashton road and destroyed it within thirty minutes. The following day another group of country people, some naked to the waist, others with blackened
faces, destroyed the turnpike at Don Cross on the Toghill road,[28] boring holes
in the posts and blowing them up with gunpowder.

The turnpike commissioners attempted to counter these outbreaks of violence by erecting a chain across the Ashton gate and continuing to collect the

toll. Farmers and laborers retaliated by driving cattle and colts through the cordon on their way to the Bristol fair. On their return, they threatened the commissioners with a horse-whipping. Three men — John Walsh, George Hickes, and John Ould — were seized in this confrontation and brought before a local JP.[29] Two were released upon the payment of a fine of £5 for deliberately evading tolls, but they were bound over to face more serious charges at the next quarter sessions. The third was sent to the jail in Shepton Mallet.

These arrests raised the tempo of protest. A "prodigious body" of country people converged on Ashton gate, this time with drums beating, shouting "Down with the turnpikes! Down with the turnpikes!" Wielding "cutting instruments fixed on long staffs," they prevented the tollhouse from being rebuilt and threatened anyone who dared to do so.[30] They also attacked the house of a gentleman whom they mistakenly thought was a commissioner, ripping out his sash windows. Another party of protesters attacked the tollhouse on the Dundry road and signalled that they would return the following day to finish off the job. Tipped off that this might happen, the commissioners marshalled a posse of constables and demobilized sailors. The posse ventured eight miles into Somerset in an effort to arrest the ringleaders, picking up one man at Backwell and bringing him back to Bristol pinioned to a horse. A couple of drummers were also arrested at Ashton gate, and, to the dismay of the country people, they divulged the names of other rioters, some of whom were taken up.

Protesters once again swung into action, this time converging on Bedminster under the leadership of two men on horseback, one "with his face black'd," the other a young gentleman farmer from Nailsea who carried a standard.[31] This group styled themselves "Jack-a-Lents" and had JL on their caps and hats, a reference to the effigy (of Winter or of Judas Iscariot) that was traditionally stoned and burnt on Ash Wednesday. As such they saw themselves as an army of redressers, revenging themselves on the social "traitors" who had affronted community norms and threatened to undermine their standard of living. Their immediate task was to tear down the Ashton gate, which had been quickly rebuilt. But they also directed their anger on Stephen Durbin, the tythingman of the hundred who had turned the three rioters over to the commissioners. They demolished his house, breaking a chain in an attempt to pull down some of the main timbers. They also raised contributions for their fellow rioters and moved toward Redcliff Hill, probably in an effort to enter Bristol and free them from Newgate. Anticipating this, the authorities closed all gates to the city, so the Jacks-a-Lents moved on to Totterdown, where they began leveling the gates and sentry boxes of the turnpikes on the Bath and Pensford roads. There they were confronted by the moving posse of the commissioners, who forced them to retreat over Knowle Hill. Sailors cut down some of the protesters with cutlasses, thirty turnpike rioters were arrested, and the Riot Act was read.

At this point the country people called on the colliers, who thus far had remained aloof from the protests. Laborers toured the smelting works and coal pits around Kingswood in an attempt to rustle up some aid, and although the colliers were divided on whether to join the agitation, some certainly did, despite efforts by the commissioners and local industrialists to dissuade them.[32] Miners helped demolish the Toghill turnpike and started raising contributions for the campaign against the turnpikes. Some called upon their fellow colliers in the North Somerset coalfield around Paulton and Clutton.[33] The liaison between the two groups was badly coordinated, and led to accusations of treachery from the Somerset group, who felt they had been needlessly mobilized. Nonetheless, more turnpikes were threatened. Some protesters declared not one would stand "in the Country," that is, in the Bristol region. One newspaper reported that the Yate (Chipping Sodbury) and Bath turnpikes were under attack "if not already down" and that rioters were demanding that those arrested be released.[34] These rumors, and the threat of approximately seven hundred country labourers and colliers descending upon the city,[35] was enough to put Bristol on an emergency footing. For two or three days its residents anxiously awaited the arrival of troops, with demobilized soldiers recruited for guard duty and many citizens enrolling as special constables. Bristol, then the second largest city in England, was essentially under popular siege, exposing the remaining turnpikes to attack. In fact, the turnpike at Yate was demolished before the arrival of the second regiment of dragoons, and another at Stokes Croft, close to the city, was saved only by the intervention of demobilized soldiers and sailors.[36]

The presence of the troops swung the balance of force in favor of the authorities. Certainly it emboldened the local dignitaries to seek reprisals. The mayor of Bristol, Michael Weekes, had been reluctant to intervene in the riots, which he felt were inflamed "not only from the inveteracy of the Country People but from the indiscreet warmth and precipitate measures of the acting Trustees," many of whom belonged to the Tory Steadfast Club.[37] Party politics was clearly complicating the response of the authorities. With the troops' arrival , however, the mayor believed peace would soon be restored, and he eagerly reported that the "gentlemen in the country" were keen to have a quick trial.[38] Since the Bristol assizes were about to begin, an effort was made to try the turnpike rioters expeditiously. But this plan was postponed at the request of the commissioners because the prosecuting witnesses were not ready to testify.

The recorder of Bristol, Sir Michael Foster, concurred with the decision to postpone the trials. He thought a special commission should be convened to deal with "such heinous and aggravating Offences."[39] The attorney general, Sir Dudley Ryder, agreed. He wondered "whether in a Case of such open publick insult upon government and the Laws, and where the Gentleman of the Country [were] immediately concerned" there was not the need for a "speedy and solemn Trial, in order to strike a Terror in the most effectual manner." It was best, he thought, to hold a special commission in a county adjacent to Somerset, where there might be a "disinterested jury."[40] In fact, the eighteen rioters at Bristol were tried at the Wiltshire assizes in Salisbury under the terms of the 1735 act against turnpikes, which made it possible to try offenders in a neighboring county. There the grand jury declared six indictments to be ignoramus. For the twelve that went to trial, the Crown prosecution encountered some difficulty. The trial of the first turnpike protester, Isaac Coles, took up the better part of the day, and although there seemed to be "very full and clear evidence" of guilt, the jury acquitted him.[41] A new jury was empanelled to hear the next case, that of William Denmeade, but once again the defendant was acquitted. The Crown counsel then abandoned the other prosecutions, sensing that the jury would be overly sympathetic to the turnpike rioters, and so ten further defendants were acquitted. The best that the Crown could manage was to bind eleven of the rioters over to the Taunton assizes to answer for other offenses.[42] Five of these defendants never came to trial because they died of smallpox while in jail.

At the Taunton assizes the prosecutions once again faltered. Several bills were not found; many turnpike rioters were acquitted. Sympathy for them ran deep.[43] The Crown was able to successfully prosecute only two men, Thomas Perry and John Roach. They were charged under the Riot Act with pulling down Stephen Durbin's house in Bedminster and sentenced to be hanged. It was widely anticipated that they would be reprieved at the intercession of some local gentlemen. Some newspapers reported they had indeed been pardoned, but in fact they were executed at Ilchester. Both refused to admit their guilt at the gallows.[44]

The executions of Perry and Roach did not mark the end of turnpike protests, nor of efforts to bring protesters to justice. Letters sent to the mayor of Bristol threatened arson if the turnpikes were rebuilt. The commissioners pressed for further prosecutions.[45] In September they asked the Duke of Newcastle for a speedy trial of those protesters still in jail, and several more people were taken up for the destruction of the tollhouses at Totterdown. In mid-September the newspapers were speculating whether these prisoners would be tried by a special commission in London, although it appears that they were prosecuted on the western circuit as before, for troops were ordered to Somerset to attend some of the trials there.[46] Meanwhile bailiffs strove to track down the Kingswood colliers who were active in the riots. When they attempted to arrest one of the "underground men" named Harborough, alias Reynolds, he barricaded himself in the upper room of his house and kept them at bay with large stones and a pitchfork.[47] After this incident, armed colliers patrolled Kingswood every night and were quite prepared to confront officers of the law who ventured into the forest to arrest them. To make the point, the patrols fired slugs into the turnpike lodge on the Toghill road.[48] As on previous occasions when they had fallen afoul of the law, the colliers used their muscle to keep officers away. Their reputation as "a set of ungovernable people" remained intact.

The turnpike riots and their prosecution ended messily and left a legacy of bitterness. They also illustrated how difficult it was to prosecute rioters locally when their actions won public sympathy. The same was largely true of the smugglers of the southeast. During the eighteenth century major areas of the counties of Kent and Sussex were in decline, especially the Weald, which had previously housed a thriving iron industry. Demographically deaths outpaced births well into the 1740s, and little work was to be had beyond grinding agricultural labor, at least outside the Medway towns.[49] The demands of the fiscal-military state, however, opened up other opportunities. Tea was a taxable commodity, an increasingly attractive taxable commodity for a government confronted with spiralling wartime expenses yet bent on reducing the land tax to placate the gentry.[50] It was a convenient tax, too, both for customs and excise, because the East India Company controlled the official trade in tea, selling it by public auction to dealers who had to store it in bonded warehouses. East India stock and East India financiers were critical to the health of public credit and to the national debt, which at the end of the war of Austrian Succession surpassed £75 million. As tea drinking became increasingly popular, both the company and the government benefited, with the tax on tea approximating its wholesale value on the Continent.

The trouble with this policy was that it was a boon to smuggling, especially in counties such as Sussex and Kent, which were closest to the Continent. Tea could be bought from Dutch and French East India companies at a third of the official British price and sold for double on the black market.[51] Even allowing for overheads and the risks of confiscation, smugglers could rake in a healthy profit of 30 percent or more. Local workers could also benefit. Agricultural laborers were more than willing to lose a night's sleep for half a guinea's work with the smugglers, especially when it represented a week's wages.[52] Some became dollop men, carrying hundredweight loads of tea to London in specially designed sleeves and pockets. Others joined the smuggling fraternities on a more permanent basis. Such was the case of John Cook of Hastings, who followed his father as a "daily Labourer in Husbandry" until the lure of smuggling took him to the gangs. And of Samuel Austin, whose father was a failed tenant farmer turned farm laborer, leaving his son little choice but to follow his father into the fields or join the smugglers. He opted for smuggling as soon as he was able to ride, rejecting "any other way of Life, or Business."[53]

Smuggling was a business. Probably half of the three to four million pounds of tea consumed annually in Britain at the mid-century was contraband.[54] A major part of that tea, worth probably £500,000 annually, was run off the south and east coasts, not to mention the gallons of French brandy brought in to satisfy an elite clientele that combined tea with spirit drinking. Many of the ports in the region had a vested interest in smuggling. John Wesley chaffed at the fact he could not wean coastal communities from smuggling, especially the one in Rye.[55] Admiral Vernon similarly bemoaned the hundreds of men who made their living from it. In Deal, he complained, there were at least two hundred "young men and sea-faring people" in the "infamous trade," which had converted "honest industrious fishermen" into "lazy, drunken and profligate smugglers."[56]

Smuggling was an organized crime. It had to be given the scale of the operations; — the need to transport huge horse-loads of contraband from the coast and find hidden sanctuaries for it before selling it to dealers. But it also insinuated itself into coastal and agrarian communities, which did not think it a crime at all. As the Ordinary of Newgate lamented in his mini-obituary of one Thomas Puryour, aka Blacktooth:

> The common People of England in general, fancy there is nothing in the Crime of Smuggling, but cheating the King of a small Part of his Revenue; and that there is no Harm done to the Community in general, or to the Properties of particular Persons: They think they have a Right to shun, as much as possible, paying any Duty for their Goods, and what they get by their Dexterity in that Manner is honest Gain, to be enjoyed as the Fruits of their Industry and Labour.[57]

This attitude among country folk made it very difficult to control smuggling. The government spent £20,000 a year trying to control this illicit traffic, and enforced its actions with formidable legislation. In the 1720s Parliament passed a series of Hovering Acts intended to prevent vessels loitering with intent outside territorial waters. Vessels below a certain size and carrying suspect cargoes were liable to forfeiture.[58] As a result over 200 smuggling boats were confiscated between 1723 and 1736, and 2000 people were prosecuted for running or receiving contraband. These successes came with a human cost: 250 revenue officers were beaten or wounded by smuggling gangs, and 6 were murdered.[59] At Ipswich smugglers had become "very numerous and so insolent in the town and country that they bid defiance to the officers and threaten their lives."[60] At Beccles, in a taste of what was to come, smugglers had hiked an officer-informer out of bed, tied him naked on a horse, then whipped him and rode him off into the night in what was clearly a kind of charivari.

In response to this violence, Parliament attempted to tighten the laws against smuggling and to strengthen the hand of magistrates and revenue officers. An act passed in 1736[61] gave magistrates the power to detain any person within five miles of the coast who was suspected of intending to run goods and hold them in house of correction for a whipping or one month's hard labor. Men transporting six pounds of unlicensed tea or five gallons of brandy within five miles of the coast or a navigable river were ipso facto considered smugglers and were thus liable to seven years' transportation. So, too, were three of more men traveling around the coast armed or masked, or those that obstructed or wounded revenue officers, or those who assembled to run the goods. Smugglers who cooperated with the authorities in disclosing two other accomplices were offered a pardon; indeed, anyone currently under prosecution before May 1736 could claim a general indemnity, although their prosecutions would be resumed if they offended again.[62]

The success of the 1736 act depended upon breaking the community's protection of smugglers and fracturing the smuggling bands themselves. It was designed to embolden revenue officers and magistrates to crack down on what looked to be an epidemic of smuggling. Unfortunately for the government, the agencies of law enforcement were too weak and too complicit with the local culture of coastal smuggling for the act to make a difference. Some of the local gentry in the southeast were upset with an act that potentially hindered their hunting activities considering it an outrageous challenge to their right to bear arms and shoot game.[63] Magistrates too frequently winked at smuggling activities, especially when they knew they were condoned or even encouraged by local people whose livelihood depended on that trade. Riding officers sometimes found the slog of detection too unrewarding for the risks it involved, even though the law guaranteed them a share in the profits of seized cargoes.[64] Although the customs commissioners in London tried to deny it, many officers had a give-and-take relationship to the smuggling fraternities. Some were not above taking bribes and ignoring midnight runs along the coast. Of one riding officer it was said: "He's as easy as can be to make him quiet, for do but dash a bottle of Brandy in his face, and he is as blind as a Beetle."[65] Others, like a collector of Faversham, were slow to alert the authorities to the known itinerary of smugglers.[66] Moreover, informers were not very forthcoming. They were clearly intimidated by the hazards of snitching on smugglers who might rough them up or worse.

The 1736 legislation resulted in an escalation of violence. Despite the fact that customs officers were often backed up with military support, "smart engagements" or skirmishes became commonplace.[67] One revenue officer from Rochester complained in 1740: "We are very much infested with Smugglers that go in such large Bodies armed with Blunderbusses and other offencive [sic] Weapons, severall of which have called at my House, swaring [sic] they would kill me or any other Officer they should meet with."[68] The Sussex supervisor, Major Battine, produced an account of fifty incidents between January 1740 and April 1745 in which armed bands of smugglers confronted the authorities while unloading and running contraband in the county.[69] The size of the gangs ranged from thirteen to one hundred men, with the most typical score being fifty.

Normally the smugglers were more than a match for the revenue officers. Smugglers fired at officers and pummeled them into submission, intimating them and preventing them from rescuing the contraband. One riding officer at Bexhill, a man named Philip Bailey, was fired on several times as the smugglers unloaded their cargo and was pursued to his own house. Later a party of one hundred smugglers ransacked his house from top to bottom, destroyed his linen and furniture, and rode off "in triumph" carrying confiscated tea.[70] Another riding officer, this time from Pett, near Hastings, was waylaid by a gang of smugglers as he was riding with his father and assistant. He was beaten "so barbarously that he lay for some time seemingly Dead."[71] On eleven occasions noted by Major Battine, smugglers confined the officers while they went about their business. At Pevensey Bay in July 1742, they forced the two riding officers to board a cutter that lay off the coast. Most of these confrontations occurred at night, but not all. In January 1742 smugglers ran their goods near the Pett racecourse at ten o'clock in the morning in open defiance of the officers. At Langley Point near Eastbourne, they unloaded their goods and confined the officers "in the Middle of the Day."[72] Act or no act, the smugglers were operating with impunity. When smugglers rode through town in large groups, locals looked the other way. On one occasion, they sent a letter to the mayor of Boston in the Fens, threatening to burn the town if they were "interrupted in their business."[73]

The most intrepid of the gangs hailed from Hawkhurst, a decaying woollen town in the Weald.[74] In October 1735 the Hawkhurst gang clashed with customs officers and dragoons at Hollington in an affray in which one of its likely runners was killed by two dragoons. Encouraged by a favorable coroner's report, the gang tried unsuccessfully to prosecute the dragoons. They also earmarked the Hastings customs officer, one Thomas Carswell, as the mastermind behind the operation, and five years later killed him when he was on a reconnoitre.[75] This episode established the Hawkhurst gang's reputation for tough, retaliatory action. Under the leadership of Arthur Gray, an ex-butcher who amassed a sizable fortune in the smuggling business, the gang embarked on some daring exploits, secure in their superiority of numbers and weapons. Riding around the country "uncommonly armed," with a brace of pistols and a carbine on their shoulders, they defied people to turn them in. In 1745 members of the Hawkhurst gang rode through Lewes, the principal town of Sussex, in broad daylight with their pistols cocked. They stopped for a pint at the White Horse Inn, directly across from the law courts, and harangued the waiter who did not serve them promptly. One of them grabbed a sergeant's halberd from the inn and waved it as some sort of standard. As they rode through on High Street they haphazardly fired at the windows to restrain the locals' curiosity of what one witness described as "a sort of rebellion."[76] Later contemporaries would describe their actions in much the same way. George Bishop used exactly the same words, "a sort of rebellion," thinking such armed cavalcades were "highly inconsistent with, and greatly reproachful to, civil government"[77]

The most daring adventure conducted by the gang was the raid on Poole Customs House in October 1747. On this occasion a party of thirty to sixty men (accounts vary) rode across three counties to recover contraband that a customs contractor had impertinently taken from one of their cutters. Around midnight on 7 October, thirty of their number broke down the doors to the upper warehouse with crowbars and hammers. They ignored the rum and brandy stored in the lower warehouse but removed the tea, all 4,200 pounds of it, save for one 5-pound bag, which was damaged. Having loaded the tea on their horses, they rode back through the country "in triumph"[78] (figure 7).

The Poole raid was an audacious act. The Hawkhurst gang and their associates congregated at Charlton Forest, the hunting ground of the Duke of Richmond, the master of horse at the Court of King George, his regent when he was in Hanover, and a close friend of Newcastle and Bedford, for whom he pulled strings in the Westminster by-election. Some of those on the October ride were outlaws of the state, with £500 rewards on their head as a result of draconian legislation passed in 1746, which outlawed them on the basis of a simple information and proclamation if they did not surrender to the authorities within forty days. Others like Thomas Fairall, of Horsmonden, Kent, a man "bred to no Business . . . but inured to smuggling," were soon to become so.[79] In assembling on the grounds of a prominent Whig patron, the sporting Duke

Fig 7: The Hawkhurst gang recover their contraband from the Poole Customs House, in *A full and genuine history of the . . . murders of William Galley . . . ,* London, 1749.

of Sussex, and in riding in broad daylight as outlaws, they were defying both the power of the state and its most prestigious magnates.

Unfortunately for the gang, at least one member, John Dymer, was identified, and a witness named Daniel Chater was subpoenaed to give evidence. Fellow smugglers got wind of this, entrapped Chater and his accompanying officer, William Galley, in a pub at Rowlands Castle, on the border of Hampshire and Sussex, and tortured them to death.[80] The elderly Galley was horse-whipped until he virtually expired and then buried, possibly while still alive. Chater was mutilated, hanged from a well, and when the cord broke, stoned to death. Even by the standards of the eighteenth century, these were particularly brutal crimes. Henry Pelham described them as "a scene of villainy and barbarity I never before heard or read of."[81] The *Bath Journal* thought the murders quite unbecoming a Christian country and concluded with a couplet from Lord Rochester. "Birds feed on Birds, Beasts on each other prey, / But SAVAGE MAN alone does MAN betray."[82]

As public opinion began to swing away from the smugglers, the Duke of Richmond went out of his way to capture the culprits. Unnerved that his former butler was seen with the Hawkhurst gang and that some of his servants were likely familiar with its movements, he made the prosecution of the smugglers his personal crusade.[83] This was easier said than done. Richmond complained that the county of Sussex had been intimidated into silence, and at one point he suggested to Pelham that outlaws not accused of murder or the raid on Poole be offered a pardon to secure the murderers' whereabouts.[84] Eventually two smugglers present at the murders turned king's evidence, and Richmond was able to organize a special commission at Chichester to try their accomplices in January 1749, even though the murder of Galley technically occurred in Hampshire. All seven men prosecuted for these crimes were sentenced to death.[85] One, William Jackson, a laborer from Aldsworth, aged fifty, died in prison the night before he was to be executed. One newspaper suggested that the thought of the gibbet totally unnerved him. The others were hanged on the Broyle, a prominent hill outside Chichester. Benjamin Tapner, who murdered Chater, was then exhibited in chains at St. Roches Hill; William Carter, who murdered Galley, was gibbeted at Rake on the road to Petersfield and Portsmouth. Two accomplices from the Bognor area, John Hammond of Bersted and John Cobby of Sidlesham, were gibbeted on Selsey Bill, in full view of the coast, a grim reminder to future smugglers of the fate that might await them. The Mills pair, father and son, at whose house Chater was confined, did not suffer the indignity of having their flesh pecked away by birds.

At the time of the special commission, prosecutions against outlawed smugglers were already underway at the Old Bailey in London. Still, the murders strengthened the government's hand against smuggling, especially when it was discovered that other smugglers had whipped an innocent man to death for purportedly stealing contraband tea. He was Richard Hawkins, an agricultural laborer, who was picked up by Jeremiah Curtis, a member of the Hawkhurst gang and a fugitive from justice. Hawkins was taken to the Dog and Partridge Inn on Slindon Common near Yapton for interrogation. Curtis and John Mills, brother of the horse-breaker and also implicated in the Chater murder, whipped and kicked Hawkins until he admitted that his in-laws had stolen the two bags of tea. Leaving Hawkins's beating to two other men, they returned to Yapton to question his in-laws, the Cockrels. The Cockrels vehemently denied any responsibility for the theft, but by the time Curtis and Mills returned to the Dog and Partridge to question Hawkins again, he was dead, his body "terribly mangled" and his head cracked open. The smugglers thought of throwing his body down a well, as they had done with Chater's, but eventually they decided to sink him in a pond at Parham Park belonging to Sir Cecil Bishop (figure 8).[86]

The Hawkins murder revealed that the smuggling fraternity was becoming more brutal in its desperation. It was also reverting to highway robbery and burglary as more and more troops returning from the war on the Continent were stationed along the coast. There had been reports of smugglers "going on account" a few years earlier, but such incidents became more frequent after 1748 as the military patrols on the coast increased and the risks of running goods and detection escalated as the navy was able to devote more energy to policing coastal waters. Henry Pelham's modification of the tax on tea also cut into smuggling profits and made highwaymen of smugglers. Prominent members of the Poole raid robbed the owner of the George Inn at Petersfield in August 1748, and several other smugglers who were gazetted as outlaws were indicted of robbery at the Kent and Sussex assizes in spring 1749.[87] They included John Brown, otherwise Jockey Brown, and Robert Fuller, who along with two well-known smugglers from Hawkhurst, Thomas and Lawrence Kemp, stole two silver spoons, a silver watch, a silver-handled cup, three gold rings and some guineas from the house of Richard Haffenden on 2 November 1749.

In this degenerative phase the Hawkhurst gang crumbled from within. One of the principal fences of the gang, Jacob Pring, turned in several of his associates.[88] He had been part of the raiding party at Poole, and once the word went around that he had betrayed some of his former colleagues, two other members of that party turned king's evidence as well. William Steele and John Race (or Raise) disclosed the names of twenty-six men who went to Poole, seven of whom were involved in the murders of Galley and Chater.

More men were rounded up as a result. Thomas Kingsmill, the leader of the

Fig 8: The fatal beating of Richard Hawkins, in *A full and genuine history of the . . . murders of William Galley . . .*, London, 1749.

gang after Gray, William Fairall, Richard Perrin, and Richard Glover were all convicted at the Old Bailey of the raid on the Poole customshouse. Glover was pardoned because it was thought that he, an apprentice shipwright, had been bullied into riding to Poole by his brother-in-law, one Edmund Richards, a notorious smuggler who was later picked up and confined in Winchester gaol to await trial. The other three were hanged at Tyburn. Kingsmill, aged twenty-eight, was regarded as a "bold resolute man" willing to risk his neck for the Hawkhurst gang and the "monied men or merchants" he served. Bill Fairall, who was three years younger, was a seasoned smuggler who had threatened to kill the gentleman who turned him in, the Sussex MP, Jack Butler, an associate of the Pelhams. Upon escaping from Newgate several months earlier, he had conspired to assassinate Butler on his way home from Horsham, and he then tried to burn down his house at Worminghurst Park.[89] This audacious behavior meant that all efforts to mitigate his sentence were refused. Both Kingsmill and Fairall were considered dangerous men and the full measure of the law was brought upon them. Their bodies were gibbeted in their Kentish villages as an example: Kingsmill's at Goudhurst; Fairall's on Horsmonden Green.

The fifth man on the indictment, Thomas Lillywhite, was acquitted and discharged. A youngster of seventeen who had gone along for the ride to Poole, he did not participate in the break-in at the Customs but was left tending the horses. Sir Cecil Bishop put in a good word for him, noting that Lillywhite had a fine reputation in his neighbourhood, good enough for him to consent to his marrying his housekeeper's daughter. He also observed: "This poor lad neither saw the Custom House nor was in the town, but attended the horses about a mile's distance. I am sensible this in the eye of the law may make him an accomplice, but in the case where there is no bloodshed, in the poor opinion of a country gentleman, ignorant of the laws, he may deserve some favour."[90] The Duke of Richmond, who heard about this plea for mercy, reproved Bishop for his leniency and wondered how he could come to such an opinion "having been lately upon the bench where you heard such a scene of barbarity and murders so evidently proved." Richmond reminded Sir Cecil that he had often said "with great truth that the common people of this country have no notion that smuggling is a crime." Lillywhite needed to feel the full rigour of the law, Richmond maintained, because

> it has become necessary to show the common people by example that accessories are to be punished as well as principals ... for you know very well that the common notion in the country is that a man may stand by and see crimes committed and even advise and assist in them with impunity, if he does not commit the fact with his own hands; this shows the necessity for examples,

without which, indeed Sir Cecil, neither you nor I, nor any good subject can live in tolerable security in this country.[91]

Lillywhite was lucky to have a gentleman vouch for him and a judge, Sir Thomas Abney, who thought the evidence against him was not entirely compelling.[92] Glover, who had participated in the break-in, was luckier still. Of the twenty-seven convicted of smuggling at the trials at Old Bailey between 1747 and 1752, only Glover gained a reprieve or pardon. Twenty of the smugglers met their fate at Tyburn. A further six were sentenced to seven years' transportation because their offenses occurred prior to the passing of the 1746 act.[93] This group included Thomas Palmer and James Monday, who were indicted in December 1749 for running goods over four years earlier, the prosecution producing an incriminating carbine belonging to Palmer on which was carved, "All you Rogues that keep me from this nation / This Carbine shall be your damnation."[94] This was enough to get them transported.

At least thirty-five smugglers from the southeast were hanged in the years 1749–50 and a further ten died of typhus or smallpox in prison. By 1751 smugglers were no longer the "public menace" they had been, although within a generation a new crop of smugglers were in full cry, as Lord Shelburne was later forced to recognize.[95] The mid-century campaign against smugglers had nonetheless demanded considerable political will and legal muscle. It demanded the full energies of a leading Whig grandee, the Duke of Richmond, who along with the Pelhams, the leading patrons of the country, had faced the embarrassment of a major smuggling epidemic in their county. It required more troops to back up a rudimentary and thinly stretched customs, something that became possible only as the war scaled down. And the campaign was made possible only because of an extraordinary statute that essentially outlawed smugglers before they had been technically indicted for a crime, simply on the basis of an information or deposition forwarded by the secretary of state to the Privy Council. As the Crown prosecutor admitted in one of the early trials under the act, the smugglers were too formidable to enable revenue officers to identify them running contraband. "Nobody could detect them [smugglers] to the Satisfaction of a Jury, " he maintained, and "therefore the Legislature thought fit to take a Method for preventing this Practice, by anticipating, if I may so say, that Offence."[96] Even its authors, Sir Dudley Ryder and William Murray (later Lord Mansfield), thought it was about as tough an act as it could legally be.[97] Initially the statute had a sunset clause; it was put in force for seven years only. To reinforce its effect, Ryder and Murray advised that both the army and the customs and excise could apprehend smugglers or suspected smugglers without any express warrant and that "necessary force" could be used in the apprehension and jailing of them. This legal war against the smugglers, and their own desperate acts of violence against informers and those suspected of betraying them, proved their undoing. Smugglers lost community support and were exposed to the full force of a state no longer distracted by war.

The years 1748–51 were nonetheless troubling for the big patrons. Jacobite revels, formidable riots in the West Country over turnpikes, and intrepid smuggling gangs in the southeast, tested the will and resolve of the Pelhams, their friends, and their clients. These events added to the anxieties of an uncertain peace and a billowing crime wave, as did the specter of a degenerate race raised on gin.

Tackling the Gin Craze

In 1734 a desperate act of violence, brought on by a craving for gin, sent a mother to the gallows.[1] In January of that year, a thirty-year-old woman of Huguenot extraction, one Judith Defour, also known as Leeford and Cullender, visited the Shoreditch workhouse to collect her illegitimate daughter. The workhouse wardens were officious, perhaps even suspicious, because the two-year-old girl, Mary Cullender, had recently been given a new set of clothes, and it was not uncommon for vulnerable children to be stripped for their clothing for the cash such items could bring in a thriving secondhand market. Consequently the officers demanded a note from the churchwardens authorizing the child's release, a request to which Judith complied, and so the child was given up to her care.

Judith Defour must have had a troubling reputation. The daughter of a Spitalfields weaver, she had worked since the age of fifteen as a silk throwster or twister, a menial job that was often farmed out to workhouse labor. After toiling at this job for eleven years, Judith had served as housekeeper to a silk master, a job she likely lost when she became pregnant by John Cullender, a local weaver. After giving birth to Mary in 1731, she returned to the twisting trade, working at night with other women. Judith liked her dram of gin as she worked away, and at the prompting of a workhouse inmate, she decided to sell the workhouse clothes of her small daughter to feed her addiction. With a shadowy character called Sukey, she took the child to the fields in Bethnal Green and stripped her of her new coat, petticoat, and stockings, leaving the child floundering in a ditch. When the child complained, Judith and her accomplice tied a linen handkerchief hard around her neck to stifle her cries. Whatever possessed her to kill her daughter is uncertain. Judith claimed she fell under the evil influence of Sukey, "one of the vilest of Creatures in and about Town." Whether this was true or not, she collaborated in strangling the child with the handkerchief and later finished her off with a blow to the head—all for a shilling and a groat to buy quarterns[2] (half-cups) of gin. The crime was too execrable to win any reprieve; Judith Defour was hanged at Tyburn in early March 1734, alongside four others. Her body was handed over to the surgeons.[3]

The tale of Judith Defour was recounted in one of the most popular pamphlets against dram drinking, Thomas Wilson's *Distilled Spirituous Liquors, the bane of the Nation,* which quickly ran into two editions in 1736.[4] Wilson did not choose to situate this narrative within the context of eighteenth-century social welfare or at the margins of the working poor. The fact that Defour's child was illegitimate and that she could not or would not support her on her own was not mentioned. The son of a bishop and soon to be chaplain to George II and the rector of a rich London parish,[5] Wilson saw the murder as a dramatic but exemplary tale of what might happen when the gin craze penetrated a manufacturing district. He described gin drinking as an "infection" that had spread deeply into the lives of the working poor of the metropolis and threatened to become a national problem of huge proportions. Gin was a "slow but sure Poyson" that entered the blood and marrow of regular drinkers, destroying the appetite, ruining digestion, weakening nerves. It was habit-forming, an opiate "both in its Nature and in the Manner of its Operations." It destroyed industry and the future generation of workers, for not only did gin drinking curb fertility, but female dram-drinkers frequently gave birth to children who were "half burnt up and shrivelled," with the symptoms of what we would now call fetal alcohol syndrome. Wilson feared Britain's social trajectory would be akin to that of the Roman Empire, which lost its virility and sank into "Effeminacy and Luxury."[6] A member of the SPCK, he was one of the most active moral crusaders against gin in the campaigns of the mid-1730s, a campaign that resulted in the Gin Act of 1736.

How did gin drinking emerge as such a challenging social problem in the third decade of the eighteenth century? One answer, paradoxically, can be related to government policy. During the wars against France after 1690 Britain placed prohibited duties on the import of French brandy had encouraged the distillation of British spirits by promoting low preferential duties on malted grain. An added advantage of this policy was that the landed classes benefited indirectly from distilling because it helped mop up the excess grain that came from good harvests and consequently sustained buoyant prices in years of surplus. In the War of the Spanish Succession this was undoubtedly a boon to the landed classes who bore much of the burden of wartime taxation, a factor never lost on anti-gin crusaders who felt obliged continually to assure the landed gentry and their tenant farmers that their fortunes would not be affected by a drop in spirit production.

Relative to beer, spirits were inexpensive. High excise duties on ale and beer had pushed the retail price of a quart to three pence or more by 1720. By contrast, gin or geneva,[7] first developed in Holland in the sixteenth century by mixing spirits with juniper berries and various citrus fragrances, was cheap. Retailers unscrupulously proclaimed one could get drunk for a penny and dead drunk for two pence. Gin production and sales were also unregulated. The Distillers Company of London lost its monopoly over the supply and quality of spirits, which meant that while the wholesale distilling of spirits remained largely in the hands of major distillers, compound distilling — the rectifying of gin and brandy with juices, spices, and juniper berries, and by all accounts disreputable substances such as fermented fruit and even urine — became a small-scale, flourishing enterprise. In the 1730s London had roughly 1,500 distillers, of whom a hundred had capital investments of more than £1,000. The vast majority had stills worth less than £100 and produced rot-gut gin for an expanding market. The retailing of gin was also unregulated for much of the early eighteenth century, unlike beer and ale, which could be sold only in licensed premises. The result was that drams of gin could be found everywhere — not only in alehouses, taverns, and coffeehouses but also in chandler's shops, cellars, back rooms, and street stalls.

Excise figures provide some indication of the scale of production and, by inference, consumption, although they are undoubtedly conservative because many illegal stills eluded the officers. According to the official accounts, the output of British spirits grew from half a million gallons in 1688, to 1.23 million by 1700, to 2.48 million gallons by 1720, roughly a fivefold increase in just over thirty years. From the twenties onward spirit production skyrocketed, reaching almost 4 million gallons in 1726, over 6 million in 1734, and soaring to 8.2 million gallons in 1743.[8] Spirit production did not fall appreciably until the late 1750s, making the period 1723 to 1757 the golden age of gin drinking, when output was consistently above 3.5 million gallons annually and in half of these years over 5 million. By contrast, the production of strong beer was remarkably consistent for the first half of the eighteenth century, barely wavering from the annual 3.6 million barrels it averaged in the first decade. This stable production of beer and spiraling production of spirits suggests a switch in consumer taste, and very probably, if the Old Bailey Proceedings offer any clues, an increasing willingness to swill down beer with gin chasers. Sometimes beer and gin were inextricably combined, for flip, a concoction of beer and spirits warmed in a pewter pot with a red hot poker, was a quite popular drink, especially among seamen.[9]

The switch in taste was noticed by contemporaries. "Dram-drinking has been a practise among the poorer sort," observed one, "because they could be made merry with distilled spirits cheaper than they could with any other liquor."[10] In the minds of the propertied classes the preference for dram drinking also registered the lamentable "luxury" of the poor. Gin was the poor man's cordial in an age when the upper class indulged itself with citron waters and cherry brandy; an example, so thought Elias Bockett, of the "little vulgar" imitating the "manners of the vulgar great."[11] Dram drinking could also be seen as a "luxury" in the sense that it signified a troubling disposable income or a disturbing leisure preference. It was not seen as a moderate gratification of desire, the way that Scottish philosophers saw it later in the century.[12] This negative view of "luxury," at least as practiced by the mechanic classes, was especially espoused by low-wage theorists, who believed that the working poor should be kept to a "middling scarcity" lest they become lazy and undisciplined. It was not adopted by people like Dr. Samuel Johnson, who thought a little luxury might profit the poor.[13]

Whether lower-class Londoners had much disposable income is difficult to assess. With the exception of three noteworthy years when the price of corn reached more than 40 shillings a bushel, Londoners enjoyed a run of relatively good harvests during the gin craze and would therefore have enjoyed lower prices on basic provisions. Yet building construction in London had stagnated and rents were high, a situation aggravated by the constant in-migration of people from the countryside looking for work. Jacob Vanderlint noted in 1734 that many people could not afford metropolitan rents, despite the vacancies, and historians have since observed that some trades were overstocked or feeling the pinch of provincial competition, including the one with which Judith Defour was involved.[14] Indeed, the increase in metropolitan mortality when winters were bitterly cold and prices high, as in 1740–41, suggests that there were many living at the margins who were extremely vulnerable to short-term shifts in living standards.[15] For those on la vie en marge, gin was undoubtedly a consolation, not a sign of leisure preference. In one satirical play recalling the agitation against the Gin Acts, Liveretta, a broken, female street seller found rotgut gin an escape from desperate poverty. "Gin dry'd her Feet," so the rhyme went, "Gin thaw'd frozen Air; Rags might let Water in, but Gin kept out all care."[16]

In what was also the age of Walpole, it was Tory satirists who saw the gin problem this way. For most reformers, especially those like Thomas Wilson who were closely associated with the SPCK, the causal flow was the other way around. Gin did not salve the pangs of poverty; it created them, and worse. The Reverend Stephen Hales, rector, physician, and Georgia trustee zoned in on the medical effects of gin drinking. From his experiments on dissected bodies, he observed that large-scale infusions of spirits into the blood congested the vessels, slowed circulation, and caused stoppages in the liver. He also claimed that slow circulation induced stagnant blood and cluttered up the heart with polyps, impairing its performance. Hales also believed, somewhat contradictorily, that the red corpuscles in the blood were burnt up and consumed by the desiccating properties of spirits, weakening vitality and causing dropsy. No one paid any attention to the inconsistencies of the theory or whether inferences drawn from corpses could be applied in vivo. What mattered was that a reputable medical authority who had presented many of his findings to the Royal Society declared gin a killer, responsible (in modern terminology) for coronary heart disease, cirrhosis of the liver, and other maladies.

Hales's pamphlet ran through five editions by the mid-century and should have been a warning to the upper class about its own intemperance and fondness for hard liquor. But only spokesmen from the middling class, men like William Hogarth, John Wesley and Jonas Hanway, seem to have agonized over this issue and the example that elite boozing set for those further down the social scale. For most reformers, the crux of the problem was not the excesses of the rich or even the deplorable social emulation that might flow from it, but the debilitating effects of gin drinking on the working poor. This was the real social problem, for it was on the backs of the workers that the wealth of the nation was built. Contemporaries were absolutely candid about this. The rich had an obligation to govern and to exercise this duty responsibly, but they did not produce the wealth of the country. Although there was a grudging respect for the industrialist and merchant in the mid-eighteenth century and a recognition of their contribution to the economy, the labor of the working poor was seen as the key to British prosperity. "Our poor labourers are the support of our trade, our manufacturers, our riches, nay our luxury, too" remarked Lord Hervey in the House of Lords during a debate on the Gin Bill of 1743. Gin threatened to destroy the laboring classes or, at the very least, compromised the tasks society assigned them. Gin "will destroy our soldiers; it will destroy our seamen" predicted Hervey. "It renders men too feeble for labour, too indolent for application, too stupid for ingenuity, and too daring for the peace of society."[17] In this manner he encapsulated many of the anxieties that surrounded the public debate on the gin epidemic. These anxieties ran high. Of "all of the Miseries and Plagues that unhappy Man has been incident to," declared Erasmus Jones, "none was ever fraught with such dire-ful Consequences to the Publick. War Plague and Pestilence rage for a while, and then they cease; but this merciless Destroyer threatens Misery, Want and Sickness to all the Generations that are yet to come."[18]

How did reformers establish the gravity of the gin problem? People were certainly aware of rising gin consumption, but it was not altogether clear how extensive the gin epidemic was. Newspapers reported examples of prodigious dram drinking outside of London, which certainly implied that it was spread-ing beyond the metropolis. In January 1736 the *Daily Gazetteer* noted the example of a gin-sodden woman dying of alcohol poisoning in a Leeds jail.[19] Yet some critics disputed whether the gin craze had advanced much beyond London and a few major provincial centers, at least in the 1730s. One letter in the *London Daily Post,* written by a "Man of Kent," reported that local farmers wondered what all the fuss was about. They baulked at social legisla-tion that might restrict their custom of taking a glass of punch to keep out the winter cold.[20]

Critics also wondered whether the social dramas about the hazards of binge drinking publicized by newspapers pertained to all members of the working class. It was all very well to cite examples of carmen, cobblers, and glaziers downing half-pints of gin in some wacky wager and paying for it with their lives, or of a notorious drunk, perhaps a journeyman blacksmith, drinking himself insensate on half-pints of gin and a few beers, but what did this signify apart from flagrant self-abuse?[21] Spokesmen for the distillers, who clearly had a special interest in disputing whether gin drinking had reached epidemic proportions, openly wondered whether the moral crusaders had not exagger-ated the dimensions of the craze. Any large city had its fair share of profligate drinkers, so the argument went, and it was unsurprising that the most demor-alized sectors of the urban poor drowned their sorrows in dram after dram. Prostitutes drank away the pain of selling their bodies; they needed spirits, suggested one poet in a mocking couplet. How else could "plying Nymphs support / The toils incessant on their am'rous sport?"[22]

Similarly, soldiers, often recruited from the most desperate sections of so-ciety, needed the rush of alcohol to sustain the rigors of the march and the sheer boredom of guard duty. In London these occupations abounded, and when one added broken porters and coal heavers, unemployed craftsmen and beggars craving oblivion, it was not difficult to see how gin could muster a ragged clientele. "Few but the very poorest sort of People are Gin-drinkers," suggested one author in the *Daily Post,* "to which Spirit their Poverty and Indigence in a manner pins them down."[23] The real problem was not gin or its availability, distilling advocates claimed. Plenty of European urban dwellers imbibed spirits without deleterious social effects. It was a definable minority, described by one skeptic as "the most abandon'd, vitious and profligate people," who gave gin drinking a bad name, and the disreputable, small-time gin retailers who encouraged excessive drinking.[24]

Moral crusaders never addressed the European comparison, although it was, and remains, an interesting question why responsible social drinking struck deeper roots on the Continent than in Britain. Yet they could point to disturbing signs that gin had become, or was becoming, a more generalized craze, something that recent historians have sought to emphasize.[25] In early 1736 the Middlesex sessions ordered an inquiry into the number of gin shops within their jurisdiction. The returns, which received a good airing in the press, revealed that there were over 7,000 establishments selling beer, wine, or spirits within this part of the metropolis, an area that excluded the City of London and Southwark. Of these over half (54.4 percent) sold only liquors, and this inquiry omitted the many cellars, garrets, and back rooms that were "not publickly expos'd to view." Moreover, of the 7,000 known drinking spots, 30 percent were unlicensed, suggesting that at the lower end of the trade there was a heavy, informal traffic in gin and other spirits. This evidence, combined with the fragmentary figures from the excise accounts about the growing popularity of spirits over beer, suggested that gin drinking had become a serious social problem that legislators ought to address.

No one had accurate figures of how many heavy dram-drinkers inhabited the metropolis. When the report was discussed in Parliament during debate on the 1736 Gin Bill, parliamentarians speculated that there were probably 20,000 drinking spots in the metropolis and a further 20,000 outside London.[26] Assuming that each alehouse or gin shop had ten excessive drinkers who quaffed half a pint of gin a day, and ten "moderate drinkers" who downed half that measure, parliamentarians proceeded to calculate how much revenue might be lost by a prohibition of spirits, a matter of some concern to the government, which had used the revenue to finance the Civil List. By these speculations, virtually every male or female over the age of fifteen in the capital was downing at least a quartern of gin a day, a ludicrous proposition that would not have been difficult to ridicule. Even so, the Middlesex report did provide detailed evidence that gin drinking had penetrated the world of the working poor: not simply the "vicious and immoral" as the report termed them, but the "sober and regular"; not simply male householders, but whole families and servants.[27] Like so much eighteenth-century evidence it was impressionistic. Even so, the discovery that workers in at least 80 inferior trades were drinking gin, and that in Bethnal Green alone, 90 weavers were selling gin on the side, did trouble contemporaries, especially when it was openly admitted that many of the constables who drew up the returns were gin retailers themselves and had a vested interest in underestimating the dimensions of the problem.

Large claims were made about the social impact of gin drinking on work and on family stability, public morals, and welfare. The Middlesex report claimed that habitual gin drinking deprived people of their "Money, Time, Health and Understanding." Here and elsewhere there was an almost syntagmic relation between gin drinking, excess, and luxury; one could not think of gin tippling without believing it swallowed up people in a vortex of vice and social disorder. Consequently, lower-class gin drinking spelt idleness and carefree irresponsibility, from the very people whose duty was to labor. Thomas Wilson echoed the Middlesex report in maintaining that gin-sodden workers could no longer sustain the heavy work required of many London trades. They were "not able to go thro' the Hardships that were, by their former wholesome Diet, easy to them." He reported that builders and coal merchants were obliged to hire more men to do the work, and that the absenteeism incident from alcohol abuse reduced the supply of labor and raised wages. What was equally troubling was that the uninhibiting effects of gin drinking had also increased labor unrest, so that employers went in fear of mischief "from a drunken, ungovernable Set of People."[28] The result was that gin drinking hindered national economic growth and international competitiveness. Since it threatened to engulf seven-eights of the population, it also undermined a critical tax base necessary for British warfare. And it foretold social anarchy. Thomas Wilson attributed the rise of collective bargaining in mechanic trades to Mother Geneva; Isaac Maddox, the bishop of Worcester, took his fears one step further. In a sermon delivered before the London Common Council and the governors of several hospitals on Easter Monday 1750, the bishop linked gin-drinking to the crime wave affecting the metropolis. Spirits released social inhibitions in disturbing ways. They emboldened men to crime and inflamed the populace "against the present Distribution of Property." Indeed, by "outrageous Overt Acts" such as the affronts smuggling gangs offered customs officers, gentry and government, the lower class revealed an alarming aspiration to social equality.[29]

Moreover, gin's attack on the social fabric allegedly penetrated deeply into the domestic economy. Commentators were keen to point out that gin tippling was not simply a male pursuit; it involved the female population as well. Female servants showed a disturbing tendency to congregate at the chandler's shop for a dram and gossip about their betters. It was feared they would not only divulge the private secrets of their households but pilfer items to slake their thirst, even tip off burglars as to when they might break and enter genteel residences. Gin-drinking servants, in effect, were seen to be serious conduits of crime. No one could trust them. Gin-loving wives were equally blameworthy.

They neglected their families to satisfy their cravings and fostered gangs of street brats who were forced to scrap and pilfer to make ends meet, ultimately gravitating from petty theft to major crime.

Gin-swilling women were viewed as an affront to public morality. "Women have been seen exposing their sex in such a condition, that 'twas an offence to every modest eye," insisted the royal proclamation of 1738. Every gin shop, Bishop Secker averred, had a back shop or cellar where men and women were thrown promiscuously together; "here they might commit what wickedness they pleased."[30] Equally disturbing was the fact that women were not producing babies in sufficient numbers or vitality. Wilson, troubled by what he saw as a conspicuous decline in christenings in the metropolis, hinted at abortions or miscarriages, for the "fruit of the womb" was too frequently "blasted before it has seen the light."[31] What progeny emerged was burnt up and shriveled, Wilson maintained, "Dreadful Monuments of their Parents Cruelty, Debauchery and Inhumanity."[32] In effect, gin drinkers were producing children whose physiques paled in comparison to "the manly and robust Constitution of preceding Generations."[33] In this respect it is worth noting that the first generation of youngsters trained by the Marine Society in the 1750s were puny: averaging four feet three-and-a-half inches (130.6 cm) at age thirteen, they were seven inches smaller than their counterparts among the gentry, and a full ten inches smaller than London children of the 1960s.[34] Many of these stunted children did not even meet the official bar that the governors of the Marine Society had themselves set, which was four feet four inches. Of the 5,000 boys recruited during the Seven Years' War, 1756–63, around 20 percent were abandoned children or children operating under no parental supervision.[35]

No one in the mid-eighteenth century attempted to use height to uncover nutritional deficiencies and consolidate the claims of punyism. The comparative data were simply not available. Even Jonas Hanway, the founder of the Marine Society and a vigorous campaigner against gin, did not choose to exploit the early figures of his own philanthropic enterprise.[36] The case against gin was largely made through the cumulative recurrence of key images and ideological themes derived from the proto-narratives of family tragedies: of gin-addicted widowers dying in debtors' prison leaving puny children on the parish, of drunken child-minders allowing toddlers to fall into fires, of gin-crazed mothers pawning their own and their children's clothes, of profligate drinkers living hand-to-mouth on the street or heaped promiscuously in back rooms to sleep off their stupor. These scenarios were standard fare in the popular press of the mid-century. They received some reciprocal validation from medical science, such as it was, and from the moral narratives of the condemned at Tyburn, in which offenders purportedly confessed their wicked

ways, including the evils of dram drinking, which always seemed to embolden
them to more desperate crimes.[37] Indeed, the familiar gravitation of the condemned from youthful pickpocketing to street robbery or worse, at least as
framed in the Ordinary of Newgate's *Account,* set off alarm bells among a
public troubled by the likelihood that dysfunctional, gin-addicted families
would only breed the next generation of criminals.

There was, however, one series that neither moral crusaders nor their skeptics could ignore, and that was the Bills of Mortality. Compiled by the Company of Parish Clerks from the sixteenth century onward these bills recorded
the baptisms and burials of over one hundred parishes within greater London
and, for those who died, the presumed causes of death. These records were
initially established to track the dimensions of the plague and other major
epidemics. From the Restoration era onward they were a very useful source for
the advocates of political arithmetic, for those who ventured to map the human resources and wealth of the state at any one time. As of 1728, the bills
featured a breakdown of burials by age cohort, which allowed contemporaries
to track the most vulnerable age groups over time, at least as a percentage of
total recorded deaths.

The bills, however, were not without their problems. To begin with, they
recorded only the baptisms and burials within the parishes of the Church of
England and thus excluded the vast majority of members of non-Anglican
denominations, not to mention Roman Catholics. Even within the Anglican
jurisdiction, the bills did not keep abreast of the growth of London. Four
parishes had to be added to the bills in the 1720s, five in the next decade and a
half, and at mid-century Paddington, Kensington, and Tottenham were still
excluded.[38] Furthermore, the causes of death detailed in the bills were frequently medically ambiguous or unsound. A significant minority of infants,
for example, were said to have died of "convulsions," whatever that meant.
Stillborn deaths were not always recorded, nor were abortions. The deficiencies of the bills were such that some nineteenth-century statisticians thought
that the recorded shortfall in burials was probably in the region of 40 percent.

Mid-eighteenth-century commentators were aware of the deficiencies of the
bills, or at least some of them, yet they did not conclude they were unusable.
Like some current historical demographers,[39] they did not believe that under-
registration would seriously affect short-term comparisons of the data. Isaac
Maddox, bishop of Worcester, allowed that the bills were "not exactly accurate, yet, when compared with themselves, one year with another, must be
supposed equally just."[40] Given the large claims that had been voiced about
the demographic consequences of gin drinking, it was inevitable that the bills
would feature in the debate over the regulation of gin.

Not everyone was prepared for this. Many commentators preferred draw-ing conclusions from other sources, from moral precept and example, per-haps, or by collating authorities that addressed specific aspects of the gin problem. Thomas Wilson's influential pamphlet in 1736, for example, drew much of its force from the authority of the church, the medical profession, and the law. He reiterated Stephen Hales's and Dr. George Cheyne's remarks on the physical effects of excessive dram drinking. The latter had commented on the deplorable effects of gin in his remarkably popular essay *Health and Long Life,* in which he maintained that the "running into Drams" was so ruinous that "neither Laudanum nor Arsenick will kill more certainly, although more quickly."[41] Wilson also quoted from Bishop Sherlock's sermon to the West-minster Infirmary about the deplorable luxurious habits of the working poor. He paraphrased the main features of the Middlesex sessions report and ap-pended the various presentments of the metropolitan grand juries. These inter-ventions were particularly concerned with the availability of gin and presumed that the high ratios of drinking establishments to houses, one in six in some jurisdictions, indicated just how entrenched and widespread the gin craze had become.

Nonetheless, Wilson did use the London Bills of Mortality to reveal that deaths outnumbered births in the British capital, unlike other European cities, such as Paris.[42] This difference in demographic fortune he attributed to gin. His use of this data was nevertheless sparingly simple: a short-term com-parison that hardly addressed the long-term degenerative effect of gin drinking on London's population. Critics quickly responded by saying that Parisian workers also had a taste for spirits and were seen drinking drams before they went to work. They disputed the assumption that spirits enervated workers and destroyed their capacity to labor. In these circumstances, they argued, any comparison of the two cities' demographic profile could hardly be attributable to spirit consumption. Moreover, a comparison of London's mortality figures during the 1720s and 1730s did not suggest gin was a grim reaper. During the 1736 debate on gin drinking one author ridiculed Wilson's "idle suppositions" about "a visible decrease of the people" by showing that the mortality figures for 1719–23 and 1724–28, when the gin-drinking was emerging as a social problem, were actually higher than in the period when gin consumption was reputedly at full throttle, namely 1728–33.[43] The author went on to show that burials were only marginally higher in 1728–33 than they were in 1714–18, when gin drinking was scarcely on the public agenda and when the population of London was thought to be smaller.[44] Judged by these figures gin drinking had not brought on a demographic catastrophe.

Wilson's anonymous critic also took him to task for asserting that gin drinking adversely affected fertility, although he backed off from verifying this in his appendix. Perhaps understandably, because the data hardly proved his point. The bills indicated a rising number of christenings to 1728, but they also registered a noteworthy decline in the period 1729–33, when the gin craze was well under way. The evidence also disclosed, rather inconveniently for this naysaying critic, a deepening demographic deficit of deaths over births throughout the period 1714–33, from an average of 6,855 per annum in the period 1714–18 to 9,415 per annum in 1729–33. Crusaders against gin quickly seized on this evidence because it illustrated the degree to which a demographically lethal London drew people from the countryside and exposed them to the pernicious habit of gin drinking. In effect, it heightened the national relevance of what some had tried to dismiss as a purely metropolitan phenomenon. Isaac Maddox subsequently took the argument one step further by revealing a disturbing downward trend of births over the whole period of the gin craze, from 1723 to 1750.[45] If the increase in deaths over this period seemed unremarkable, and Maddox went out of his way to suggest they were actually underreported, the decline in christenings did not. Unlike Paris, London was not only draining the countryside of people by the thousands, it was enlarging the deficit by a shocking decline in fertility; by the most conservative estimate, an overall loss of 10,000 every three years, if not 15,000. The deepening deficit, Maddox argued, was "coeval with gin" so that whatever other causes might be assigned to the demographic failure of the metropolis, gin drinking had to stand high on the roster. In more modern phraseology, Maddox sensed that gin addiction had a serious impact on the nation's reproductive capacity at precisely the point where Britain had to gird itself for further imperial wars against France.

Maddox's interventions in 1750–51 probably won the argument for the moral crusaders: certainly his sermon and subsequent shilling pamphlet reached a large audience, running into three editions in six months. Newspapers alerted readers to the fact that the first edition of the sermon contained no statistics from the Bills of Mortality and reminded them of the conspicuous deficit of births during the gin craze.[46] Yet many unresolved matters about the bills had not been adequately aired in the heat of the debate. Consequently, in March 1751, in the wake of Maddox's pamphlet, a Shropshire economist and government client by the name of Corbyn Morris offered some acute observations on the bills that not only highlighted their deficiencies but promoted the argument for launching a national census to facilitate a more accurate and informed debate about Britain's population.

Morris hoped his reflections would engage the public "independent of all Party and Prejudice."[47] He began by offering some straightforward revision of the bills, suggesting the Dissenting congregations deliver monthly account to the parish clerks so that a wider population would be recorded in the series. He also demanded more accurate ages for those who had died, and a listing of what diseases, so that it would be possible to chart age-related diseases in a more meaningful way. Like modern demographers, Morris was particularly interested in early infant mortality, which he rightly surmised was only partially attributable to the debilitating affects of alcohol. Infant mortality was lower in the countryside, and its higher toll in London was partly owing to poor urban sanitation and air, air because Morris had a thoroughly miasmic view of how disease was transmitted.[48] This led him to recommend widening and straitening many streets and removing the accumulated filth of the kennels into barges on the Thames.

Morris also offered a complex explanation of the decline in fertility in mid-century London. Like his contemporaries, he certainly thought gin drinking a factor in why christenings had fallen conspicuously in the mid-century decades, but he also developed a more comprehensive and satisfactory explanation of this phenomenon. The high cost of living in London and the allure of metropolitan lifestyles inhibited early marriages and even marriage itself, as did London's vast and expanding servant economy, which deterred large numbers of nubile women from marrying in their most reproductive years. Indeed, Morris thought great households of servants were a "trespass upon National growth," a misapplication of labor and industry, which ought to be taxed.[49]

Morris sensed that any inquiry into London's demographic dynamic was greatly complicated by in-migration, and he struggled to unravel this problem. He thought that London's population, resident and migrant, would quickly reproduce the shortfall of the previous year, not simply in total numbers but in terms of its reproductive capacity. He assumed this because the Bills of Mortality in the seventeenth century suggested a rapid recovery after each outbreak of plague. At the same time Morris recognized that he needed better data if London's demographic profile was to be clearly understood.[50] If the vital statistics of births, deaths, and marriages were collected on a national basis, Morris argued, then it should be possible to calculate the age structure of the population at any one time and, by extension, the actual rates of mortality. Morris recognized that the current figures for calculating mortality through the bills applied only to ratios. Hence it was possible to ascertain just how many infants died as a proportion of all deaths in any one year, which for those under five, was never below 41 percent in the first half of the eighteenth century. But it was not possible to calculate the actual mortality rate by age cohort, which for London infants under five is now thought to have run at around 350 per 1,000, if not higher.[51] Eighteenth-century commentators were correct in thinking that the gin age saw a deepening mortality in the metropolis; they could not see that it had a lot to do with infant mortality and the vulnerability of infants to gastric diseases in their first year, and smallpox thereafter. Bad water rather than bad gin killed babies, although it is very conceivable that the gin epidemic impaired the survival capacity of many small children.

Morris's dissatisfaction with the London Bills of Mortality, a dissatisfaction that certainly emerged from the controversy over gin, pushed him to promote a national census. He laid the groundwork for the bill that Thomas Potter presented to the House of Commons in 1753. Potter asked for a "general register" of the people, including births, marriages, and deaths, and also an account of those receiving parochial and extra-parochial relief. The data were to be collected by the overseers of the poor in each parish and delivered once a year to the county authorities, who would then pass them along to the Commissioners for Trade and Plantations.[52] Potter maintained such information would allow policymakers to detect the growth areas of the country, both economic and demographic, and where dependence on the poor rates was highest. It would allow them to gauge the efficacy of immigration or emigration, an issue that had flared up in the light of demands for the naturalization of foreign Protestants and Jews.

Potter had government support for his venture, but many MPs didn't like it. They feared such a census would serve as a pretext for more taxation, or for conscription into the army and navy. One of the most vocal critics of the bill, William Thornton of Yorkshire, saw it as a flagrant attack upon British liberties, establishing a nation "en police."[53] Others were troubled by the expense of the plan, which Potter estimated at £50,000 per annum. And they worried that the annual returns, for that is what was envisaged, would put too much power into the hands of local officials. Defenders of the bill thought a census would abet government strategy at a critical time in international affairs. It was a necessary initiative in the context of Britain's ongoing rivalry with France, when the country would likely need to remobilize the navy at short notice and to frame a policy that would reconcile the needs of war with commerce. Yet all the evidence suggests that MPs were not particularly interested in the bill, which sometimes could not proceed for want of a quorum. Ultimately the bill slinked through a third reading in the Commons in early May 1753, only to get lost in the Lords,[54] where members were too preoccupied with Hardwicke's Marriage Act to endorse another bill that addressed vital statistics.

The passing of the Marriage Act satisfied some of the concerns of the moral reformers and political arithmeticians. Because couples were now obliged to publish the banns of marriage weeks before the ceremony, the act would regularize plebeian nuptials and forestall those impetuous unions that had formerly been legal within the rules of the Fleet Prison and elsewhere. The new law might arrest what contemporaries perceived as a disturbing trend toward erratic and often irregular matches among the working poor.

Even so, Harwicke's act fell short of a civil registration of marriage, which would have provided the authorities with comprehensive data on age-specific nuptiality, today regarded as the key to Britain's demographic growth in the eighteenth century. And it did nothing to resolve the ongoing debate about the overall status of Britain's population, which many believed was declining. Indeed, despite the defeat of the census bill, calls for a general "recension" of the population continued to appear. In 1754, a French political economist of the Gournay Circle named Louis-Joseph Plumard de Dangeul again advocated a census, if only to clarify the size of Britain's population, especially that of the metropolis, which many feared was sucking up the human resources of the country. Dangeul took his cue from the clergyman and economist Josiah Tucker, who had been actively involved in the debate over Britain's international competitiveness and the political economy of gin. Tucker had argued that the potential loss of gin revenue through tighter regulation and fewer tipplers could be more than made up by increased labor power and consumption, which in turn would improve Britain's international economic standing.[55] If people could be weaned from gin, they would eat more food, drink more beer, and work more regularly and efficiently. Certainly Tucker believed that tight fiscal and legislative controls were necessary to channel plebeian consumption into socially desirable directions, but a few years later he thought government's role in this regard might be less obtrusive than the usual roster of prohibitions. What were needed were preventive strategies to meld the worker's self-interest with the human disposition to benevolence. "The distinguishing Characteristics of a People," Tucker declared, depend on "their National Police," that is to say, broad strategies of governance, not simply upon the coercive aspects of the law. In other words, social policy should necessarily encompass the routine regulation and monitoring of populations; it could not be based exclusively or emphatically upon the exemplary punishment of malefactors and the deterrent effects of the law.[56] Dangeul's ideas moved along the same path. He saw the need for a "social economy," a project to map the distribution of skills, land, and wealth in the country. A census was critical to this monitoring process since it would give bureaucrats the opportunity to plan, specifically to uncover socioeconomic and demographic trends so that new strategies could be devised to supplement and improve Britain's natural advantages. A census, he maintained, offered the state the opportunity to "multiply the means of employing its subjects."[57] Diehards might deprecate such enumerations as the armature of an inquisitorial state, but the idea of the census as an important instrument of social planning would not go away.

Gin drinking thus brought to the fore the vexed question of what Michel Foucault would call "biopolitics"[58] at an important conjuncture in Anglo-French rivalry. It prompted people to consider strategies for improving the reproductive capacity, health, and wealth of the population, including as we shall see later, ramping up the resources of orphan charities, such as the Foundling Hospital. These goals are conventionally associated with the early nineteen century, when the quest for social data quickened and allowed bureaucrats and politicians to map the resources of the population. Yet the notion of what is now known as "governmentality,"[59] that is, the strategies and technologies of rule that are part and parcel of the art of government and are intimately linked to managing populations in market economies, was present at this earlier juncture.

In some sense "governmentality," which shares a commitment to social regulation similar to the older notion of "police,"[60] was part of English statecraft from the Tudor age onward. One could argue that the Statute of Artificers and creations like the Bridewell Hospital were critical to the strategies of rule in the Elizabethan era.[61] With the problems incident upon the gin age and Anglo-French rivalry, critics began to ponder the question of governmentality in new ways, to consider expanding the parameters of governance and knowledge about the economy and population in order to mobilize more efficiently for war. The quest inevitably came up against an ingrained skepticism of larger government that was conventionally part of the libertarian canon. Nonetheless, governmentality was imagined even if it could not be effectively implemented. And it continued to be advocated. During the Falkland Islands crisis of 1771, Arthur Young once again made a case for a five-year census to promote economic growth and mobilize populations for war. In his view it was imperative that "decisive certainties" rather than "random ideas" become the "parent of great national measures."[62]

The gin craze also raised questions of governance in a more conventional sense, that is, in terms of law enforcement. Between 1729 and 1751 Parliament passed eight gin acts in an attempt to control the informal trade in spirituous liquors. Initially the government hoped to reduce the sales of gin by raising taxes on compound liquors to 5s a gallon and by insisting that anyone retailing the product had to take out a license at the substantial rate of £20 a year. In other words, it hoped that prohibitive taxes would stifle gin drinking among the general populace. Almost immediately the act was a dead letter. Very few people took out a license, particularly after the first six months when retailers were a little apprehensive as to how the act might be enforced.⁶³ Enforcement, moreover, was ineffectual and sporadic, with very few prosecutions. Some distillers evaded the act by promoting cheap, uncompounded gin known impertinently as "parliament brandy," which fell outside its purview. The consumption of gin did fall a little in the first year, but it quickly rebounded to its pre-1729 rate.

By March 1733 both the government and the City magistrates urged the repeal of the act on the grounds that it simply was not working. In its place came another that rolled back the taxes on gin but sought to crack down on the street trade by offering informers £5 for every successful conviction, the money to be raised from the £10 fine levied on every offender. Unfortunately the new act made no provision for compensating informers where convicted hawkers were too poor to pay the penalty, with the result there was very little incentive to enforce the law. The consequence was a significant spike in the consumption of British spirits, from 4.8 million gallons in 1733 to over 6 million per annum in the next three years, which led moral crusaders once again to try to eradicate the sale of cheap gin by slapping a prohibitive tax of 20s a gallon on all retail sales and requiring publicans to take out a license of £50 per annum. In effect the government and moral reformers like Sir Joseph Jekyll, the Master of the Rolls, who was widely recognized as the driving force behind the act, sought to restrict the sale of gin to only the most prestigious establishments. To police the sale of gin, the 1736 act once again used informers, but this time it allowed them to denounce established retailers to the Excise Office, where their chances of getting a reward were improved.

The 1736 act encountered some protest. Some consumers reveled away their last hours of low-taxed gin, encouraged, perhaps, by poems and broadsides that saw the act as an attack on the pleasures of the poor. In London, Bath, Bristol, and Norwich, publicans and distillers staged mock processions of the death of "Madame Geneva." At Norwich, "several People made themselves very merry on the Death of Madam Gin, and some of both Sexes got soundly drunk at her Funeral, for which the Mob made a formal Procession with Torches, but committed no Outrages."⁶⁴ In London, one JP arrested the mourners of a potential gin wake in Swallow Street, St. James, and another took up a few drunkards in Newgate Street who had the audacity to cry out "No Gin, No King."⁶⁵

On balance, the fears of disorder were grossly disproportionate to what took place. Sir Robert Walpole was apprized of rumors that the Jacobites in Scotland would send arms to London to take advantage of the protests, which some anticipated might be as formidable as the excise agitation of 1733. One writer thought the act "Sticks hard in the Stomachs of the meaner sort of

People."[66] Consequently, Sir Robert, who feared that he might once again be burnt in effigy, called out the troops, doubling the guards at St. James, Kensington and Whitehall. Yet as the *London Daily Post* reported, there were no serious disturbances, "Mother Gin having died very quietly."[67] What resistance there was came in the form of mock funerals and the invention of new drams outside the ambit of the act: among them Sangree (presumably Sangria), Tow-Row (usually slang for drunk and disorderly), and cider boiled with hot pepper.

New concoctions were unnecessary because many street sellers continued to ignore the act. Some of the larger distillers complained to the government that gin was still being hawked about the streets in open defiance of the act and recommended that JPs galvanize their constables to enforce the legislation. In fact, between September 1736 and July 1738, 12,000 informations were laid against irregular retailers, leading to some 4,896 convictions and 4,000 claims for the £5 reward. Most of the early claims resulted from the prosecution of middling retailers, who under the 1736 act could afford to pay a £10 fine to avoid two months' imprisonment in a house of correction. For informers, at least, there was no incentive under the 1736 act to prosecute poor people who could not afford to pay the fine. That became the responsibility of constables if they were so inclined. Under two subsequent acts in 1737 and 1738 the Commissioners of the Excise were ordered to pay informers the £5 reward when convicted retailers refused to pay their fines, hoping thereby to encourage private prosecutions. The result was that the sweep of prosecutions was broader and its incidence higher, pulling in thousands of petty retailers, especially in 1738.[68]

The prosecution of retailers encountered resistance. Contemporaries deplored the underhanded way in which informers enticed retailers to sell them gin under the terms of the 1736 act. The opposition *Craftsman* fuelled this unpopularity by reminding readers that pervasive informing typified the disreputable eras of Caligula and Tiberius and that many a jurist had warned how reward-mongering perverted the course of justice.[69] Retailers who exposed informers in the streets often gathered sympathetic crowds, crowds that had little compunction about humiliating and punishing people they regarded as predators. Suspected informers were pelted with stones and dirt, rolled in the kennels, dumped in dung hills, dragged to the pump, and sometimes ducked in the Thames. According to the *London Evening Post*, one informer caught by the mob in the Strand was forced to drink a pot of piss.[70]

Predictably, a few informers were subjected to rough music, a ritualized humiliation imposed on community transgressors, whether their offenses were social or more strictly sexual. Skimmington rides had been directed at adulterers, wife beaters, henpecked husbands, and strikebreakers.[71] It was unsurprising that they would be imposed upon informers who threatened to unsettle local informal economies and incriminate respected neighbors. One informer was "set upon an ass . . . while other beat and pelted him, leading him up and down Bond Street." Another, a chairman called Pullin, was carried in effigy around several streets in St. George, Hanover Square, for informing against a victualler in Princess Street. After the procession, the effigy was "fix'd upon a Chair-Pole in Hanover Square, with a Halter about his Neck, and then a Load of Faggots [was] placed around him, in which Manner he was burnt in the Sight of a Vast Concourse of People."[72]

Most of the attacks against informers seem to have occurred in Westminster and the City rather than in the Middlesex or Southwark, although this might well reflect the fact that publishers and printers were better informed of the goings-on in their immediate neighborhoods. The victimization of informers certainly impeded the prosecution of gin retailers, and in 1738 Parliament decided to make it a felony to assault informers, punishable by transportation. After this act, the attacks on informers and collaborating constables declined. Prosecutions against illegal gin retailing resumed, but the authorities did not process them as vigorously as they might have. No doubt the magistrates and constabulary were disposed to act this way because there was a noticeable rise in the prosecutions of informers for perjury and extortion. Indeed, it appears that legal prosecutions against informers rose as street assaults declined.

Certainly the well-publicized incidents of perjury fired the already strong hostility toward informers. One well-known informer named Henry Gaffney was committed to Newgate for robbing Cornelius Cannon of two guineas or more, an episode that prompted the *London Evening Post* to recommend that magistrates "inquire more narrowly into the Characters of those vile Fellows who plead the Law as a protection for their Roguery."[73] Six months later, an exciseman named Edward Parker, who reputedly had thirty people on his payroll and had claimed hundreds of pounds from turning in retailers, had to be interred privately upon his death for fear that the mob would tear his body to pieces.[74] Professional informing was seen to be so profitable that one wag worked up a broadside from a notoriously corrupt lord chancellor advising the highwayman, Joe Clincher, to quit the pad and turn to what was obviously a more lucrative game.[75]

By 1738 the unpopularity of informers was such that some justices were openly refusing to prosecute offenders under the Gin Acts, among them Clifford William Phillips. He was a JP for Tower Hamlets, but he was also a distiller with a pecuniary interest in the gin trade. When one of his hawkers, Mary Bryan, was arrested for selling gin without a license, he endeavored to have her released and fell out with a fellow justice, Richard Farmer, who had sentenced Bryan to two months' hard labor in a house of correction. His open disagreement with Farmer heightened the opposition to the Gin Act in the eastern parishes of London. He also openly criticized the excisemen who were active in the campaign against illegal sales of gin, suggesting that the commissioners employed "Scoundrels and Rascals" who "made the Excise stink in every persons nostrils."[76]

By 1738 the popular resistance to informers and the open disagreements among justices about the virtues of the Gin Acts led to the first major riot against the legislation. In January of that year Elizabeth Beezley and Martha Sawyer took a woman before the Bow street magistrate Sir Thomas De Veil for selling spirits without a license. In retaliation one Edward Arnold went to Beezley's house and threatened to kill her and pull her house down. Beezley then gave evidence against Arnold, and he was committed to jail on a misdemeanor. Nonetheless, the incident drew a very large crowd before De Veil's office, reputedly a thousand people, who besieged the two informers in the Bow Street premises. De Veil read the Riot Act in an attempt to disperse the mob, but for three hours crowds surrounded his house threatening hell and destruction. Eventually De Veil was forced to call in troops from St. James to bring the situation under control. He also arrested a man named Roger Allen who had encouraged the crowd to pull down his house in Bow Street and kill the informers. Allen was indicted under the Riot Act, a capital offense, but at the Court of King's Bench he was acquitted after a six-hour trial on the grounds that he was really too simple to have masterminded a large-scale riot. "Westminster Hall was so full," one newspaper reported, "you might have walked on the People's Heads; and the Mob on hearing that he was acquitted, was so insolent as to Huzza for a considerable time, whilst the Court was sitting."[77]

The Allen trial proved to be a major test of the enforceability of the Gin Act. The prosecution was led by the attorney and solicitor generals, which shows how seriously the government took this anti–Gin Act riot. The acquittal of Allen (who also had counsel) had a chilling effect on the Westminster judiciary and the constables, who subsequently proved very reluctant to enforce the acts. The leading excise prosecutor, Edward Parker, complained that "witnesses were so terrified on Allen's Acquittal that he could not prevail on many of them to appear as usual."[78] The result was that after the trial prosecutions under the Gin Act started to decline. Where they were pursued, they encountered diffident juries, especially on charges of assaulting informers, where the penalty was now stiff. In September 1738, for example, the London alderman Sir William Billers committed three women to Newgate Prison for rioting against an informer, only to learn that the grand jury was troubled by the plaintiff's testimony and found the bill of indictment ignoramus.[79]

After the Allen trial, the apparatus for regulating the Gin Acts began to collapse. The excise commissioners had already reduced the fines of smaller retailers in an attempt to mollify the opposition to the acts, an option first exercised in May 1737. Now they discouraged prosecutions by refusing to address the complaints of professional informers unless they were supported by firm evidence and backed up by character references. In the immediate aftermath of the anti–Gin Act riot, the Privy Council urged JPs to hold special petty sessions to address prosecutions under the acts. This brought about a flurry of activity, but even in Westminster, where the justices were more assiduous in upholding the law, the number of JPs who attended these sessions fell from ten in April 1738 to four in January of the following year. In effect, the JPs were unwilling to commit the time and energy needed to address the thousands of prosecutions. At the same time, middle-class vestrymen of the London parishes did little to encourage litigation under the acts and began returning their portion of the reward money to the poor retailers who had been fined.[80] They realized that gin hawking was often the only recourse of poorer people trying to make ends meet, women especially. Quite apart from the disquiet it would promote in the courtyards and alleys of the working poor, the vigilant prosecutions of these hawkers would only push them on the parish and raise local rates.

By 1740 the Gin Acts were pretty much a dead letter. Prosecutions had dropped to a trickle, and the consumption of gin increased, reaching an all-time high of 8.2 million gallons in 1743. In that year the government adopted a different tack. It repealed some of the objectionable clauses of the previous Gin Acts and chose to derive as much taxable revenue as it could from what had proved to be extremely unpopular legislation. Licensing fees were reduced dramatically, from £50 a year to only £1, and the excise on spirits was levied at the still-head to provide extra money for the war effort.[81]

Some noteworthy noblemen, among them Lord Hervey, opposed the bill on the grounds that gin bingeing would dissolve the deference so necessary to their hierarchical society. Others feared the government's change of tactic signified a deplorable capitulation to popular pressure. Now the mob was dictating to the legislature, a state of affairs that meant an end to all subordination.[82] Moral reformers were predictably outraged by the government's flagrant admission that dram drinking could not be eliminated and by its plan to tax the people's vices. If the new law passed, charged Bishop Sherlock, we shall "have defeated any endeavours for the suppression of wickedness."[83]

The bill did become law, despite efforts by the bishops to block it in committee. In essence it reduced licensing fees in the hope that publicans would police their establishments if they wished to stay in business. Some thought the new act might encourage social drinking. As Lord Bathurst rather tendentiously argued, accessible gin would now be drunk in "Houses visited by publick Officers, observed by the neighbouring Inhabitants, and frequented by Persons of Morals and Civility, who will always endeavour to restrain all enormous Excesses."[84] Whether the act really regularized gin drinking is an open question. What is clear is that the number of annual licenses soared to over 200,000 a year and that gin consumption declined from its all-time high in 1743, falling by more than 25 percent by 1750. What is less clear is whether the illegal trade in gin was really brought under control. As with previous acts, there was a flurry of initial prosecutions against hawkers for selling gin without a license, both from excise commissioners and justices of the peace. Over time, however, the vigilance of the JPs declined, despite prompting from the Duke of Newcastle, leaving it to the commissioners to crack down on illegal retailers.[85] The decline in judicial activity is evident from the Middlesex House of Correction calendars, which registered just two committals for selling spirits without a license between 1745 and mid-1751.[86]

The 1743 act might be seen as a fraught compromise between financial opportunism and social regulation, but in the light of the persistent failure to control the gin epidemic, it might also be seen as a modest success. Excise taxes were replenished; consumption leveled off, albeit at levels well beyond those of the 1720s and early 1730s; and the illicit street trade was to some extent curbed. So why, eight years later, were there demands for a new gin act?

The answer lies in the postwar context, in the panic over crime, and the real fear that Britain might not be able to compete in the next war against France. In mid-January 1751, Henry Fielding published his *Enquiry* in which he reiterated a point made by Thomas Wilson in the 1730s, namely, that gin emboldened people to commit more desperate crimes. It also inhibited industry, Fielding claimed, destroyed health, and undermined the groundwork for Britain's next confrontation with the French by failing to supply the nation with good soldiers and sailors.[87] "What must become of the Infant who is conceived in Gin?" asked the Bow Street magistrate. "Doth not this polluted Source, instead of producing Servants for the Husbandman, or Artificer; instead of providing Recruits for the Sea or the Field, promise only to fill Alms-houses and Hospitals, and to infect the Streets with Stench and Diseases?"[88]

In the wake of Fielding's *Enquiry*, Bishop Isaac Maddox lent his weight to the anti-gin campaign. Revisiting a sermon he had earlier delivered to the City aldermen and governors of the London hospitals, the bishop highlighted the "dispeopling" of the country during the gin era and cited evidence from the Bills of Mortality that revealed an alarming decline in christenings in Britain's vast metropolis. In Maddox's opinion gin drinking was a more serious problem than the plague; it was a blight on Britain's future and required preventive measures to keep cheap spirits out of the reach of the poor. It also imperiled the very notion of government, claimed Maddox, "by transferring to the inconsiderate Will and Pleasure of the Multitude, that Power and Authority which belong only in Law and the Civil Magistrate." Indeed, he feared that the success of the mob in resisting the Gin Acts might well produce a "Populace *enflamed* against the present Distribution of Property, and discovering by outrageous Overt Acts, the strongest *Inclination* to being it nearer to an Equality."[89]

William Hogarth added his name to the chorus of anti-gin campaigners. In mid-February 1751 he produced a pair of prints that depicted the evils of gin and the regenerative qualities of beer (figures 9 and 10). In *Gin Lane* Hogarth presents a picture of desolation, despair, and degradation. In a scene of tumult, anarchy, and near-madness in the parish of St. Giles, a gin-sodden, syphilitic mother drops her baby while taking snuff. Further down the steps, a cadaverous ballad singer and possibly gin hawker, dressed in secondhand army clothes, takes his dying breath with a dram in hand. Behind the mother, ragged residents pawn their last items, including the cherished kettle, and impoverished gin addicts gnaw on a dog's bone. To the mother's left, before the distiller's, men jostle one another and fight under the influence of gin while two charity girls take a dram. A baby and an old woman are also silenced by gin, and an addicted mother is laid in a coffin, leaving the beadle to ponder what to do with her abandoned child. A child nearby has a crueler fate. He or she has been skewered by a gin-crazed chimney sweep.

Gin Lane is not a realistic portrait of what went on in St. Giles-in-the-Fields, even allowing for that parish's reputation as the epicenter of the gin epidemic.[90] It is essentially an "iconotext," a collage of images representing the evils of gin as they were developed in the popular press: images of degradation, of economic ruin, of child neglect, of family breakdown, of a spirit commonly thought to induce madness. Hogarth said he produced cheap versions of the print to expose "the dredfull consequences of gin-drinking." In *Gin Lane* "every circumstance of its horrid effects are brought into view, in terorem, nothing but Idleness, Poverty, misery and ruin are to be seen, Distress even to madness and death, and not a house in tolerable condition but Pawnbrokers and the Gin shop."[91]

Ronald Paulson has suggested that the poor of Gin Lane are victims of the "unholy trinity" of church, state, and pawnbroker.[92] It is doubtful that Hogarth saw them this way, not to mention his readers. The pairing of *Gin Lane* with *Beer Street* suggests Hogarth was first and foremost caught up in the debate over Britain's future, its capacity to marshal its resources in a future war with France. Certainly a *Dissertation* on Hogarth's prints, published months later, believed this to be the case. In that document, gin is presented as

Fig 9: William Hogarth, *Gin Lane,* engraving, 1751. © British Museum.

Fig 10: William Hogarth, *Beer Street,* engraving, 1751. © British Museum.

a substance that had undermined the "regular industrious Subject" and imperiled British competitiveness in trade and war.[93] This was also the central motif of the petitions to Parliament that followed hard on Hogarth's prints. In the petition of the City of London, it was claimed that gin had destroyed "the Health, Strength and Industry of the Poor of both Sexes and of all Ages." It had obstructed the reproduction of "a most useful Class" and consequently threatened the trade, navigation, and power of the country. In the petition from the City of Bristol and its Merchant Adventurers, the same point was made.[94]

In this context *Gin Lane* registers alarm at the effects of gin drinking on national capacity. It is admonitory, drawn to warn the public of Mother Geneva's debilitating effects. In contrast, *Beer Street* depicts industry and jollity, hand in hand. In the first state of this print Hogarth included a miserable Frenchman heisted high by a brawny blacksmith, thus reversing the fear that gin-inflicted punyism would damage British competitiveness in trade and war by invoking the hearty effects of good old English ale, something that Thomas Wilson had advocated in his popular pamphlet against gin.[95] Hogarth subsequently changed this image to the pair of lovers, whose union would presumably produce a healthy crop of children and further the patriotic project of fostering a healthy nation. Patriotism, in fact, abounds everywhere in the print. It is the king's birthday, yet there is a harmonious fusion of industry and merriment that stands in marked contrast to the immiseration and confusion of *Gin Lane*. In *Beer Street,* builders and tailors toast the king, and the only failing business is the pawnbroker. Most topically, two fish-women read John Lockman's broadsheet promoting the British herring industry, a project designed to reduce the poor rate, create a nursery of seamen, and bring a disaffected, Highland Scotland within the British capitalist fold.

Hogarth was perhaps exceptional in his realization that the gin craze could be satisfactorily resolved only by a change in consumer taste. In this respect his insights were prescient. The Gin Act of 1751 offered little that was new to the battery of regulations that had been tried over the course of almost two decades. Taxes at the still-head were raised to 4½d a gallon and licensing fees were doubled, and to ensure that the registered premises were not lowly dives, licenses were issued only to public houses rated at £10 per annum. None of this likely made much difference to the balance between the legal and illegal trade. Although the act allowed excise commissioners to try petty hawkers as well as publicans, it was once again dependent upon informers for its enforcement. Judging from reports in the press, their activities were sporadic and ultimately ineffectual. What was new about the 1751 act was a provision barring distillers from the retail trade, something they had gained in 1747, and the prohibition of gin in prisons and workhouses. At least in controlled environments the law had a measure of success. Otherwise it was more of the same. Certainly the hopes of moral reformers that gin could be regulated out of the reach of the poor remained unrealized.

The gin epidemic was ultimately contained by changes in consumer taste, not by regulation. Poorer harvests and higher prices gradually weaned workers away from gin, the consumption of which fell precipitously after the harvest failures of 1756–57. Cheaper beer, and especially porter, stepped in to take its place. Yet the fact that the gin crisis was resolved by economics rather than social regulation underscored the huge difficulties of policing consumer tastes that did not jibe with the official national project. Parliamentarians recognized this problem very clearly in the debates of 1743, which were well reported in the press. The problem was also recognized by Henry Fielding in his role as a journalist and Bow Street magistrate. In the *Covent Garden Journal,* Fielding expatiated on what he saw as the rise of the mob to the status of a "Fourth Estate." One of the hallmarks of this disturbing phenomenon, disturbing, that is, to Fielding, was the ability of the populace to control the execution of the laws. The glaring example Fielding cited was the Gin Acts, which, unlike the protests against turnpikes, were resisted not so much by force as by evasion, obstruction, and by the intimidation of informers on whom the legal process depended.[96] How Fielding confronted the gin craze and the social problems of the postwar era is the subject of my next chapter. Suffice to say that the gin era raised important issues of governance, with respect both to healthy, productive populations and to policing. These two themes, so clearly articulated by Maddox and Fielding in the early 1750s, distinguished the debate on gin in the aftermath of the War of Austrian Succession.

7

Henry Fielding and Social Reform

Henry Fielding was at the center of the demobilization crisis of 1748–53. He became a magistrate first of Westminster and then of Middlesex as the crisis was breaking, and being at the center of things, briefly in Soho, then at Bow Street, he had to deal with much of the fallout. Within four months of taking office he was involved in the examination and committal of several members of the Hawkhurst gang, whose vulnerability had increased at the end of the war with the redeployment of troops to the coast. In July 1749 Fielding was called in to deal with the bawdy-house riots on the Strand, the collective reprisals of demobbed sailors who felt they had been cheated by whores. As we have seen, the consequences of those disturbances were to haunt Fielding well into the next year, for he defended the government's decision to execute Bosavern Penlez for his part in the disturbances. Indeed, he cast the riots themselves, which some saw as little more than rough justice against bawdy houses, as a formidable attack upon property.

Fielding was also involved in the efforts of seamen to get their prize money. A group of angry sailors approached him when they failed to recover their bounty at a meeting in a tavern behind the Royal Exchange in early 1751. An advertisement had been circulated that the prize money would be distributed, but the sailors, frustrated to find it pertained only to the relatives of deceased sailors, collared the author and took him first to the Admiralty, then to St.

8

James, and finally to Fielding at Bow Street. Fielding examined the culprit "while a multitude of sailors attended" but decided the case was outside his jurisdiction. He referred the seamen to the authorities in the City of London. As it turned out, troops had to be called in to restrain the tars, who threatened to ransack the houses of several bankers in Lombard Street where it was rumored the bounty money was stored.[1]

As a Bow Street magistrate, Fielding predictably had to deal with the criminal effects of demobilization. In December 1749 he sent a demobbed soldier to Newgate Prison on suspicion of coining and then committed a former steward aboard a man-of-war, one Dighton, for breaking into the house of an apothecary in Bloomsbury. Early in 1750 Fielding also sent two soldiers to Clerkenwell Bridewell for attempting to break into an inn in St. Giles-in-the-Fields, but perhaps the most interesting case with which he had to deal in his first year of office involved a demobilized sailor named Thomas Lewis, alias Captain Flash. Lewis had worked in the merchant marine and then the Royal Navy for seven years or so. Early in 1749 he was discharged, and after almost a year's unemployment, he joined a street gang robbing genteel passersby in central London. Arrested in February 1750 and committed to Clerkenwell Bridewell and subsequently Newgate by Henry Fielding, Lewis turned king's evidence to save his own skin and was discharged. Yet within a month he was implicated in several other robberies around St. Pancras and again committed to Newgate by Fielding. This time he was hanged for robbing a Mr. John Matthews behind Montagu House of two gold rings and some small change, jamming a pistol into his victim's jaw with such force that his gums bled.[2] Lewis epitomized the kind of thief that deeply troubled the public in the years after the Peace of Aix-la-Chappelle. He was young, aged twenty-two, flashy, violent, and reckless. "A young Fellow of an undaunted Spirit" was how the Ordinary described him. He was prepared to rob the rich to survive the challenge of demobilization. Among his victims were Lord Bury, the Countess of Albemarle, John Beard, the future manager of the Covent Garden theater, and the dean of Peterborough, whose wig was singed by a pistol ball and powder as Lewis and his gang relieved him of his gold watch and chain.[3]

As one of the most active magistrates in London, Fielding was well placed to comment on the crime wave. His credentials, however, were not impeccable. He was, after all, a trading justice, one whose livelihood was partly sustained through the fees of office. Although Fielding does not appear to have connived or profited from illicit activities, as did some of his contemporaries, he never fully lived down the taint his profession carried in an age that habitually linked impartial justice to independent wealth.[4] His promotion to the bench also smacked of political favoritism. As Opposition critics rightly recognized, his magistracy was a reward for services rendered in defense of the Treaty of Aix-la-Chapelle and, more generally, in the trenchant satire of government opponents, whom he had regularly smeared as Jacobites, republicans, and disloyal scoundrels. As his role in the tumultuous Westminster by-election was to reveal, his partisanship did not disappear with his appointment to the bench. Dependent on the good will of the Duke of Bedford to retain the property qualification necessary for a magisterial position, Fielding had to support the duke's political interest in Westminster and play a partisan role in the support of his lordship's son-in-law.

Fielding's ambition to become a respected spokesman on crime and social problems was evident in July 1749 upon the publication of his charge to the Westminster grand jury. In this charge Fielding clearly defined his role as a "censor of the age," one whose task was to improve the moral fiber of society as much as adjudicate its crimes.[5] His address did not deal with crimes against property directly; that would come with his next tract. Rather, he urged jurymen to curb "the licentious and luxurious Pleasures" that had become "the Characteristic of the present Age."[6] This necessitated a crackdown on brothels, gaming houses, fairs, and masquerades, the latter resembling "Temples of Iniquity" rather than sites of "innocent Diversion." Fielding favored such an initiative because he was particularly interested in curbing vices that promoted idleness and immorality among the "lower sort of people," who, unlike the rich, had to labor for their living and fulfill their role as "the most Useful Members of the Society."[7]

Some critics thought his charge both pretentious and hypocritical: pretentious in that it was liberally laced with legal quotation to affirm Fielding's aptitude for the job; hypocritical in that Fielding posed as a moralist when his earlier career suggested otherwise. One critic tartly remarked that one of Fielding's plays, the *Golden Rump,* was so licentious that it had prompted the licensing act of 1737. Another taunted Fielding by alluding to "the refuse of the Playhouse and Grub street Renegades" who now acting out "their Tragi-comic parts" upon the "Law-Stage " and wondered whether Tom Thumb might now "come properly under your Cognizance and Censure."[8] Yet the *Monthly Review,* at least, was complimentary. "This ingenious author and worthy magistrate has, in this little piece, with that judgment, knowledge of the world, and of our excellent laws (which the publick, indeed, could not but expect from him) pointed out the reigning vices and corruptions of the time, and the legal and proper methods of curbing and punishing them."[9]

Fielding's quite conventional call for a reformation of manners set the scene for a lengthier discussion of social ills some eighteen months later: *An Enquiry into the Causes of the late Increase of Robbers.* This tract coincided with the formation of a parliamentary committee to investigate the pressing problem of crime and received considerable public attention when it first appeared in January 1751. It was generously summarized in the monthlies and more frequently cited than any other social pamphlet in the fifties. Josiah Tucker thought it a "very seasonable judicious treatise," and at least two members of the 1751 Select Committee, William Hay and Charles Gray, commended its proposals for countering crime.[10] Fielding's tract was probably not as influential as some have proposed. There is no hard evidence that it definitively shaped the committee's recommendations, despite the fact that among those on the sprawling committee were two of his former schoolmates, George Lyttelton and William Pitt. Many of the committee's more active members were experienced social administrators in their own right, JPs familiar with the local problems of crime and poverty and men who had been preoccupied with the social problems of gin drinking for over a decade.[11]

Nonetheless the *Enquiry* was an important intervention in the public debate about crime. It begins with a statement of urgency. The crime wave is far from over, Fielding insisted, and if something is not done about it soon, "the Streets of this Town, and the roads leading to it, will shortly be impassable without the utmost Hazard."[12] He is troubled by the political implications of this state of affairs: he is astonished that in a country famed for its liberties, and he is particularly emphatic about the liberty to accumulate and preserve property, people should "tamely and quietly support the Invasion of her Properties by a few of the lowest and vilest among us."[13] In the circumstances, Fielding asks, what was essentially the difference between a libertarian Britain under siege from armed gangs of highway robbers, and an absolutist state under a standing army?

Fielding ascribed this dire state of affairs to three principal causes: the luxurious habits of the poor; the ineffectual provision for the poor, by which he meant the need to regulate labor, because "poor" is defined in the broader sense of having to work for one's living, in Fielding's own words, "those capable of gaining a comfortable Subsistence";[14] and finally the defects in the criminal law. In effect, his analysis centered on the issues of how the criminal code might reinforce order and deter crime and, beyond that, how one might regulate the morals of the poor to encourage honest labor and prevent the formation of criminal subcultures. Interestingly, what Fielding declined to address was the demobilization crisis itself, despite the fact he witnessed its effects as a London magistrate. Beyond situating his analysis within a discourse of luxury, he refused what we would call a social or sociological explanation of crime. Why he did this in the light of his clear engagement with the repercussions of demobilization remains unclear. Fielding, certainly, had little liking for sailors. While he begrudgingly acknowledged their contribution to making Britain a preeminent maritime power, he regarded them as a feckless, dissolute lot: coarse, surly, and quite willing to play the market when it came to taking or breaking contracts. In his eyes they epitomized the qualities of plebeian self-assertion he feared and despised. They were the prototypical plebeians who thought liberty meant "the power of doing what we please."[15]

Fielding probably felt that the sailors' grievances had already been addressed. Although there had been pressure to create a naval reserve in the aftermath of the war, Henry Pelham resisted the pressure, even the parliamentary motion to produce a small reserve of 3,000 sailors in 1749. In that year, however, demobilized seamen and soldiers were given the opportunity of resettling in Nova Scotia, where the government was troubled by the French presence in Acadia and Louisbourg.[16] Parliament also endorsed the plan by several philanthropists of creating a British herring industry to re-employ discharged seamen and win over disaffected Highlanders. Like the settlement in Nova Scotia, this was promoted as an enterprise in the national interest because a good pool of fishermen would smooth the course of remobilization, provide jobs for British tars, and deter them from joining foreign fleets. It would also keep them from "begging from Door to Door," even "plunging into Crimes that may bring them to a fatal End."[17] Wildly optimistic figures were produced about the potential benefits of this enterprise; some thought anywhere from 78,000 to 100,000 seamen might be gainfully employed in this fishery, whereas in practice little more than 3,000 men were employed in the industry in any one year before 1782.[18] Fielding clearly knew of the plan. He told Thomas Wilson in December 1750 that as many as 200,000 men, women, and children might be involved in making herring nets for the new industry and that charity children and paupers might be accommodated within it.[19] As indeed they were. In May 1751 it was reported that children of the Foundling Hospital and other charities were making nets, as were the paupers of St. Andrew, Holborn. Some hoped this scheme would substantially reduce the poor rate.[20]

It is quite possible that the promotion of these schemes so absolved the conscience of people like Fielding about the plight of Jack Tar that demobilization was dismissed as the central social problem of the postwar years. If servicemen had opportunities to accommodate themselves to civilian life, then taking to the road could not be a product of need but evidence of the deplorable dissoluteness of the lower orders. Such a line of reasoning reinforced those conventional explanations of crime that centered on the idleness, insubordination, and immorality of the poor and the threat such vices posed to honest labor and the security of property. That labor, one clergymen affirmed in 1750, was "the main Support of the Advantages and Blessings of higher life, and a Common Benefit of all." Consequently "such members as are unemployed, or employed in Mischief, are a common Burden and Nuisance, wasting the Public Stock which they are, by their Rank and Station, fitted to augment."[21] In this way the question of crime became umbilically linked to the question of regulating the poor, to monitoring their manners, morals, and pauperism.

In the *Enquiry*, Henry Fielding addressed these linkages squarely. The growth of trade and the consequent commercialization of leisure had created tastes and expectations among the "lowest sort of people" that were not only socially inappropriate but politically damaging. "To be born for no other purpose than to consume the fruits of the earth is the privilege . . . of the very Few," Fielding averred. "The greatest part of mankind must sweat hard to produce them, or society will no longer answer the purposes for which it was ordained."[22] Public diversions, the gin craze, and the popularity of gaming had destroyed industry and morality in favor of idleness and crime. In this Fielding shared much with contemporary clerics, who were also concerned with what they saw as the moral lapses of the lower orders, and the potential damage that a drug culture of gin could do to national well-being. Like Isaac Maddox, the bishop of Worcester, Fielding was very troubled by the effect gin drinking had on the present and future manpower of the nation and how its addiction was an inducement to crime. Gin removed "all Sense of Fear and Shame," he insisted and emboldened the "poorer sort" to commit "every wicked and desperate Enterprize."[23] William Hogarth would have shared the same moral view. As we have seen, his *Gin Lane* is a veritable hell of depravity, immiseration, and anomie, although in *Beer Lane* he clearly revealed a more indulgent attitude to the petty recreations of the poor and a more relaxed attitude to work discipline. Fielding, by contrast, assigned the worker to unremitting labor and was quite perplexed by the number of holidays, including execution days in London, that society had to endure at the expense of honest toil.

Predictably, Fielding was troubled by the poor laws, one of the cornerstones of social regulation in eighteenth-century society. He believed that the original intentions of the Elizabethan statutes, which were intended to provide work for the able-bodied and allotted full relief only to the infirm and impotent, had been compromised by administrative indifference, neglect, and misplaced charity. He was keen to return to those original objectives and to buttress them by enforcing the Statute of Artificers of 1563 and subsequent acts that allowed justices of the peace to compel people to labor. If this bundle of statutory controls could not be promoted to instill work discipline, then Fielding wondered whether a voluntary system of charity might not prove a more successful method of relief, because it would increase the discretionary power of the employer class as to which laborers deserved charity.[24]

Fielding was reluctant to admit that the statutory revisions to the poor law in the late seventeenth century gave the mobile poor some rights if they fulfilled their contracts with respect to apprenticeship and servitude. He was not interested in plebeian entitlements so much as plebeian discipline. He ignored the fact that the whole economy of London — particularly its servant economy — would have been inoperable had not more flexibility been applied to the poor law. This seems a remarkable oversight, especially since Fielding must have periodically been called upon to adjudicate claims to welfare and settlement that by the mid-century had generated a substantial amount of case law. But this was an oversight quite in keeping with his conservative, even reactionary social philosophy.[25]

In contrast, Joseph Massie was far more sympathetic to the plight of mobile workers seeking employment, especially in London. Writing in 1758, Massie believed that many workers flocked to London with the best intentions, but unemployment, sickness, and "other misfortunes" brought "great numbers of those people to Poverty when they are far from Home, and frequently, in Places where they are not known."[26] In these circumstances the poor law ostracized them, forcing them back to their native parishes and inducing many to beg or pilfer to make ends meet. In Massie's view the rigidity of the poor law, which was originally framed for a more static society, was damaging to the commercial environment of the eighteenth century, stigmatizing precisely those workers who gave it buoyancy.

Massie saw the poor laws as inhibiting the progress of capitalism, just as he saw the vagrancy laws as criminalizing the mobile worker. Such a vision was foreign to Fielding. He consistently evoked the image of the unfree laborer whose wages ought to be regulated, mobility restricted, and leisure supervised. Despite the erosion of the paternalist controls over labor that were enshrined in the Statute of Artificers of 1563, despite the usefulness of a mobile labor force to agrarian capitalism and industry, Fielding continued to cherish a very traditional vision of society.[27] Fielding advocated a low-wage theory of labor discipline at a time when social commentators were debating whether material incentives to labor were not ultimately more productive than near-starvation wages. In the mid-thirties Bishop Berkeley had asked, "Whether the creating of wants be not the likeliest way to produce industry in a people?" and "Whether the way to make men industrious be not to let them taste the fruits of their industry?"[28] Similarly Jacob Vanderlint believed that workers might socially profit from a rise in real wages even though dram shops and alehouses proved "so great a Snare to the poorer sort." Working people did idle their time away, he admitted, but "they nevertheless do work enough, and too much too, as things now stand: and . . . they would do more if it were provided in a way that would encourage their industry."[29] Fielding would have found such attitudes too indulgent and accepting of plebeian work habits, which were very often shaped by a demand-driven putting-out economy in which frenetic schedules of work were interspersed with periods of unemployment or underemployment.

This was essentially the rhythm of many trades in London, whose industry was shaped by the season, when the parliamentary gentry and their retinues flocked to town. It was also the rhythm of the port, still the largest in the country, where the loading and unloading of ships were determined by sailing schedules, weather, and the available pool of casual labor. Fielding ignored this reality. In his view workers had to be metaphorically (and sometimes literally) kept at the shuttle; any small advance in wages would result in absenteeism and debauchery. Josiah Tucker, the rector of St. Stephen's, Bristol, and later dean of Gloucester, sometimes adopted this view. In his assessment of British and French competitiveness, he was very troubled by the higher cost of British labor, to which he attributed the leisure preferences of the poor. Great numbers of British workers of both sexes refused to work "while they have anything to spend on their vices," Tucker declared in 1749.[30] At the same time Tucker did believe that "the artificial wants, refinements and decorations of social life" encouraged industry and commerce; unlike Fielding, he was not prepared to deny the lower classes these aspirations. All segments of society were motivated by self-love to labor for the goods and honors they wanted. It was the task of governments to facilitate the accommodation of such selfish drives with public-directed benevolence.

Tucker's philosophy anticipated, if it did not entirely endorse, a high-wage theory of labor. In his reflections on the gin craze Tucker recognized the benefits of lower-class consumerism and developed an argument that differentiated the responsible worker from the addict, whose false values were so detrimental to the domestic economy.[31] Tucker's repudiation of cheap gin, in fact, and his answer to the possible loss of tax income from stricter controls over its sale, was predicated on the compensatory benefits that skilled artisans would bring to the economy through the higher consumption of provisions and clothing. Fielding did not make these distinctions. His social policy was rooted in a past age. He wanted general wage regulations where maximum levels were set, even though this part of the Statute of Artificers was rarely invoked by the middle of the eighteenth century.[32] Those clauses of the statute that were applied were principally designed to mediate disputes between masters and men, as was the act regulating the London tailoring trade, with which Fielding was involved as a Middlesex magistrate.

The labor disputes in tailoring stretched back to the beginning of the century, when the journeymen first organized themselves into box clubs to combat the growing power of their employers.[33] The possibility of journeymen becoming master tailors was slim. It took at least £100 to set up a business, and perhaps two or three times that sum to be assured of a regular income in a trade that was volatile to changes in fashion and required extensive credit to address the notorious reluctance of quality clients to shop now and pay later. Most journeymen had to reconcile themselves to the lot of lifetime workers in a trade that was overstocked and susceptible to competition from country tailors who were prepared to work on the cheap. "They are as numerous as Locusts," remarked Campbell of the journeymen, "are out of Business about three or four Months in the Year, and generally as poor as Rats."[34] Journeymen tailors worked long hours, from six in the morning until eight at night, with only an hour's break for dinner, which meant that in winter they worked six hours by candlelight to the ruination of their eyes. Sitting cross-legged and hunched over, they were very susceptible to spinal deformations and bronchial diseases.

Journeyman tailors could sustain a modest living only by organizing collectively. In 1720 the master tailors attempted to break the closed shop by setting up alternative houses of call and enticing tailors to leave their combinations. The honorable section of the trade, the "Flints" went on strike and closed down several of the masters' houses, but the employers responded with legal action and pressured Parliament for an act regulating the trade.

This they achieved in 1721, but the collective strength of the journeymen tailors was such that the going rates of pay were frequently in excess of those set down by statute. Consequently in the mid-forties the masters once more attempted to break the combinations that defined the conditions of employment, only to be confronted with a strike of 15,000 journeymen during the summer and early fall of 1744. The Privy Council ordered the magistrates to intervene, and although several journeymen were convicted of contravening the 1721 act, little headway was made. In January 1745 the journeymen took their grievances to Parliament, "setting forth their Masters large profits and what Wages they might allow them."[35] In their view the 1721 act had held down wages and destroyed their eyes by the time they were forty. They wanted fewer hours working by candlelight, and they resented the manner in which the bigger masters, whose pretensions to gentility they duly noted, had kept them on short time in order to maximize their profits.[36] They wanted "a just and equitable Subordination" between master and journeymen, a "Birth-Right secured to them by Magna Charta and the ancient Constitution of their Realm."[37]

The dispute between masters and journeyman smoldered on. It resurfaced in 1751 upon the death of the Prince of Wales. Taking advantage of the temporary spike in demand for mourning dress, journeymen dug in their heels about basic wages, hours, and the dilution of skilled labor from inexperienced tailors outside London.[38] Under the terms of the 1721 act, the masters requested some arbitration of the dispute, and as the chairman of the Middlesex sessions in July 1751, Fielding was very involved in the deliberations. Two months previously Fielding had sent several journeymen tailors to the Clerkenwell Bridewell for not completing an order contracted with a master in Norfolk Street,[39] and while he was prepared to make some alterations to a statutory rate that had remained unaltered for thirty years, he, like other members of the Bench, was not prepared to tolerate quasi-unions and baulked at the pressures workmen might apply. At the July quarter sessions the justices announced a going rate of 2/6d a day in the high season and 2 shillings per week for the rest of the year, an advance on the official rate, and a reduction of one hour to make it a six-day, thirteen-hour week.[40] The journeymen were unhappy with these concessions, having petitioned for 3 shillings a day, which they calculated was actually worth only 9 shillings a week in a trade that was susceptible to the fluctuations of the London season. The journeymen's clubs thus defied to order. According to the masters, who complained to the Privy Council about journeymen violence, the workers sent letters to tough-minded masters and threatened to burn their premises.[41] In the light of these "Riots, Tumults and Outrages," magistrates were ordered to clamp down on strike-prone or recalcitrant journeymen. In October 1751 a Westminster JP reprimanded three journeymen for refusing to work at the new rates. He did not imprison them under master-and-servant law because they recanted, but his colleague on the bench, Henry Fielding, certainly did so. Later the same month Fielding committed more journeymen to one month's hard labor in the Tothill Fields Bridewell for leaving their masters before their work was finished.[42]

Fielding deplored the freedom that many workmen had over the labor process. He attributed this freedom to "the idleness of the common people." He bristled at the thought of skilled workers reaping even a momentary advantage over their employers. In *A Journey from this World to the Next*, written by Fielding in 1743, Julian the master tailor is taken to task by his "skilled servant," in effect, his journeyman. The journeyman "knew it was easier for him to find another taylor such as me than for me to procure such another workman as him," Julian recalled. "For this reason he exerted the most notorious and cruel tyranny, seldom giving me a civil word; nor could the utmost condescension on my side, though attended with continual presents and rewards, and raising his wages, content or please him."[43] One wonders what he thought of the journeymen shoemakers, who in a suit of trespass, assault, and false imprisonment, with which Fielding was involved, were savvy enough to defend themselves from a pawnbroker who was collecting upper soles and illegally farming them out to be worked up as shoes.[44] He probably found their knowledge of the law presumptuous, as no doubt he did of those tailors who were disconcertingly frank about how the old Tudor statutes and tradition of magisterial supervision were stacked in the masters' favor.[45]

Fielding was a thorough traditionalist when it came to labor relations. His explanation for the crime wave of 1749–53 was also quite conventional. To attribute the rise in crime to the luxury-loving habits and idleness of the poor was quite commonplace in the eighteenth century. In 1750, for example, an anonymous country JP linked the current spate of disorders and felonies to "that torrent of Gaming, Extravagance, Lewdness and Irreligion which has appeared amongst all Ranks of People."[46] In broad terms this argument had been reiterated for more than ten years in the context of the gin craze, in which legislators, magistrates, and parish officials had wrestled with the problem of how to control the resilient street trade in gin and the thousands of petty shops and stalls that provided it.[47] In a provocative if not perverse way, the argument had been present in Bernard Mandeville's notorious *Fable of the Bees;* only Mandeville put a positive spin on luxury, interpreting it as an index of a vibrant consumer society, with crime the inevitable consequence of such prosperity.

In one respect Fielding went further than his contemporaries. Whereas most social critics used the crime wave to advance their pet project — whether it be tighter controls over bawdy houses, or gaming, or gin drinking, or better-regulated workhouses — Fielding contextualized the crime wave as a structural, not contingent, crisis of order. In his preface to the *Enquiry* he writes of the long-term erosion of vassalage and the concomitant rise of independent labor as fundamentally altering the balance of forces in English society, creating a crisis of governance. Precisely why Fielding felt this way is unclear. Perhaps his early experience as a magistrate alerted him to the daunting prospect of controlling the habits of the lower orders. Perhaps the sheer intractability of some social problems, gin drinking, for example, was deeply troubling; troubling in that magistrates had been too frequently overwhelmed with the task of policing illicit sales of liquor in the context of unpopular informers and sporadically active vestries.[48] Whatever the reason, Fielding argued that in the more libertarian, commercial environment of the mid-eighteenth century, the powers of government had become too weak to contain the licentious, insubordinate habits of the common people. The rising crime rate was the consequence. Hence his call "to rouse the civil power from its present lethargic state."[49]

In the *Enquiry* Fielding did not specify how reform might be achieved, although he hinted that he had brought a suitable proposal before the government. This was the plan he submitted to Lord Hardwicke in July 1749, which eventually found its way into the Duke of Newcastle's papers.[50] Fielding's plan called for five metropolitan commissioners or magistrates to reorganize the parish watch into an efficient and accountable police force, with the finances drawn from extra parish taxes. By the standards of the day it would be a massive policing operation, with as many as forty men on annual watch and ward duty in any one parish. Its goal was to crack down on street crime, sweep the streets of vagrants and the unruly, and root out rookeries of immorality and thievery. For its efficacy, it depended crucially on the vigilance of the magistrates and their ability to revivify a watch that had too frequently lapsed into complacency and corruption. In 1750 this was a daunting challenge. Fielding's proposal would have extended the responsibilities of justices to those of police commissioners at a time when the Middlesex Bench was better known for its lethargy than energy. His ideas were concordant with those of Lord Chancellor Hardwicke, who was concerned with the absence of active magistrates in some parts of London.[51]

Accompanying this recharged form of parochial policing was a range of legislative interventions designed to enhance the prosecution of crime and promote respect for law and order. Many of these emanated from Fielding's practical experience as a magistrate. He advocated tougher laws against the receivers of stolen goods, especially their ability to advertise offers to return them without any questions asked. He wanted the rules of legal testimony changed to allow implicated thieves to testify against receivers, who were currently shielded from prosecution as accessories. In other words, he wanted to establish the independent liability of receivers, who could then be held to account without first incriminating the thieves who fenced the goods.[52] Fielding also wanted to extend the Vagrancy Act of 1744 to allow magistrates to detain suspicious persons for up to three days so that potential victims might have the opportunity of identifying them, in effect, a "sus" law, which enhanced the discretionary powers of JPs and constables to pick up potential "trouble-makers." Fielding wanted to extend the Vagrancy Act to those "idle persons" who frequented taverns and alehouses late into the night so that high constables, such as his friend Saunders Welch, could root out potential rookeries of crime. In other words, Fielding wanted the Vagrancy Act to serve as a more efficient instrument of policing and detection, one in keeping with his plan for an enhanced role for the justice of the peace.

Disturbed by the public's reluctance to prosecute felons on account of the cost, Fielding recommended that the county reimburse the plaintiff. He also wanted to streamline the prosecution of property offenses by removing the prejudice against thief-takers, knowing full well how critical ex-thieves were to providing the evidence necessary to expose organized crime. He disliked the trial jury's predisposition to partial or reduced verdicts, a "foolish Lenity," he thought, even though the evidence suggests that such verdicts were on the decline in the mid-eighteenth century as more varied forms of punishment became available.[53] And he wanted to restrict the number of pardons, believing that they detracted from the judicial terror of the law and its deterrent effect. As we have already seen, Fielding wanted to rid public executions of the rituals that undermined the solemnity of the law and the terror of its example. He rhetorically asked his readers whether they "hath beheld a poor Wretch, bound in a Cart, just of the Verge of Eternity, all pale and trembling with his approaching Fate" and "whether the Idea of Shame had ever intruded on his mind."[54] In Fielding's view, the procession to Tyburn dissipated any sense of shame, for the malefactor was swept up in what had become a holiday for "the Mob." The best way to restore the solemnity and terror of executions was to eliminate Tyburn and conduct a prompt execution, in relative privacy before the judges, in the courtyard of the Old Bailey. This form of execution would emulate those conducted in Holland, where the incredible solemnity of the occasion was upheld. "I leave it to any Man to resolve himself upon Reflection," Fielding concluded, "whether such a Day at the Old Bailey, or a Holiday at Tyburn, would make the strongest Impression on the Minds of every one."[55]

By eliminating Tyburn, Fielding hoped to curb the plebeian irreverence for the law; he also hoped to control the spaces in which plebeian culture throve. In all his later writings Fielding was troubled by the degree to which "the Mob" had become a power unto itself, a veritable "Fourth Estate" commanding public space and compromising the policies of its superiors. "None of the other Orders can walk through the Streets by Day without being insulted," he claimed in the *Covent Garden Journal,* "nor by Night without being knocked down." Were it not for the magistracy and the military, the crowd would "have long since rooted all the other Orders out of the Commonwealth."[56]

Fielding's aversion to plebeian culture was in some sense part of his personal agenda, concurrent with his gravitation toward the Whig establishment since the early 1740s. Yet his fears about plebeian insubordination and disorder undoubtedly resonated throughout the propertied public during the crime wave of 1748–52, when, as we have seen, reports of street robberies were accompanied by accounts of smuggling affrays, riots in the West Country and Cornwall, Jacobite revels in the West Midlands, and keelmen's strikes on the Tyne. In Newcastle, at the height of a strike in 1750, keelmen declared for the Pretender; in Wiltshire troops had to be called in to deal with industrial protests from the weavers, adding to an already tense situation in this part of the West Country, where colliers and farmers were defying the authorities and smashing turnpike tollgates.[57] Even at the London fairs, the common people were said to be "audacious, insolent and ungovernable."[58]

However conservative his perspective, Fielding's alarmism touched a raw nerve. No newspaper ribbed his credentials to pronounce on crime in 1751, unlike 1749. The *Monthly Review* was once again laudatory, declaring that Fielding had risen to the task of explaining the crime wave with "spirit, judgment and learning."[59] The *London Magazine* summarized the main points of his tract, without comment, so that they might reach a wider audience than the middling or upper-class readers who were prepared to fork out 2/6d to read it. Fielding's *Enquiry*, in fact, inspired William Draper to pen a long poem in blank verse on the degradations of the metropolis.[60] It was also cited by Isaac Maddox as grist for the argument that drink disposed the lower class to rob and steal.[61]

To be sure, there were some disclaimers. Writing under the nom de plume of Ben Sedgly, Richard Rolt was troubled by several of Fielding's recommendations. He was suspicious of Fielding's attempt to augment to the role of the magistrate in English society, sensing that this would undermine the long-standing conventions of liberty enshrined in such documents as the Bill of Rights. It would increase the powers of the Crown and executive at the expense of the House of Commons. Rolt saw little purchase in attempting to revivify the old laws about wage regulation, however troublesome combinations had become, as indeed they had in both London and proto-industrial areas of the countryside. Nor did he think voluntary charity could address the larger issue of poverty, however usefully it was applied to particular issues. Rolt also berated Fielding for suggesting that upper-class luxury was socially inconsequential and irrelevant to the task of reforming manners and morals. The South Sea Bubble had set new standards of prodigality and risk taking, Rolt maintained, and the slavish adoption of French fashions by the upper class and its obsession with gaming was having a destructive effect on London society as a whole. Basically, Fielding was wrong to sidestep the responsibilities of the rich in promoting a more sober, responsible society; something that he did, for when some "young gentlemen of fashion" were caught in a raid of a masquerade at the Exeter exchange, Fielding chose not to expose them and therefore was obliged to release some women of dubious reputation at the same time.[62]

Some of Fielding's suggestions for reforming the criminal process opened the door to corruption and authoritarianism, or so Rolt thought. The liberal use of rewards to discover malefactors would allow unscrupulous informers or thief-takers to incriminate the innocent, of which, one might add, there were some glaring examples in the smuggling trials. Hanging people within the confines of the prison smacked of secret government and undermined the transparency of the law. If this proposal were adopted, Rolt opined, "A giddy multitude will then be apprehensive of tortures, forced confessions and compulsory accusations which are the harbingers of arbitrary power."[63]

Yet Rolt could find common cause with Fielding on a number of issues. Like the author-magistrate, he was very concerned with the problem of drunkenness, because it both undermined work discipline and encouraged insubordination, "exalting every man to an equality with his master or governor" and "repressing all that awe which retains men within the limits of their proper sphere."[64] Rolt was very troubled by the "idleness," "insolence," and "debauchery" of "the common people of both sexes," which was daily observed "in every part of this great metropolis." Consequently, like Fielding, he strongly endorsed the need to crack down on gin drinking and gambling, which he thought the root causes of crime, and to strengthen the deterrent effect of the law. Here he differed from Fielding, believing that the discretionary use of pardons and fewer executions would offer a more compelling theater of justice than quick executions in a courtyard, although he suggested that violent criminals should suffer dismemberment — the chopping off of their incriminating hands — either before or immediately after execution.[65] Rolt also believed that transportation could be more effectual if it were directed to new colonies like Georgia and Nova Scotia under official superintendence and not left to private enterprise, something that was eventually adopted in Australia.

Rolt was Fielding's most vocal critic. He was most troubled about the authoritarian implications of Fielding's program of reform and skeptical that some of the old laws on the statute book could be revamped so effortlessly. But, like others, he was certainly prepared to entertain a conversation with the Middlesex magistrate about a public agenda of reform. So, too, was "Philo-patria." He thought Fielding had not spent enough time condemning debauchery and thinking of ways to eliminate prostitution, which Philo-patria saw as one of the principal causes of crime. Yet he commended Fielding for his thoughts on the poor laws which he hoped the legislature would consider.[66]

There was in fact a broad consensus about the need to address such pressing social issues, especially the gin epidemic, which was widely seen as a contributory, if not major, factor in the breakdown of social order. Most public spokesmen advocated new laws to monitor pawnshops, alehouses, and places of amusement, only occasionally voicing concern that such regulation might be perverted for political ends. To counteract this, some writers proposed that all substantial men of property should be promoted to the bench, not simply those sympathetic to the government. Such a recommendation was hardly needed, for Henry Pelham and the lord chancellor, Lord Hardwicke, had already begun the process of promoting Tory landowners to the commissions of the peace, sometimes in the face of local Whig opposition. By the early 1750s, appointments to the bench were becoming increasingly nonpartisan as the government sought to mobilize gentry resources to combat crime and disorder.[67]

Part of the publicity accorded Fielding's *Enquiry* had to do with timing. His pamphlet came out two days after the king's address to Parliament. It urged MPs to consider measures "for enforcing the Execution of the Laws and for suppressing those Outrages and Violences which are inconsistent with all good Order and Government."[68] Within a month a committee was struck to consider these issues. Led by the lawyer and leading government supporter, Sir Richard Lloyd, it was broadly based. It included members of the Leicester House faction; MPs from the City of London; Tories, such as Charles Gray, the MP for Colchester; and philanthropic-minded MPs who had backed the new colony in Georgia and had enthused about a British herring fishery. It was by no means a partisan committee, but it reflected a broad swathe of parliamentarians interested in the problems of social reform and committed to addressing them in what was the "grand inquest" of the nation.[69]

The first set of resolutions that the committee penned addressed the perceived deficiencies of the Westminster watch, its finances and salaries, recommending that the watch take up "every suspicious Person" found "loitering or lurking about the Streets, Passages and Alleys" and link up with JPs to advertise rewards for the conviction of robbers.[70] These very practical resolutions were embodied in a bill managed by Lloyd and Sir John Strange, the Master of the Rolls. More general resolutions followed — about lower-class idleness, diversions, and gaming as the causes of crime, with recommendations to regulate pawnshops, to crack down on disorderly houses, to reform houses of correction, and to toughen the law against those who tried to rescue those sent into custody. As we have seen, the latter was a continuing problem in London, where sailors, in particular, had rescued fellow tars from the law.

Further resolutions echoed some of the concerns voiced by Fielding in his *Enquiry*. There was a need to revamp the laws against receiving stolen goods, to subsidize private prosecutions, and to strengthen the hand of magistrates in detaining suspicious persons.[71] These were to be included in a bill drawn up by Sir Richard Lloyd, Sir John Strange, and two other well-known government supporters, Henry Bathurst and Nicholas Hardinge, the latter the former clerk to the Commons. Finally, in June, Lloyd's committee included the poor laws in its mandate, as had Fielding, suggesting that the laws of settlement should be reviewed and that proposals should be considered for reducing the expense of the poor law and for reinvigorating its work provisions to inculcate habits of industry and offset the emergence of welfare cultures.[72]

No further progress was made on these resolutions in 1751. The only legislative achievement of that session was the Gin Act, which doubled the fee on retail licenses and taxed gin at its source by raising the duty on spirituous liquors.[73] In this way it was hoped that the working poor could be weaned from gin to beer, a beverage considered far less damaging to their health and to the economic health of the nation. This well-supported initiative went some way toward allaying ruling-class fears of lower-class decadence and drug dependency, but it did not directly address the crime wave that had preoccupied the public since the peace. The urgency to do so was underscored in the king's speech of November 1751, when Parliament was pressed once more to ponder "some effectual Provisions to suppress those audacious crimes of Robbery and Violence which are now become so frequent, especially about this great Capital."[74] Accordingly, several bills were drawn up to address specific issues noted by Lloyd's committee, although some projects, such as reforming the houses of correction, went by the board.[75]

Not all of these bills were successful. One bill recommended that some categories of male felons be sentenced to hard labor in the royal dockyards rather than transported abroad, for there were growing complaints on both sides of the Atlantic that felons were escaping servitude and returning home before their sentences expired.[76] Badged and chained, dockyard felons would do some of the laborious jobs required to build up the fleet, thereby turning "disgraceful criminals" into "useful members of society."[77] In this legislative proposal it was not assumed that felons could be rehabilitated; rather it was hoped that by working in chain gangs they might deter others from serious crime, adding another variation to the existing panoply of public punishment.[78] This bill, the Dockyards Bill, passed the Commons but was rejected by the Lords. Precisely why is unclear. Jonas Hanway later surmised that their lordships thought the policing requirements of such chain gangs dangerous and inoperable.[79] Some may have thought chain gangs too redolent of continental galley slaves, an inappropriate punishment for liberty-loving Britons; although at least one commentator proposed both galleys and chain gangs as alternative punishments for felonies precisely because there was a deep aversion to slavery.[80] Perhaps their lordships agreed with an anonymous pamphleteer who thought transportation to America allowed for a stricter supervision of felons than a dockyard experiment, which threw unruly convicts together. In this commentator's view there was a greater possibility of reclaiming convicts through coerced labor in the New World than by having them do casual work for the British navy.[81]

A pawnbrokers' bill, drafted under the chairmanship of Sir William Yonge, also foundered, despite the fact that it quickly passed through the Commons.[82] It recommended that pawnbrokers be licensed in the same manner as the vendors of spirituous liquors., They should also be known ratepayers who kept routine hours and records of all business transactions, respectable people willing to detain anyone suspected of passing stolen goods. These recommendations did not find their way to the statute book until 1757, having failed to pass in two successive sessions.

Yet three bills did pass in 1752. Benefit of clergy was denied to those who stole goods on wharves or navigable rivers, which meant that riverside theft was more likely to become a hanging offense. An act "for the better preventing thefts and robberies" broadened the licensing regulations to places of entertainment "for the lower sort of people" and strove to facilitate the prosecution of disorderly houses by plugging loopholes in the existing laws. This act emboldened JPs and constables to prosecute offenders at the request of as few as two local inhabitants. It also fined those advertising rewards for the return of stolen goods with no questions asked and allowed justices to hold "suspicious persons" for up to six days.[83]

Finally, Parliament passed an act to extend the judicial terror for murder. Known as the Murder Act, it isolated convicted murderers from the public and subjected them to a spare regimen of bread and water during their final days in jail. In effect, no one was allowed the opportunity of sensationalizing his or her crime. To facilitate this and to amplify the judicial terror, the act demanded quick sentences upon conviction and gave judges the option of recommending that the corpses of the executed be publicly dissected or hung in chains. Although a few commentators at the time advocated galley slavery as an alternative to hanging, largely on the grounds that it would strike punishment terror in a liberty-loving populace, the general consensus was that chain gangs and galleys were punishments more appropriate to continental regimes than to the British system of justice.[84]

No great change of principle underscored these legislative proposals. It is difficult to agree with Sir Leon Radzinociwz that the Dockyards Bill signaled a significant departure from the prevailing doctrine of "maximum severity" enshrined in the Bloody Code.[85] Certainly, the assumptions underlying the Dockyards Bill indicated that legislators thought that a greater variety of punishments for property crime might encourage private prosecutions and obviate the need for trial juries to downsize indictments when they felt a particular case did not merit the prescribed punishment. As John Beattie has shown, the introduction of transportation in 1717 offered juries a viable alternative to capital punishment for property crime, sometimes as a reprieve from execution.[86] Now legislators were prepared to revisit that calibration of justice from the standpoint of public utility, from a belief that thieves should be forced to make a contribution to society rather than face banishment, or from a conviction that petty offenders might be rescued from more serious crimes and, through hard labor and discipline, sent on an "honest course of life." A greater range of punishing options, in other words, would facilitate the efficiency and efficacy of criminal justice. None of these precedents undermined the belief that hardcore examples of judicial terror should be employed from time to time as a critical deterrent to crime. Indeed, in the aftermath of the War of Austrian Succession, the debate turned on what was the best way to achieve this given the disconcerting scenes at Tyburn. In the end legislators opted for the high visibility of public executions, not for official, semi-private ones as Fielding had advocated in his *Enquiry*.

Essentially the proposals of 1751–52 were pragmatic, ad hoc responses to the crime wave. There were designed to plug loopholes in the law and to use the existing machinery of justice to do so. Fielding must have been delighted with the introduction of the "sus law," which would have aided his new experiments in criminal detection. He was no doubt pleased with Parliament's decision to prevent indictments against disorderly houses being moved to higher courts on writs of certiorari, something he had advocated in the *Covent Garden Journal*. He must have been disappointed, however, with the rather tepid solutions to receiving stolen goods, which did not address the difficulties of prosecuting fences and receivers as accessories to crime. And he was surely less than satisfied with Parliament's indecision over the poor laws, which formed part of the discussion about crime because legislators hoped to rescue young offenders from habits that would inure them to a life of crime, especially crimes of a more serious nature. No doubt the gin craze, which highlighted the prospect of drug-addicted dysfunctional families spawning lawless guttersnipes, did much to focus social critics on the educative possibilities of welfare legislation in meeting the challenge of such "delinquency."

As the Commons' resolutions of June 1751 clearly revealed, three issues informed the mid-century debate on the poor law.[87] The first was the spiraling cost of poor-law relief and the need for cost efficiency. The second was the need to promote habits of industry among those on relief and to find a profitable method of employing pauper labor, for both moral and fiscal reasons. The third was to train young dependents to be self-supporting subjects who would not become "a new Race of chargeable Poor" and possibly petty criminals. Many thought these objectives could be achieved only by dismantling, or at the very least radically revising, the parochial system of poor relief. In fact, the Commons, troubled by the litigious nature of poor-law removals and the diversity of existing poor-law practice, approved a resolution abolishing the laws of settlement, the regulations that determined where a pauper might receive relief.[88]

The mid-century debate thus turned on a question that had engaged administrators and politicians since the late seventeenth century: whether larger administrative units would provide a more efficient and economical system of poor relief than the parish. Advocates for change argued that larger unions would provide a better range of facilities to handle the different problems of poverty, be it better provision for the sick and infirm, labor for the able-bodied, correction for the indolent and disorderly, or the reclamation of their progeny, potentially the next generation of criminals. Some saw the possibility of using houses of correction to institute more efficient regimes of disciplined labor, and to punish petty offenders more thoroughly and appropriately. As Joshua Fitzsimmonds put it in 1751: "Such punishments as Branding, Whipping and even Transportation might be very properly changed to hard Labour and Correction, suitable to the nature of the Crime."[89]

Critics of the Poor Law claimed that the existing system undermined the mutualities of rich and poor so essential to the social order and subjected the poor to the vexatious rivalry of individual parishes and to the petty tyrannies of local officials, some of whom had misappropriated funds for their own ends. "Every Parish is in a State of expensive war with the rest of the Nation," claimed William Hay, the MP for Seaford and a member of the 1751 committee. It "regards the Poor of all other Places as Aliens; and cares not what becomes of them if it can but banish them from its own Society."[90] Joseph Massie even thought that the parish system encouraged crime because it forced well-intentioned laborers on the tramp to pilfer and steal to make ends meet when overseers refused them occasional relief. These problems could be resolved only by abolishing the settlement acts and allowing JPs the opportunity to set up new unions, managed by propertied guardians, under whose supervision new hospitals and houses of industry would be established. Only then, argued Hay, would the problems of crime, labor discipline, and itinerant poverty be brought under some semblance of control and "Examinations, Passes, Duplicates, Certificates, Orders, Appeals, and a thousand other idle Trumperies . . . dispersed like the Sybil's Leaves."[91]

Two bills were actually drawn up to revise the poor laws in 1752, but neither got off the ground. Parliamentarians remained unconvinced that larger institutions were necessarily more efficient or less corrupt. Even Charles Gray, who chaired the committee that drew up the so-called poor children's bill, admitted that some of the Corporations of the Poor had not been successful. While he applauded the administration of the Bristol Corporation of the Poor, he cited others, including the one in his own constituency of Colchester, where "party views and private purposes" had intervened.[92] He also felt that the promiscuous character of many large institutions was detrimental to the morals of the poor, exposing the better sort to the depravity of the "vagabond and idle." Larger units were also open to legitimate libertarian and financial objections, to a deep-rooted suspicion of new centers of power, and to their problematic expense. Such skepticism from potential reformers reinforced the opinion of those who were far from convinced that the poor laws were operating as disastrously as their critics claimed, even in London, where the City parishes were said to be competent managers of their poor. "The best, the safest, and the most rational means" of employing the poor, one merchant asserted, was to continue the old policy of erecting local workhouses "where the poor are well looked to, kept industriously employed, and managed under all the parishioners' inspection in the most frugal as well as honest manner."[93] One commentator claimed that the efficiency of poor relief was not really a question of size so much as the fusion of self-interest and benevolence within particular, knowable contexts. This was especially the case with pauper employment, which could prosper only where there was a resilient demand for labor and a readily available stock of material. In the eyes of this commentator, labor discipline could sometimes be better instilled by contracting out the poor than by subjecting them to mundane tasks in parochial or county workhouses.

These reservations sealed the fate of the two bills. The more radical, a bill "for the more effectual Relief and Employment of the Poor" proposed by Lord Hillsborough, sought to substitute the county for the parish as the fundamental unit of poor relief. It planned to build multi-functional hospitals to accommodate the poor, financed from the county rate, and to phase out the old system of parish provision within two years. It reached the second reading in March 1752 before it was ground down in committee.[94] The other, a bill "for the better maintenance and employment of poor children," was moved by Sir Richard Lloyd, one of the central players on the committees of 1751–52. It sought to establish countywide corporations of the poor managed by a board of guardians consisting of JPs and wealthy freeholders elected by lot. The guardians would provide work for the able-bodied pauper, principally though not exclusively in large houses of industry, but their main task was to ensure that marginal children — whether orphans, vagrants, bastards, or simply pauper children — were given an adequate training to save them from a life of crime. To offset the expense, the houses of industry would be financed by charitable benefactions and a lottery, relying on the poor rates only as a default position. To avoid interfering with thriving poor-law projects, the new institutions would supplement rather than compete with facilities established under the 1723 Workhouse Act and the existing Corporations of the Poor. In effect, the project sought to buttress the existing system by providing greater institutional care for vulnerable children and ensuring that they did not germinate a criminal subculture.[95]

This proposal satisfied neither reformers nor traditionalists, even when it was proposed that the new houses of industry be established in more limited jurisdictions, defined by county hundreds or subdivisions. Thomas Alcock thought Lloyd's bill too "narrowly bottomed." It concentrated on a minority of the poor and ignored the existing facilities for marginal children, such as charity schools and foundling hospitals. Moreover, most parents would refuse to send their children to the new houses of industry, he predicted, but "would rub on without this assistance."[96] Besides, workhouses without adjoining hospitals and houses of correction were hardly worth the effort, for what was need was an efficacious mix of welfare paternalism and penal discipline. A poorhouse without a house of correction, in particular, would not resolve the problem of suppressing the "idle, daring, wicked poor," Alcock averred, who were "the most troublesome and dangerous to the state."[97]

For their part, traditionalists continued to believe that charity began at home and balked at the prospect of diverting their funds and committing their pauper children to large impersonal institutions over which they had limited control. In the end, all the could be recovered from the reform drive of the early 1750s was a flood of local acts on poor-law relief, including two statutes establishing workhouses in Chichester and Spitalfields, where legislators were assured that the poor could be more cheaply provided for and efficiently employed.[98] Efforts to launch a general scheme for larger workhouses or hospitals and to modify the settlement acts floundered in the face of localism and a deep skepticism of big government. With them went one of the central underpinnings of the regulatory drive to combat crime and disorder in the aftermath of the War of Austrian Succession. Despite the warnings of Fielding, Hay, and others that the war on crime could only be successfully waged by reforming the morals of the poor, and that meant the poor laws as well as the criminal code, divisions within the propertied classes frustrated a broad legislative strategy.

If there was sometimes little consensus about the social reform agenda of the early fifties, that agenda was not unimportant or inconsequential. The fact that Parliament was enjoined to consider social reform with such insistency between 1751 and 1753 speaks forcefully to the fact that issues of social policy were regarded as matters of national interest. They were not simply the preoccupation or hobby of a few parliamentarians; nor did they only form part of the many private bills that Parliament routinely enacted for the better administration of towns and parishes. Parliament had a mandate to address matters of social policy when the occasion arose, even if they were not normally part of the legislative agenda.[99] The conventional view, that such matters became important only when the impact of large-scale industrialism wrought profound changes upon an essentially agrarian society, is clearly incorrect. As a number of historians have recently shown, there were a series of regulatory drives throughout the century, some of them synchronized to the dislocations of war and the problems of reintegrating servicemen back into society.[100] During the mid-century, and again after the American war, the upsurge in propertied crime was the occasion for a broader assessment of the problems of social regulation, generating demands for a reform of the criminal code and the poor laws, and also for a reformation of manners. It was no accident that the amalgamated poor-law unions, the penitentiary, the police, and moral reform should form part of the social agenda after 1783, just as crime, poverty, and the "luxury" of the poor formed part of the agenda at the mid-century. All formed part of the discourse of social regulation, impinging directly upon the social reproduction of labor and the patterns of domination that sustained the social order.

That discourse did not mark a shift from a bloody code toward penal sanctions that emphasized preventive strategies and toward analyses of crime that stressed environmental factors. The Bloody Code remained with its hangings, gibbets, and dissections. As we have seen, there was more, not less, severity in the punishment of violent crime, and much of the mid-century discussion turned on what extra or new sanctions might be added to the criminal code to produce a more efficient choreography of judicial terror. Social reformers were in broad agreement on the need to vindicate the majesty of the law and to enhance the deterrent effect of the gallows, which in London at least, had been significantly undermined by the surgeons' riots and the counterculture of Tyburn fair. New capital punishments were added to the statute book. A spate of coastal wrecking along the south coast that attracted the attention of the attorney and solicitor general resulted in a new act which made it a capital offense to plunder any cargo from a ship or to hinder anyone attempting to escape from it, or even to put out false lights to lure ships onto dangerous coasts.[101]

There was nevertheless a serious quest for preventive strategies to meet the existing crime wave. Reformers looked for ways to instill labor discipline and to curb those leisure preferences of the poor that were widely believed to be conducive to crime. These efforts proved contentious. As we have seen, Thomas Potter's proposal for a census in 1753 was opposed by diehard libertarians who feared an extension of governmental influence. Not even the suggestion that such information might rationalize state policy and highlight the growth areas of the economy could assuage their suspicion of central government. Major shifts in governmentality were not something mid-century politicians were ready to endorse even if the seed had been planted. If Anglo-French rivalry sometimes pushed social reformers to consider new strategies of planning and surveillance, Anglo-French differences cobbled them. Too much centralism still smacked of unpopular French regimes.

Even so, projects designed to enhance the visibility and efficiency of work-houses were aired publicly. In the wake of the call for larger workhouses by the 1751 committee, Henry Fielding produced a pamphlet that signaled a change of heart about poor-law reform.[102] Whereas in the *Enquiry* Fielding argued that the current system could be redeemed if reformers returned to its original premise of providing relief for the impotent and work for the able-bodied, two years later he had decided that only a change in governance would achieve this goal. Rather than rely on the parish, Fielding proposed that Middlesex create a county workhouse and house of correction to address the work-shy habits and moral laxity of the London poor.

Fielding's proposal went far beyond the Corporations of the Poor that had been launched in London and several provincial towns earlier in the century. The one in Bristol, for which we have detailed information, housed only four hundred inmates and allowed for a healthy provision of outdoor relief.[103] Fielding's plan was more like the nineteenth-century workhouse after the Poor Law Amendment Act of 1834. Outdoor relief was banned. The pauper population was huge, some five thousand inmates, segregated by sex. They worked ten hours a day with two hourly breaks, half an hour for breakfast, and an hour for dinner. The work was tedious and disagreeable: beating hemp, chopping rags, "the hardest and vilest labour."[104] For this labor inmates would receive 2 shillings a week advance until their work was sold, at which point they were expected to be self-sustaining, a condition in the proposal that was clearly designed to meet the objection that large workhouses would be exorbitantly expensive. Apart from Sundays, inmates were allowed twelve days off a year, principally the Christian high holidays and royal anniversaries, but they could not leave the workhouse for any length of time without special permission. Suitably badged on the left shoulder of their clothing and able to move about only with official passes, they were stigmatized for their poverty.

In addition to the work assigned to them in the workhouse, inmates could be legitimately farmed out to employers within twenty miles of the metropolis. They could be hired out for as long as a year, but always in highly regulated circumstances. Inmates could get permission to leave the workhouse only if they had completed their assigned work and if they had repaid any advances of money. And then they could go only to their lawful place of settlement within the metropolis where there was some guarantee of work, for Fielding did not see his county workhouse as accommodating the many people who came to London from outside. The "license of departure" from the governor would also specify whether they had been industrious and well-behaved inmates, for as the title of the tract revealed, it was intended to amend the morals of the poor and render them "useful members" of society.

Fielding's scheme was a massive policing operation of the London-based poor, designed essentially to root out rookeries of crime and inculcate habits of industry among the lower class. His institution was designed not only to deal with London's pauper population; it contained prison cells and a court-yard for as many as six hundred to one thousand reprobates. Fielding saw his prison-workhouse as a huge disciplinary institution to deal with London's idle and work-shy, under conditions of incarceration that would deter the tem-porary unemployed from wanting to go there. In this respect it echoed the nineteenth-century policy of "less eligibility," making workhouses unattrac-tive places to live in. One of the weaknesses of his proposal was that it was not designed to deal with those workers who tramped to the metropolis in search of work beyond insisting that they had appropriate passes. They would pre-sumably be dealt with under the vagrancy laws, although the logistics of this surveillance and the degree to which it might involve some brief incarceration in a workhouse or house of correction remained unclear. Those who resented this near-prison house of work, or who were regarded as defiant or disorderly, were subjected to harsher treatment. This could include a mean fare of bread and water and a whipping before hard labor, a period in solitary confinement, and for aggravated offenses, transportation or compulsory service in the East or West Indies, where the drain in manpower was great because of tropical diseases.[105]

Fielding's *Proposal* never adequately addressed the complexities of Lon-don's in-migration and service economies. It did not confront the fact that London was both a large manufacturing sector that was subject to seasonal spikes in demand and an imperial port that continually spilled men on to its wharves and ropewalks. Unlike Joseph Massie who recognized the volatility of metropolitan work, Fielding wanted to rivet men and women to their as-signed settlements and place in society, and to punish those who ventured beyond them. Consequently his *Proposal* was rigidly formulaic in its applica-tion of the existing laws. It accepted the current status quo about settlements, even if Fielding really wanted to bypass them as far as possible.

The *Proposal* was wildly optimistic about the enforcement of a poor-law

regime. With their salaried officials, their regimen of labor and religious in-
struction, their solitary cells and sex segregation, Fielding hoped these massive
institutions would mold the mind as well as punish the body of the reprobate
and idle worker. In his imagination he saw these places as "cities" of correction, spaces where the reprobate could be disciplined and the work-shy redeemed. They were not designed like a panopticon, where warders might
survey the inmates at will; rather the plan of the county workhouse was not
dissimilar to the old almshouses, with the different sexes congregating in open
courts and with workshops constructed just beyond them.

Within this space Fielding hoped that the wardens would be able to invigi-
late regimes of sex-segregated work in an effective way. To add to its effective-
ness, he proposed to eliminate the customary fees and perquisites that blunted
the disciplinary imperative of old institutions.[106] To amplify the disciplinary
effect, Fielding calibrated the punishments of the inmates, beginning with
moderate punishments designed to reprove rather than shame the culprit, "to
persuade the Offender that he is corrected only for his own Good." Exemplary
punishments were reserved for recidivists and the incorrigibly reprobate. They
were intended "rather to raise Terror in others than to work the Reformation
of the party itself."[107] This mixed regime of punishment, then, calibrated
severity by the offense and disposition of the inmate. It was prepared to deploy
the theatricality of punishment in all its old-regime goriness, but it did not
neglect "the Correction of Mind." Citing Archbishop Tillotson, Fielding believed that the wrath and fear of a magistrate was "a weak and loose Principle
of Obedience, and will cease whenever Men can rebel with Safety." Obedience
to the law was ultimately a matter of "Conscience, which is a firm, and constant, and lasting Principle, and will hold a Man fast when all other Obligations will break."[108]

Fielding's institution stood in marked contrast to the conventional workhouse or house of correction, which threw together different delinquent populations in a promiscuous fashion, paid less attention to regular work schedules, and doled out physical punishment in a discretionary but essentially
reactive manner.[109] In this respect it was not so different from that proposed
by Thomas Alcock in 1752.[110] Like Alcock's three-tiered workhouse, which
included a hospital and a house of correction, it held fast to the ideal of a
corrective prison that had sometimes been associated with the bridewell and
the newly designed workhouses of 1723. Like those institutions in their most
utopian form, it was imagined as an engine of social transformation.[111]

In the broadest terms, Fielding's model county workhouse gestured toward
the "Bastilles" of the nineteenth-century welfare system and also to the penitentiary.[112] Yet for all the emphasis Fielding placed on the persuasive powers

of religion, his plan was not infused with an evangelical optimism about the regenerative potential of the religious conscience. Fielding imagined that his house of correction would employ a chaplain like the Ordinary of Newgate, whose conversations and prayers with prisoners were designed to bring them to a becoming repentance of their crimes. Consequently his *Proposal* did not quite meet the regimen so central to corrective institutions in the age of the penitentiary: solitary confinement, discretionary sentencing, and prison work as a source of character formation. While Fielding recognized the utility of solitary confinement in bringing the "most abandoned profligates to reason and order," he did not construct a continued and comprehensive routine of solitude to induce inmates to repent their sins. Rather, he assigned the fasting room to induct inmates to a regime of hard labor. As for discretionary sentences attuned to each criminal's progress toward rehabilitation, such an individualizing mode of prison surveillance had yet to be conceived. The nearest Fielding came to this was in the governor's testimonials of good behavior and in the broad powers given authorities to discipline the reprobate and the recalcitrant. Even so, Fielding's scheme signaled a break with the permissive, self-regulating prisons of the past and a shift toward more professional, centralized institutions devoted to reshaping the character of the individual. The age of the penitentiary had yet to arrive, even if there was a desire for a more intensive carceral regime.

In the end the propertied classes opted for relatively conventional solutions to the crime wave in the aftermath of the war: stricter licensing, local workhouse regimes, philanthropic hospitals, a retuning of the criminal code, and wider powers of detaining the idle and disorderly. These were not without some efficacy, although after an immediate flurry of activity, enforcement ebbed and the legal difficulties of policing the streets, in particular, reasserted themselves.[113] A few pleasure gardens were closed in the wake of the Disorderly Houses Act. Ranelagh was refused a license in 1754. There were intermittent raids on gaming dens, sometimes with the help of troops. Sabbatarian legislation was enforced, at least in parts of east London. And there were dramatic, if brief sweeps of vagrants and prostitutes. In the parish of St. Clement Danes, the scene of the bawdy-house riots of 1749, seventy women were charged as common streetwalkers, prostitutes, or simply as loose, idle, and disorderly in the period 1752 to 1756, and thirty-one of them endured a public whipping.[114] Fielding even sent an apprentice to prison for taking a pint of gin into the Savoy Prison at the request of a soldier-guard.[115]

Politicians had not been able to agree on a policy for pauper children beyond farming them out as apprentices in lowly trades and domestic service, but there were proposals in the public domain that recommended that vagrant and orphaned children should be institutionalized until they were of a suitable age to be employed in manufacture, the fishery, or the navy. Thomas Alcock saw the need for more efforts on this front to complement the charity school movement and to ensure that children would not become part of that "bad Culture" from which "a considerable Part of the yearly Crop of unhappy Felons has grown."[116] Like others, he linked the debate on crime to public morals, punishment to welfare. The concept of what David Garland would term "penality," that is, a cluster of strategies in which penal sanctions were intimately bound up with broader issues of welfare, was central to the mid-eighteenth-century debate on social reform as it was to the nineteenth.[117] It was not as well articulated, and it lacked the same legislative effect, but it was certainly present in the discussion of the demobilization crisis of 1748–53 under the rubric of "police."

One issue that did resonate with eighteenth-century commentators was the potential mobilization of street urchins for the navy. At least one proposal sought to corral these children for sea service, first as boys, and then as part of a national register of eligible seafarers to minimize the need for naval impressment.[118] Within an institutional setting this proved to be an impractical solution to a public committed to public parsimony and sensitive to the potentially spiraling expenses of large institutions. Even so, the basic goal was taken up by the merchant-philanthropist Jonas Hanway within a matter of years. At the onset of the next war, when the country sought to mobilize its marine manpower by extending naval impressment ashore,[119] Hanway raised money by subscription to create a Marine Society in which male urchins would be recruited into the navy and rescued from a life of crime. Like other ventures in the mid-century, this initiative was inspired by patriotism and Christian benevolence, with the benevolence, one might add, firmly subordinated to national imperatives. At a time when people were fearful that the population was declining in the face of a major drug scare, such ventures were designed not only to inhibit crime and the emergence of criminal subcultures but to raise Britain's stock in future imperial wars (figure 11).

Raising Britain's stock for future wars was one of the central preoccupations of the preventive measures to confront the crime wave of 1749–53. The long struggle against the gin craze had convinced public-minded Britons of the essential profligacy of the laboring poor. They were troubled that the leisure preferences of this class were potentially detrimental to a nation whose prosperity rested in large measure on international competition with the French and Spanish. Many were convinced that the next generation of Britons would not be able to provide the necessary manpower required of international rivalry. Virtually all of the preventive measures aired in the 1750s were shaped

Fig 11: Giovanni Battista Cipriani, frontispiece to Jonas Hanway, *Three Letters on the subject of the Marine Society*, 1758. © British Museum.

by these anxieties, whether it meant rescuing orphans, prostitutes, and street urchins or finding means to return a profligate lower class to worthwhile labor.[120] As did those proposals, which pertained to the welfare of sailors. While there was some recognition of the patriotism of the tar, there was more anxiety about his recklessness and antisocial behavior. Sailors were slotted into national projects. There was no attempt to accord them any special status for work done and victories achieved, only efforts to shore up their potential contribution to future war efforts. How this worked out in the wastes of Nova Scotia, where seamen were sent as part of a Protestant bridgehead in a precarious peace, is a subject we must now address.

8

From Havana to Halifax

In March 1749 the Board of Trade offered land in Nova Scotia to demobilized soldiers and sailors. According to the terms, every soldier and sailor who agreed to go out to this maritime outpost was offered fifty acres of land, in fee simple, with no obligation to pay quitrents or taxes for ten years. A similar offer had been made in 1719, after the War of Spanish Succession, when Britain wrestled with the problem of what to do with Nova Scotia, which it had acquired under the terms of the Treaty of Utrecht. Few servicemen acted on that offer, perhaps because the province was unknown and the aboriginal presence formidable.[1] In 1749, by contrast, there was every indication that Britain would invest resources to develop and safeguard its territory; and indeed, further douceurs were offered to those that would join the enterprise: an additional ten acres were allotted to every family member who accompanied the servicemen; the passage out was free; and every settler was offered twelve months' subsistence along with arms and ammunition for his own defense.[2]

The window of opportunity for this settlement was narrow. Rumors of the offer had circulated in the newspapers in October 1748. According to these reports, a bill would be introduced in the Commons giving faithful servicemen the chance to own land in Nova Scotia, with free passage and subsistence for a year. Yet there is no evidence in the Board of Trade minutes that this was acted upon in the ensuing months.³ Instead, everything was done with haste. The terms of the offer were not published in the main London newspapers until mid-March 1749, yet the transports for the expedition were scheduled to leave on 10 April: potential recruits thus had about a month to volunteer for this venture. Although four hundred people signed up in Whitehall within days of the official notice, the deadline proved impossible to meet.⁴ Agents for the expedition had to be contacted in Boston as well as in London, where Chauncey Townsend was contracted to deal with the subsistence allotments. The recruits, who also included artificers in the building trades, for carpentry skills were especially coveted, were scarcely mustered before the due date. The first volunteers did not sail until mid-May, to be soon followed by others. Even so, the expedition was organized in such haste that some seamen who had seen duty under Admiral Boscawen in the East had no opportunity to take up the offer.

The hasty arrangements had much to do with the international situation. Nova Scotia was contested territory. Officially it was a British province, but the British presence in Nova Scotia before the mid-century was minimal and predominantly military. As one disgruntled officer sarcastically put it, "We had not an English Inhabitant nor a Rood of Land in our Possession throughout the whole Country." Annapolis Royal was there solely "to keep up our right to the Bay of Fundy."⁵ The fort had little influence over the rest of the province. The bulk of the resident population, in fact, consisted of Acadians who farmed the salt marshes of the Bay of Fundy. They numbered roughly 7,500 by 1750, having grown exponentially since the early decades of the century.⁶ These Francophone farmers and fishermen professed neutrality in the rivalry between Britain and France, although language, religion, economic ties, and their proximity to New France pushed them toward the French. In the war that flared up in 1744, the Acadians found themselves in a precarious position. Under the influence of the French missionary Abbé Jean Louis Le Loutre and his Mi'kmaw allies, who had their own grievances with the British, the Acadians had connived at French incursions into Nova Scotia. A minority were persuaded to participate in raids on British forts, although the French were not impressed by their participation. The commander of the 1744 expeditions, Duvivier, attributed Acadian neutrality to his lack of success.⁷ Indeed, the efforts of the Acadians to carve out some space between two international rivals satisfied no one. Even the British governor at Annapolis Royal, Paul Mascarene, who was usually sympathetic to their predicament, sometimes vented his frustration. In August 1748 he warned the Acadian deputies "that the Contempt and Disobedience of some amongst you" would adversely affect relations with the British. Indeed, their reluctance to rein in disloyal Acadians made them "much greater foes than friends to the Gov[ernme]nt to which you have sworn obedience."[8] To his superiors in London Mascarene was more frank: "I would be happy could this province be rid of these Inhabitants, especially [those] who have openly declared themselves for the Interest of the Enemy; but as this cannot be done at present without sending so many Inhabitants to the French settlements of the islands of Cape Breton and St Johns [now Prince Edward Island] . . . it is a perplexing Dilemma which requires speedy Instructions."[9]

At the time Mascarene wrote to the Board of Trade two factors complicated the dilemma of which he wrote. The first was that the British needed the Acadians to provision any settlements they contemplated in Nova Scotia. The second was that such settlements became more necessary under the terms of the Treaty of Aix-la-Chapelle. Although Britain had managed to retain Nova Scotia during the War of Austrian Succession, the decision to return the fort of Louisbourg to the French made the British presence in the region precarious. Louisbourg was a critical site for defending the empire of the St. Lawrence. Its deep harbor sheltered many vessels in the thriving cod fishery around Canso and beyond. By returning the fort, the British risked losing fisheries to the French as well as boosting the French naval presence in North American waters.[10] Most significantly, Britain risked losing its toehold in Acadie, thus exposing its colonies to the south. For the British, some counterpoint to the Cape Breton fort had to be found, both militarily and commercially. Furthermore, the presence of the Acadians in Nova Scotia had to be counterbalanced by Protestant subjects whose loyalty was beyond dispute. For years Governor William Shirley of Massachusetts had been agitating for an influx of quintessentially British subjects to swamp the Acadians. He had hoped that over time the Acadians would be assimilated into a more diverse but predominantly Protestant population. As far as he was concerned, that task was now an urgent one, although members of his General Court were less enthusiastic.[11]

The task of resettling Nova Scotia fell to Lieutenant-Colonel Edward Cornwallis. He was a scion of the aristocracy, the sixth son of Baron Cornwallis, well connected at Court, and in his early years at least, he was something of a high-society officer in and about London. Yet unlike some society officers, he did see active service. Cornwallis fought at the Battle of Fontenoy in 1745, and the following year participated in the Duke of Cumberland's "pacification" campaign in the Scottish Highlands. Cornwallis presided over trials of soldiers who surrendered forts. He was remembered for his "unrestrained violence" in the cleanup operations in Cameron and MacDonald country. His men were allegedly allowed to rape with impunity. They killed diffident Highlanders and summarily executed those whose weapons were found in their houses.[12] Com-

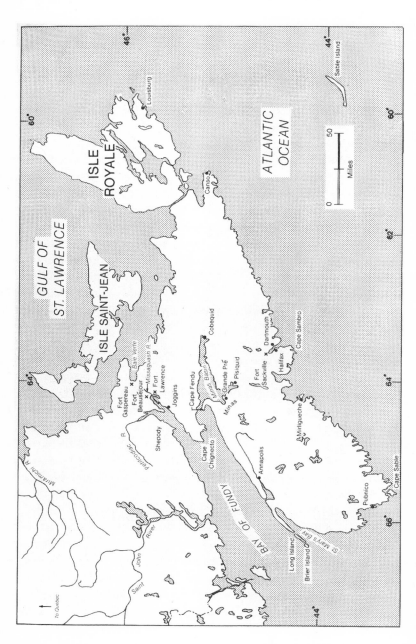

Fig 12: Map of Nova Scotia, c. 1750.

mended for the "satisfactory manner" in which he brought the Jacobite rebels to heel, Cornwallis was deemed very appropriate for the Nova Scotian assignment, for which he received a salary of £1,000 per annum.

Cornwallis's immediate task was to establish a base at Chebucto Bay to contain French incursion into Nova Scotia. In the continuing negotiations over the boundaries of Nova Scotia and Acadie, the French asserted sovereignty over the north shore of the Bay of Fundy, the Chignecto isthmus, and parts of Nova Scotia that lay south of Île Royale (Cape Breton) and broached on Canso. Cornwallis was instructed to settle these contested areas with British inhabitants as fast as possible. As a corollary, he had to test the loyalty of existing residents in the province, including the Acadians and the Mi'kmaq.

As soon as he had anchored at Chebucto Bay and had set up a council, Cornwallis gave orders to clear the land on the western shore of the outer harbor, to be named after Lord Halifax of the Board of Trade. He also had an audience with some of the Acadian deputies, who had customarily taken a qualified oath to His Majesty, qualified in the sense that they would not be required to take up arms on his behalf. Initially Cornwallis, perhaps on the advice of Paul Mascarene, did not press for an unqualified allegiance, but when the next delegation arrived, Cornwallis insisted on an unconditional oath, to be taken by mid-October, by all Acadian communities. Moreover, Cornwallis demanded that if they would not take the oaths, they should leave the province without their effects. They could no longer benefit from the relocation terms of the Treaty of Utrecht, which had long expired.

Cornwallis talked tough, but he was in no position to press his case upon the Acadians in the early months of settlement. He could not afford to lose an important supplier of provisions at this critical juncture, when there were no other farms in the province. He also reluctantly recognized that a mass exodus of Acadians would benefit the French, who were already attempting to entice them across the Chignecto isthmus into territory they occupied on the other side of the Bay of Fundy. Needless to say, Cornwallis was frustrated by the Acadians' refusal to swear unqualified loyalty to the British Crown. He also disliked the fact that they chose their own deputies without his approval. He accused them of being an independent people. "It appears to me," he told the deputies in October 1749, "that you think yourselves independent of any government; and you wish to treat with the king as if you were so."[13]

Cornwallis was probably right, but there was little he could do about the intransigence of the Acadians in the fluid, uncertain conjuncture of 1749. His difficulties, moreover, were compounded by the quest for peaceful relations with the local Amerindans, some of whom had actively assisted the French in the previous war. At first this did not seem an insurmountable problem. When Cornwallis first arrived in Nova Scotian waters he was told by some of the

Francophone settlers of Mirliqueche Bay (Lunenburg) that the "Indians were quite peaceable and not at all to be feared."[14] His early encounters with them led him to believe this was the case. Several chiefs had an audience with him, and he offered them friendship and small presents, with the prospect of more once they had abandoned their allegiance to the French and entered into a treaty with the British.[15] A month later, in mid-August 1749, Maliseet deputies from the St. John River visited the governor and ratified the 1726 treaty on behalf of themselves and the Passamaquoddy and Chignecto bands. They confessed that their warriors had killed some of Captain John Gorham's rangers while they were reconnoitering the St. John River, but they pleaded that the braves had not been cognizant of the new peace treaty between Britain and France. This explanation seems to have satisfied Cornwallis, who renewed the 1726 agreement with a present of an extra thousand bushels of corn. The Maliseet, who looked exotic to the British with their vermilion smeared faces and black markings, their ears adorned with ribbons and tobacco pipes, danced on one of the men-of-war after the signing of the peace and were given a seventeen-gun salute on their departure.[16]

It was not the Maliseet who were the main opponents of the British presence in Nova Scotia; it was the Mi'kmaq of the peninsula. They were troubled by the buildup of the British presence after 1749, which had been hitherto confined essentially to Annapolis Royal. To a migratory, hunting and fishing nation, one fort did not immediately infringe on its pattern of living, but the British proposed to build a new citadel on Mi'kmaw ancestral land and to occupy land along the coast, even at Chezzetcook, Lunenburg, and Minas, where the Mi'kmaq had cleared land for summer fishing.[17] The Mi'kmaq assumed that under the terms of the 1726 treaty, by which they had been granted hunting and fishing rights, the British would consult them about any new settlements. But Cornwallis was predisposed to believe that the Mi'kmaq were savages who should abide by his definition of the treaty and British sovereignty. He was not prepared to modify the treaty or use it as a template for ongoing negotiations. He had been instructed by the Board of Trade to cultivate "a strict Friendship and good Correspondence with the Indians," but there was also the expectation that the aboriginals would "become good Subjects."[18] In the post-1748 situation, in which the British were determined to augment their presence in Nova Scotia to counteract the regional influence of the French, there was very little room for what Richard White would consider "a middle ground," a site for developing reciprocities, between British and Mi'kmaq.[19]

British incursions thus meant hostilities. Invasions were met with invasions. In mid-August the Mi'kmaq seized twenty New England fishermen at Canso and ransomed them to the French governor at Louisbourg. When the British moved in to fortify Minas, one of the key sites of contention with the French, Mi'kmaw warriors surprised two British ships in the Chignecto isthmus, killing three of the crew.[20] By late September 1749, with encouragement from their priests and a renewed understanding with the French, the Mi'kmaq formally declared war on the British. "The place where you are," one sachem told the British, in a letter that was probably drafted by Abbé Pierre Maillard, "where you are building dwellings or a fort, where you wish to enthrone yourself and make yourselves absolute master, this land belongs to me. I have sprung from it as certainly as the grass. It is the very place of my birth and my home. This land belongs to me, the wild one, yes, I swear, it is God who has given it me to be my country for ever."[21]

Within a week, forty Mi'kmaw warriors ambushed several of Major Gilman's party who were cutting wood at a sawmill close to Halifax. Two of those killed were beheaded and another scalped. A fourth soldier, from New Hampshire, went missing.[22] In response to these actions, the council in Halifax was quickly convened. It did not deign to declare war on the Mi'kmaq. That would "own them a free people," the minutes recorded, "whereas they ought to be looked on as Rebels to His Majesty's Government, or as so many Banditti Ruffians."[23] Instead the council ordered the officers at Annapolis Royal and elsewhere to annoy and distress the aboriginals, and 10 guineas were offered for every scalp taken. Later the reward was raised to 50 guineas, a very significant sum by eighteenth-century standards, enough to feed a leatherstocking's family for a year or more. As Cornwallis's chaplain, the Reverend William Tutty, explained to his superiors in London, scalping Indians might seem inhuman, un-British, and certainly "an extraordinary way of making war," but self-preservation, aboriginal cruelty, and the circumstances of bush warfare demanded it.[24] For the bounty hunters in Captain Gorham's rangers or Major Gilman's new company, for basically any leather-hosed adventurer, it was open season on the aboriginals, even on the group from St. John that had renewed its treaty with the British but was now thought to be complicit in the hostilities that had broken out. Whatever reservations Governor Cornwallis had about this policy, and one doubts he had many, he was now convinced that Nova Scotia was a "Frontier to the other Colonys" that had to be defended at all costs in the continuing, unofficial war against France and her allies.[25]

The settlers who ventured into this uncertain situation in June 1749 were a mixed group. Including wives, children, and servants, they numbered 2,576 in the thirteen transports for which we have detailed information.[26] Of these 2,576 passengers, 1,406 (54.6 percent) were women, children, or servants. One of the women, Ann Medlicot, was a midwife who came with her son and a female servant.[27] She was likely very useful, for there were ten or twelve births on the long but relatively healthy passage over, and by the time the transports had landed there were several others "ready to lie in."[28] The rest of the women on the expedition accompanied men. Of these 1,170 men[29] (excluding servants and teenage children) 555, or 47.4 percent, came alone, and 42.6 percent sailed with wives, common-law wives, or children. Their occupations were in line with the original proclamation, which had offered land to demobilized servicemen and to artificers in the building trades and husbandry. Although the settlement scheme was promoted first and foremost as an opportunity for demobbed soldiers and sailors, the artificers proved as numerous as the target group.[30] Half of the male settlers were artificers of some kind, with a noticeable number of carpenters, joiners, smiths, and shipwrights. Some of the workers were not in "essential" trades, as defined by the proclamation. They included seven bakers and brewers, four shoemakers, a furrier, a bookbinder, a weaver, wool comber, and pipe maker. One wonders whether they were added to swell the initial shipment of recruits, or whether some form of petty favoritism found them a berth.

Among the servicemen, mariners and other naval personnel vastly outnumbered those in the army. It is not clear why. Perhaps the word had passed down the regiments about how inclement the Maritime winters really were, at least relative to those in Britain and Europe. In his account of his days as governor of Louisbourg, Charles Knowles wrote of mountainous drifts of snow and garrisons crazed with liquor in their efforts to keep out the cold. "Words are wanting to Represent it [Louisbourg]" Knowles had written in January 1746, "the Severity of the Weather being now such and the Miseries and Sufferings of the Troops so great as to be beyond Expression or Comprehension: many have been Frozen to Death, and the Sentrys though relieved every half hour frequently lose their Toes and Fingers."[31] Whatever the reason, there were few army privates and corporals among the applicants for Nova Scotia. Indeed, a rumor circulated London that Chelsea pensioners would be forced to join the expedition,[32] so few were the volunteers from the ranks. Consequently the military contingent aboard the transports was small, only 10 percent of the male settlers. A third of them were of the officer class, with a good smattering of lieutenants and ensigns. Most servicemen hailed from the navy. They included lieutenants, midshipmen, surgeons, and a few gunners, boatswains, and their mates. The mariners were undoubtedly the most conspicuous group, both within the navy and among the expedition's volunteers. They numbered 390, or a third of the male settlers who were aboard the transports.

To what extent the settlers were aware of the uncertain international situation in mid-1749 is a debatable and speculative point, speculative in that the records are silent about their aspirations and knowledge of the region, save for a few of the educated elite. Seamen were the most likely to have some familiarity with Nova Scotia, and from the muster books we can guess who they might be. Some sailors had been part of Admiral Knowles's squadron in the Caribbean. They included nine seamen from HMS *Lenox* under the captaincy of Charles Knowles, seven from Digby Dent's ship the *Plymouth,* and five from Captain Clark's ship the *Warwick,* all of whom were among the crew in 1747 when Knowles used it as his flagship.[33] No doubt these mariners picked up some knowledge of the Maritime provinces from the admiral's tenure as governor of Louisbourg. What they might have learned from the upper-deck conversations that circulated below may well have been more about weather than politics, for Knowles was an unhappy administrator of the frozen north, desperate to leave Louisbourg's penetrating cold for warmer climes.

The early summer passage across the Atlantic amid fine weather no doubt pushed those stories of snowdrifts and frostbite into the background. Mariners who had been with Knowles, and some had been with him at Santiago de Cuba and Havana, were probably more interested in the officers' quarrels that had broken out in the fleet and the impending courts-martial. Whatever might be said about Knowles, he was a colorful character who created enemies as much as friends. Like Sir Peter Teazle in Sheridan's *School for Scandal,* he was the sort of man who left his character behind him.[34] He was fodder for gossip. Would his disagreements with his captains prove as controversial as those of Admirals Mathews and Lestock? Those admirals had fallen out over conduct of the battle of Toulon in early 1744, and their recriminations against one another and against several subaltern officers had reverberated through Parliament. In fact, the Toulon affair became a matter of national anxiety about the indiscipline of the navy. The talk of the town from 1744 to 1746, their quarrel was quickly memorialized after the peace and deepened the context of Knowles's fracas with his officers.[35]

A few seamen certainly had direct experience of Nova Scotia and Acadie. Several had been on the *Launceston,* one of the ships in Sir Peter Warren's squadron during the Cape Breton expedition of 1745. Others had been active in intercepting French commerce to Canada. Among them were the captain and lieutenant of the Duke of Beaufort's privateer, which had captured several vessels sailing to Quebec, including *La Trompeuse,* later sold along with her cargo at Lloyd's coffeehouse in June 1748.[36] Even so, it is doubtful that many seamen had a keen understanding of the complexities of the Nova Scotia situation with its multiple players, confusing names, and unfamiliar terrain.

Governor Cornwallis rather cynically thought this was inconsequential; he did not expect most seamen to stay long in this colonial outpost. He considered most seamen to be perfect scammers, taking advantage of the expedition for a free ride, a year's free food and lodging, and perhaps even some kind of rum fest. Whatever might be said about young, feckless tars, this was certainly a caricature. A very significant minority of mariners, some 41.5 percent, came out with wives and children, which does imply a disposition to resettle. A few even came out with servants. This was true of William Whiteacre, who came out on the *Charlton*, along with his wife and a female servant. And of William Rowles, formerly of HMS *Exeter*, of Thomas Drury of the *Tavistock*, Stephen Hill of the *Tilbury*, and of Thomas Bryant, who brought two servants with him, one male, one female. It is possible that these men were warrant officers of some kind, and that their status had been overlooked by the clerks responsible for entering their occupations and wartime affiliations. It is noteworthy that relatively few gunners, boatswains, coxswains, or even ship's carpenters are mentioned in the lists.

Mariners may not have been overly eager to convert swords into ploughshares as some of the promotional literature of the expedition propounded, but they were no doubt hoping to take advantage of the commercial and maritime prospects that the new colony seemed to offer. Chebucto harbor was reckoned to be "one of the finest in the world" one settler claimed, "and has Conveniences and Advantages for a Fishery, superior, as I am told by Persons of Knowledge, to any other Place they ever saw." From the beginning, sloops and schooners came in from New England "like a swarm of bees," not only to provision the emergent colony but to trade with the French as well.[37] The prospect of a burgeoning maritime complex in Nova Scotia was doubtless attractive to shipwrights, such as Thomas Hardwell, who came out with two male servants, and Daniel Sullivan, who came out with one. Although the Halifax yard would not open for almost a decade, they were very likely men who had an eye for an opportunity. If the Nova Scotian coast was to be critical to the consolidation of the British Empire in America, and some certainly argued this was the case,[38] then maritime and shipbuilding skills would be at a premium.

Governor Cornwallis typified the seamen as ne'er-do-wells, "idle abandon'd fellows" who were "most troublesome and mutinous."[39] Some of them certainly had troublesome war records, especially for seamen whose service to the nation was supposedly vetted when they applied for the Nova Scotia scheme. Several had deserted from the navy. They included John Bickmore of the *Lenox*, John Moore of the *Warwick*, and William Morgan of the *Tilbury*, who was pressed in May 1748 and ran three months later at Port Royal, Jamaica.[40] Clearly in its haste to mount the expedition, the Board of Trade and Admiralty officials did not inquire too closely into the record of these or other men; they simply did not have the time.

This did not mean, of course, that other seamen would not have met the most stringent conditions of service. Some of the maritime settlers had served in one ship for almost the duration of the war. William Bliss and William Cammel of the *Revenge,* for example, entered their ship in 1742 and were there until they were discharged in 1748. So, too, did Thomas Perry and Thomas Shaw.[41] Others served two or three years before they were invalided. The few mariners from the *Oxford* who took up the settlement scheme — Thomas Proctor, Robert Walthall, and Richard Leveridge from the carpenter's crew — had stuck it out on a ship noteworthy for its desertions and near mutiny. So, too, did John Reeves and John Evans of the *Royal Oak,* where Martin Murphy and Christopher Drake were hanged in April 1747 "for Talking Seditious & Treasonable Words, and Drinking Treasonable Healths."[42] Augustus Caesar Harbin, who came over on the *Roehampton* transport, first entered his ship as an able seaman and by dint of regular service amid a sea of desertions was promoted to assistant surgeon.[43] By official standards they were deserving men, and so it would be inaccurate to characterize the settlers as recalcitrant opportunists, willing to avail themselves of any state subsidies that came their way.

Cornwallis's remarks did, nonetheless, address some of the points of tension that all settlers encountered upon arriving in Chebucto harbor. The proclamation of 1749 announcing the new settlement declared that a civil government would be established "as soon as possible," at which time the colonists would "enjoy all the liberties, privileges, and immunities enjoyed by His Majesty's subjects in any other of the Colonies and Plantations in America." The promise of some sort of representative government was, however, delayed until 1758, with Cornwallis and his emphatically military council acting in an executive capacity and issuing ordinances when the occasion arose, even divorcing couples who did not get along.[44] One London newspaper feared this would happen and remarked that military governors had a tendency to laud it over settlers in a manner that was "pernicious to civil Society and a Spirit of Liberty."[45] It cited the case of General Joseph Sabine, governor of Gibraltar, who illegally established a court-martial to try a worker in the Ordnance Yard who had assaulted an officer for consorting with his wife. The poor man received 300 lashes, which were said to have been "shockingly executed," to a point where the man could not work. He eventually sued the general at King's Bench and was awarded £700 in damages.[46]

Cornwallis was clearly no Sabine. He did not flagrantly abuse his military powers, but he did have a tendency to see the new settlers as simple instruments of a broader military strategy for Nova Scotia. As his recent biographer put it, he approached the Nova Scotia assignment with the "vigour and directness of a soldier."[47] One outcome of this directness was that settlers were not treated as subjects who were free to come and go as they pleased. Early in July Cornwallis issued a proclamation that any settlers who left Halifax without permission would forfeit their rights and be banished from the colony. He quickly implemented this policy with respect to "eight fellows that had gone off in Canoes."[48] Nor were settlers able to benefit unconditionally from their labors, as had been publicly anticipated.[49] In the strictest terms, the initial passengers were certainly freer than many of the German Protestants who came over a year later, of whom many were indebted to agents for their passage. These immigrants were known as redemptioners, committed to working off their debt by fulfilling specific tasks. Yet Cornwallis did treat the first settlers as if they were his to dispose of. Settlers who had to be provided with shoes, stockings, and shirts had to repay their debt by building storehouses and hospitals. All who were offered a year's allowance, that is every settler on the first transports, were more or less required to help the Twenty-Ninth and Forty-Fifth Regiments build wharves and palisades and to clear land on a site that Cornwallis admitted was "one continued wood."[50] They were admittedly paid for this work, yet there is no suggestion they could easily refuse it, especially those tasks for which they were actually mustered. One letter from a settler revealed that the newcomers were organized by ship's company in an effort to inculcate competitive team work. Later, as we shall see, they were compelled to join the militia and were assigned jobs building the fortifications of the town.[51] In effect, they were requisitioned as if they were part of an army. In his letter to the Duke of Bedford in September 1749, Cornwallis wrote as if the settlers were servicemen. They had of late behaved "very well," he said patronizingly, and "I hear of no complaints of riots, mutiny or disobedience."[52] For their part, their lordships replied that they had expected the settlers to be irregular and indolent on arrival and were pleased that Cornwallis had "brought them to a decent behaviour."[53]

Building Halifax, then, was more or less done on the basis of forced labor. Settlers were fined or imprisoned if they did not complete the construction of their log cabins in a timely and efficient way. They were organized into work parties for what were predominantly military tasks. Hemmed in by Mi'kmaw warriors, they were a captive labor force within the Halifax compound. If settlers had hoped for some yeoman's paradise, or an open society of sorts on a new frontier, they were sorely mistaken. Contrary to the ballads that circulated about the glorious benefits of Nova Scotia, settlers were not freed from old-world work habits; or, for that matter, from old-world hierarchies.[54] The officer class was allotted larger tracts of land from the very beginning. That was made very clear in the original proclamation: minor officers were offered 80 acres, ensigns and surgeons 200, and army and naval captains as much as

600, with an extra 30 acres per family member. These members of the "better sort" were not expected to work themselves but to manage the rest.[55] They were the "overseers" of the ships' company.

If status determined the allocation of lands and tasks in the new territory, war service counted for little beyond a free passage and the promise of a fifty-acre lot of brushwood and forest, at least for the army privates and mariners who constituted the majority of servicemen. Those concessions were given to other men, carpenters and the like, even to the few wig makers, shoemakers, and furriers who joined the expedition. Although the settlement scheme was touted as a reward for services rendered,[56] in actuality seamen and soldiers were not given any advantages over the artisans and husbandmen who also came to Nova Scotia. If anything they were not considered as valuable as the sawyers, carpenters, and joiners who could build log cabins and palisades efficiently, or the butchers who would dress the meat for the new community. Settlers with families, moreover, were privileged over single men, and most sailors, in particular, were single. Married men were given their own log cabins whereas the single men were thrown promiscuously together in the transports or long huts. Sailors were used to cramped conditions and hard work, but this was a different rhythm of work, a different space, a different seascape.

These circumstances probably explain why some settlers did not attend to the task of building Halifax and its harbor with a becoming enthusiasm and deference. It explains why Cornwallis complained that beyond the three hundred willing soldiers, sailors, and "tradesmen" there was a rag-tail of "poor idle worthless vagabonds" who shirked hard work. It also explains why that oily chaplain of Cornwallis, the Reverend William Tutty, talked of the courageous and generous governor battling a sea of "idleness, obstinacy and perverseness."[57] Some settlers skulked in their tents and seemed to pay little heed to the oncoming winter. One officer reported that they were "so very indolent that most of them now lie in their Tents, not considering that the Winter is at Hand, and the Weather very severe; they never trouble their heads about building themselves Houses."[58] Many took to drink and perhaps consorted with the whores the merchants brought in from New England. By November, as the first frosts appeared, John Salusbury reported, "Abundance of poor wretches starv'd in the snow by getting drunk and lying out," adding, "It can not be said that the severity of the weather could Kill any of them."[59] If intemperance did not kill them, disease might. Although one settler reported in August that lying under canvass was "not attended with any cold Shiverings or Disorders," a typhus epidemic broke out the in the fall and winter of 1749–50, taking over two hundred lives, and there were more fatalities the following year when sickly soldiers from Ireland joined the settlement and when German settlers arrived without adequate supplies.[60] One gets hints of this in the council minutes, where it is noted that settlers were ordered to bury the dead quickly and inform the clergymen. Carpenters were ordered to ensure that each coffin was labeled with the initials of the deceased, an ordinance that implied a substantial death toll.[61] Cornwallis would continue to profess to his superiors in London that the first Nova Scotia winter passed "without complaints of any kind,"[62] but the reality was very different.

As far as the actual settlement in Halifax was concerned, the early reports claimed that the work went on "very briskly." A letter in October 1749, published in the *Boston Evening Post,* stated that "every Body seems to be very resolute about the Settlement . . . and have made a great Proficiency, considering the Time they have been about it."[63] By that time about three hundred logwood huts had been built and two small forts completed. Yet there were conflicting accounts of just how much progress had been made. One officer recently arrived from Louisbourg painted a more disconsolate picture of the new settlement. He thought the settlers were poor, ill equipped, and indolent and noted that the fortifications were falling behind schedule. "We are not," he confessed, "in the happiest Situation in the World."[64] In fact, the lethargy of some settlers, and their distaste for the servile status imposed upon them, meant that Halifax remained vulnerable to aboriginal attacks, far more vulnerable that Cornwalllis and his circle would have wished. In January 1750, fearing renewed raids from the Mi'kmaq, the council organized a militia among the men aged sixteen to sixty to encourage the building and guarding of town defenses. A home force of 840 men was envisaged, mustered into ten companies, with night patrols. Those who refused to join up were fined 5 shillings and sent to jail for twenty-four hours.[65]

No force of this kind could be successful unless Halifax was adequately fortified. This took time. The early plan to have five stockades and a picket line around the town stalled. The fortifications were not completed until December 1750, months behind schedule. A fire among the existing buildings set off rumors that the Acadians working in Halifax were responsible, stoking stories that there were enemies within.[66] To add to the uncertainty, individuals who strayed beyond the boundaries of the town were picked off by indigenous warriors. As one settler reported, "The Indians dislike our settling here, and destroy all Stragglers that they pick up in their Way."[67]

In July 1750, six men who ventured three to four miles beyond the stockades were ambushed. Among the party were Cornwallis's own gardener and son, both of whom were killed.[68] The vulnerability of people on the periphery of the Halifax settlement was underscored in May 1751 when the Mi'kmaq conducted a series of raids on the satellite settlement at Dartmouth and virtually razed it to the ground. Reports of just how many settlers were killed vary; it seems that at least eight were slain with a further six taken captive in one of the early skirmishes. The account that found its way to the London press fed on stereotypical reports of savagery. It depicted a mini-massacre of men, women, and children and the burning of their homes. "The whole town was a scene of butchery," reported the *London Magazine,* "some having their hands cut off, some their bellies ripped open, and others their brains dashed out."[69] Nearly two years into the settlement, Halifax remained under siege. Even when the Mi'kmaq failed to attack stragglers, one observer remarked, they kept Haligonians "in such a State of continual Alarm and Dread, that they cannot apply themselves to make any lasting or considerable Improvement."[70]

If progress in Halifax was slow and hazardous, elsewhere it was as bad if not worse. Cornwallis had been instructed to establish townships at Minas, Baie Verte, at Whitehead to the south of Canso, and Le Have, west of Halifax. He was strongly encouraged to push settlement north of the Nova Scotia peninsula, especially on the St. John River. These goals proved elusive. A rough wooden road, some eighteen feet wide, was built from Halifax and Minas in an attempt to facilitate contact with the Minas Basin and beyond. But the French were bent on impeding British progress and continued to foment their aboriginal allies to assist them in this task. In November 1749, three hundred Mi'kmaw and Maliseet surprised and captured a detachment of British soldiers outside Fort Edward at Minas. The fort was attacked as well, which led Cornwallis to believe that the French were behind the raid. The fact that eleven Acadians from Pisiquid were among the party added to his suspicions, and Captain Gorham's rangers were sent there to arrest them.[71]

The November ambush and the previous engagement of aboriginals with two British vessels at Chignecto alerted Cornwallis to the urgency of securing the northwestern parts of the peninsula. In January he dispatched Sylvanus Cobb of the *York* sloop to victual and arm his vessel in Boston and sail to Chignecto to apprehend the French priest Le Loutre and his Acadian accomplices. Cobb compromised the secrecy of the expedition, however, by advertising for volunteers, and so the plan was scotched.[72] Nonetheless, Cornwallis did increase the military presence in Chignecto by sending Captain Joseph Gorham, younger brother to John, to investigate the disappearance of a courier supposedly taken hostage by Le Loutre and his allies. Gorham and his men searched for arms and confiscated weapons from Acadian settlers in Cobequid, where Le Loutre had been seen. The deputies there and the parish priest, Jacques Girard, were arrested and taken to Halifax, where they were examined by Cornwallis and his council. Nothing conclusive emerged from these interrogations, but the response to the raid was the capture of three British hostages by pro-French Acadians and Mi'kmaq in Pisiquid, an event that sent Captain John Gorham and his rangers to confront them at the St. Croix River. Gorham was ordered to remain in Pisiquid to sustain the British military presence in the area, and Acadians were threatened with arrest if they contemplated moving to the French areas of the country.

The following month, April 1750, Cornwallis decided to erect a fort in Chignecto to counter the French military presence there under the command of Louis de La Corne, who had fought colonial troops at Grand Pré in the Minas Basin three years earlier.[73] Cornwallis sent Colonel Charles Lawrence and four hundred men to do the job, but La Corne, who held the ground on the northern side of the Missaguash River, sent Le Loutre and the Mi'kmaq to evacuate the Acadians to the south around Beaubassin. The Acadians refused to abandon their homes, and so Le Loutre had them burnt to the ground, forcing the residents across into French-held territory. This did not augur well for the Acadians, who were already suspected of treachery and disloyalty. It also led to a standoff between La Corne and Lawrence at the Missaguash River. La Corne told Lawrence that as far as he was concerned the north shore was French territory and would remain so until the commissioners had resolved the boundaries between Nova Scotia and Acadie. Lawrence retired in the face of a thousand well-positioned French, Mi'kmaw, and Canadien troops. Even so, the confrontation defined the spheres of influence that characterized the unofficial armed contest between Britain and France for the next few years. The British secured their position at the Missaguash by building Fort Lawrence near Beaubassin; the French responded across the river with Fort Beauséjour. They looked at each other across what is now the boundary between Nova Scotia and New Brunswick.

Despite a military buildup in the Chignecto Basin, the British proved unable to move beyond the Missaguash. More troops and transports were brought in, but La Corne held his ground. Edward How, who was one of Cornwallis's main intermediaries with the French and also a member of his council, attempted to secure the release of some hostages and bring some semblance of order to the dirty bush war that was enveloping Minas and Chignecto. But in 1751 he was shot under a flag of truce, "an instance of treachery and barbarity not to be paralleled in history," railed Cornwallis to the Lords of Trade.[74] To add to his frustrations, Cornwallis was unable to gain a foothold on the St. John River. Sylvanus Cobb ventured there in late July 1750. He attempted to intercept a brig that had supplied the French fort there, but the French retaliated by capturing him under a flag of truce and refusing to release him until the brig was three days' sail out of the river. All Cobb achieved was a messy standoff in which each side took hostages.[75] The commander of the fort, the Canadien ensign Charles

Deschamps de Boishébert, backed by two hundred Abenaki, once more insisted that the British were interlopers in French territory.

After two years' tenure in Nova Scotia, Cornwallis was complaining of "distresses and disappointments." He was ready to resign. He had spent nearly £174,000 fighting the Mi'kmaq, a lot more than had been allotted by Parliament, and he had little to show for it.[76] Most important, Cornwallis had built no new townships outside the Halifax area, where his own settlers were hemmed in by Mi'kmaw warriors. As one officer complained, "their dastardly Hedge-Fighting gives them often the advantage, as they generally rush out of the Woods, superior in Number three-to-one, to the Party they attack."[77] Although 1,800 or more settlers from England, Switzerland, and Germany had come in 1750–51,[78] not to mention the thousand or so who sailed north from New England, the plan to plant loyal Protestants in this new colony had stalled. Cornwallis had hoped to send the European newcomers to Pisiquid or Chignecto to counteract the presence of the Acadians,[79] but they were stuck in bustling Halifax where pilfering was endemic, brawls frequent, and rum drinking so rife that unlicensed retailers were whipped or placed in the stocks for encouraging public inebriety.[80]

There were other problems as well for early Haligonians. Among them was the fluctuating price of public labor, brought about by the influx of foreign redemptioners who had to pay off their passages, and the threat of disease. The German Protestants who arrived on the *Ann* in the fall of 1750 were suffering from some form of typhoid fever and created a crisis of near-epidemic proportions. They were also cheated of their rations, which forced Cornwallis to dismiss the commissary and chief storekeeper in Halifax for "shameless irregularities."[81] Fortunately for the settlement, most of the new immigrants were provided with lodgings in the northern suburbs, away from the main population. They were assigned the task of rebuilding Dartmouth after the aboriginal raid of May 1751, or of constructing blockhouses and a patrol road across the isthmus between the Northwest Arm and the Bedford Basin.[82] They remained in the northern part of Halifax until the move to Lunenburg in spring 1753.

How did the original settlers fare in what was clearly a disturbing and seemingly intractable situation? The July 1752 roll of settlers offers some clues. This list reveals that of the 1,174 families that arrived in the summer of 1749, roughly 657 (or 56 percent) had disappeared within two years. Many people had died of typhus or were lured to Boston by the New England merchants who traded with Halifax and were responsible for much of the rum running. On some days, up to twenty schooners from New England ports entered Halifax.[83] According to Esther Wright, as many as 2,000 people left within two weeks' of arrival, although this seems very unlikely given the fact that the total settler population in July 1749 was just over 2,500.[84] This conclusion is derived from a chance comment of Cornwallis to the Lords of Trade, stating that there were 1,400 men, women, and children in Halifax. Where this figure came from, whether it referred to heads of households or to the number then settled in tents and cabins, remains unclear. Had it been a straightforward headcount, it would certainly have driven Cornwallis to despair and have been so registered in his letter.

Boston and its neighboring seaports were the obvious exit for many sailors disgruntled with their situation in Halifax. The merchant marine offered them work, and the possibility of high wages as opposed to the forced labor of the Cornwallis regime was too attractive to pass up. Stowing away on the Boston-bound brigs or schooners that crowded Chebucto harbor was not difficult, especially for a single man. In this context it is noteworthy that of the 906 males on the 1752 list (and it appears to exclude some of those living in Dartmouth) only 27 or 3 percent were single men, although a further 168 anonymous men, 18 per cent and mostly single, one suspects, were employed in the fisheries at Ketch harbor, Cornwallis Island, Cross Island, Sambro Island, and St. Margaret's Bay.[85]

In 1752 only one in six seafarers remained from the original group that accompanied Cornwallis. Less than 5 percent were single, if Esther Wright's valuable inventory of settlers is any guide.[86] They included Barnaby Cavanagh, very likely an Irish Catholic, who had sailed on the *Stafford* from 1745 to 1747 but had been invalided. He was probably unfit for future service at sea and likely hoped that living in a frontier town was a better prospect than begging in Britain or Ireland. Another was John Ferguson, the midshipman of the *Lenox,* who came over with his daughter in 1749 and was presumably willing to give the new colonial outpost a try, if only for the sake of his offspring. He was unusual in that he had not found another mate, for among the other single seafarers whose marriage record can be traced, and this is admittedly a small group, all seemed to have done so. They included Thomas Fugett, a shipwright who married quickly once he came over, and James Kelly of HMS *Feversham,* who married Katherine and had two children by her within two years, Kelly and Eunice. William Watson, the midshipman of the *South Sea Castle,* also married quickly, as did Darryl Smalt, a mariner who came over on the *Merry Jacks.* He married Hannah Hammond soon off the boat, but died within two years of taking his nuptials. Perhaps the most intriguing case in this category was Joseph Palmer, a mariner who had served on HMS *Rupert,* very likely at Toulon in 1744. He was single when he arrived but married and had a child by April 1752. On the July 1752 roll he is listed as "in the hospital" but as the head of a household of twenty males over sixteen and one female. Could it be that he is simply the first patient on a long list? Or was he a hospital administrator or orderly?

A few of the seafarers had children born in Nova Scotia, a fact that likely disposed them to staying in the new province. They included William Williams, the lieutenant of the *Bellona,* who arrived in Halifax with a wife, two male servants, and a female, and who appears to have had at least two daughters by 1752. And James Welner of the *Launceston,* whose son was born late in 1752. Yet from what can be gleaned about these households in the parochial records, deaths outweigh births by a large margin, by a ratio of more than two-to-one. A quarter of these deaths were attributable to children. Alexander Hay, the surgeon's mate on the *Revenge,* brought his wife and two children to presumably start a new life in the colony, where his skills were something of an advantage in a wartime environment. His son, Richard, died within six months of arrival. Precisely how old Richard was is impossible to say, but predictably some settlers in the service had children die as infants, in an age when infant mortality was spectacularly high. George Popplewell, who had seen service on the *Chesterfield* off the coast of Africa, where one of the lieutenants organized a mutiny and took possession of the ship,[87] came to Nova Scotia with his wife and daughter and later had a son, George, who did not survive. Lewis Hays, purser of the *Carcass* sloop, arrived in Halifax with his wife, Elizabeth, his son, and one female servant. He seems to have prospered, for in 1752 he had extra servants in his household and perhaps a clerk. His wife gave birth to a son within six months of their arrival, one Thomas Perriman Hays, who died quickly. The same was true of Charles Mason, the midshipman of the *Serpent* bomb who came over to Halifax in the *Canning* frigate. He increased the size of his household by one servant, having three males and one female above sixteen years of age in 1752. He married soon after his arrival, but his first son died relatively quickly. As was often the case in the early modern era, infant mortality was no respecter of wealth. Members of the officer class saw their infants die like anyone else's.

What is particularly striking about the experience of these families is the rapid rate at which wives died in Halifax in the first two years of settlement. Half of the resident maritime families in 1752 experienced the death of a wife or a mother. Thomas Fugett, a shipwright who traveled on board the *Canning* frigate arrived alone in Halifax. He married quickly, but his wife was dead by May 1750; he married again, this time to a woman who bore him two daughters in two years. William Green the quarter gunner with the *Russell,* a ship that had engaged the Spanish at Cartagena and the French at Toulon, lost his wife quickly as well. As did Richard Greenhill of the *Sunderland,* Richard Hollis of the *Revenge,* and James Jones of the *York.* John Matthew, a shipwright, saw his wife die in a little over a year; James Neal experienced the loss of his spouse some eighteen months after their arrival. In this case a child survived, which makes one suspect that his wife, Hannah, died in childbirth. The same fate likely befell Jane, the wife of Samuel Tanner, a mariner from Deptford. She and her husband arrived with three daughters in 1749, and Jane gave birth to another in 1751, but by 1752 Samuel was alone in a house of three women, two of them minors, and a male who was either an apprentice or a lodger.

Wives died, children came and went, and some tars succumbed to the cold and sickness. Family bereavements were a more common feature of early Halifax than the joy of new births. Moreover, relatively few servicemen had large households than when they came over. Among those who did were Thomas Greenock, the mate of the *Nassau,* and Charles Mason, the midshipman of the *Serpent* bomb, who came to Halifax with two male servants and one female. Once married, he added another servant to his household. Along with Lewis Hays, these examples suggest that some men of the officer class did prosper in the early years of this colonial outpost. Others did not. Lieutenant John Steinfort of the *Salamander* privateer profited from the French prizes his ship took in Atlantic waters, including some rich cargoes of indigo, cotton and sugar.[89] He came to Nova Scotia with an impressive household that included four male and two female servants, but by 1752found himself with only two servants. Apart from the intriguing case of hospital Joe Palmer, only one mariner is known to have headed a larger household. He was Stirker Nelson of the *Monmouth,* who arrived in Chebucto Bay with only his wife. By 1752 he had three males and two females over sixteen in his household and one male under sixteen, who may have been his son. Whether these adults were lodgers or servants is unknown. The fragmentary record provides no clues about their status.

What can one conclude about the sailors who went to Halifax in 1749? One thing is certain: very few of them remained there for long. Perhaps they felt deceived by the promotional literature that cast the new venture as a golden opportunity for fishermen and sodbusters. Certainly the large claims made for the colony, of its rich fishing banks, mild winters, and fertile ground, must have seemed rather hollow.[90] The ground around Halifax was formed of shale, unsuitable for husbandry and not at all like the rich Acadian farmlands of the Bay of Fundy, which had been meticulously drained and dyked over the generations. The fishing opportunities were a lot better, but it was back-breaking seasonal work in a tricky international situation. As for the winters, well, as one settler admitted, they were more severe than those in Scotland.

Settlers must have cast a jaundiced eye over ballads that invited them to

"*New Scotland,* where Plenty sits queen." They must have been astounded by the promises of "a Pleasant Life / Free from all Kind of Labour," or at the very least, appreciative of its irony. Seamen, in particular, baulked at the regimentation to which they were exposed in the early days of settlement, when they were expected to help clear land and build wharves and palisades without any consideration for their wartime record. This humiliating work was another incentive to quit this colonial outpost. So, too, was the gnawing realization that they had not escaped the service of the state, that far from being rewarded for their contribution to the war effort, they had been corralled once more into state servitude in a manner analogous to impressment. Bonded to the state in war, they were now little better than the European redemptioners who were indebted to the government for their passage. In what must have sometimes appeared as a bewildering war zone, with multiple players, not least of whom was the warlike Mi'kmaq, they predictably sailed south to a more predictable maritime world, to ports that had a reputation for protecting seamen from the hazards and whimsies of wartime service. As we saw in the first chapter, Boston in the 1740s developed an awesome reputation for defying press gangs and trumpeting the freedom of the seas. Admiral Knowles learned that to his cost, as did Governor Shirley. Some seamen may have seized the opportunity of funding their passage to this haven of maritime liberty on government pay. Others often found their way there, for the promise of peace and prosperity eluded ordinary seamen on the Nova Scotian peninsula. Dubbed the "first production of our Infant Peace,"[91] the Nova Scotia settlement scheme of 1749 was always shaped by state imperatives, by the desire to create a Protestant bridgehead on a frontier that was politically precarious but strategically vital to the security of the North American empire. Veteran seamen had seen enough of the war and had no desire to continue to fight its battles. So they sailed south. Their "progress" was not like Hogarth's: no moral tale, no nemesis. It was an itinerary of survival in a fluid, confusing world where one old European power (France) and one emergent one (Britain) faced off for a further round of colonial wars and where hostile aboriginals resented the intrusive presence of new settlers.

Conclusion

This book has been an exercise in micro-history, not in the conventional definition of the term, where a strange event is used to illuminate the social and cultural contexts of a particular moment by unraveling the rules and norms that were threatened by the exceptional. Rather I have tried to capture the anxieties of the period following the War of Austrian Succession in a series of specific interlocking narratives that, I hope, illuminate the complexities of that conjuncture. They begin with the last battle of the war, where the expectation of spoils was frustrated by officer ineptitude and rancor, and where captains were prepared to defend their honor in a series of irregular duels that brought little credit to the Royal Navy. They conclude with a hastily contrived expeditionary force to Nova Scotia, where war veterans found themselves quite unable to convert their weapons into ploughshares in what remained a veritable war zone for the conquest of Canada and the North American interior. In between, chapters address the demobilization of thousands of unemployed soldiers and sailors and the social problems it created or intensified — intensified because the period immediately after the war also witnessed a surge in troubling labor relations and the continuation of a seemingly intractable problem of gin drinking, which, to contemporaries at least, generated fears of imminent degeneration and decline among a working population on whom Britain's future wealth and preeminence rested.

The years 1749–53 produced something of a crisis in social relations in Britain. To some the notion of a "crisis" might seem hyperbolic. At the level of formal politics, these years bridged two of the most uncontested general elections in British history. Among the twenty-eight largest urban boroughs in England, conventionally the most contentious within the British electoral system, a minority actually went to the polls in 1747 and 1754, revealing how pervasive the grip of oligarchic control could be among voters not particularly noted for their deference. The years immediately following the Peace of Aix-la-Chapelle also enabled Henry Pelham to restructure the national debt and reduce the rate of interest on long-term annuities. This was surely one measure of investor confidence in British high finance. Another was the relatively stable level of stock prices amid escalating crime rates. As the graph reveals, there was no strong correlation between the movement of bank stock and the ebb and flow of prosecutions for theft at the Old Bailey in London (see graph 3). If demobilization prompted social anxieties, it did not generate a financial crisis. The nearest Britain came to that occurred somewhat earlier, during the Forty-Five, when the Jacobite army eluded British troops and ventured within 120 miles of the capital.

And yet to talk of a crisis seems apt. At the level of international affairs Britain entered the peace unsure of its ability to wage another vigorous war and fully expectant that it would be forced to do so on disadvantageous terms. Quite apart from the legacy of unresolved problems that remained in 1748, not least of which was the French reluctance to vacate potentially profitable sugar islands, Britons wondered whether they had the capacity to renew hostilities with a nation whose population was three times their size. With historical hindsight we know these anxieties were misplaced. Britain's financial capacity to wage war and to collect taxes to do so was superior to that of France. Her agricultural productivity allowed for a greater diversification of economic endeavor that ultimately benefited trade and commerce and boosted domestic consumption.

Yet contemporaries, and reasonably well-informed contemporaries, thought otherwise. They did not have the benefits of historical hindsight. In one of his last publications, Henry St. John, Viscount Bolingbroke, agonized over the accumulated debt and feared for the decline of a landed class who were the "true owners of our political vessel."[1] So dire was the situation that he toyed with a voluntary default of the national debt to clear the deck of formidable encumbrances to state enterprise. From a different political perspective, the Whig Josiah Tucker was deeply troubled by Britain's lack of international competitiveness with France, which he attributed to trading monopolies, electoral corruption and its effects on labor, and to the high-wage demands of British

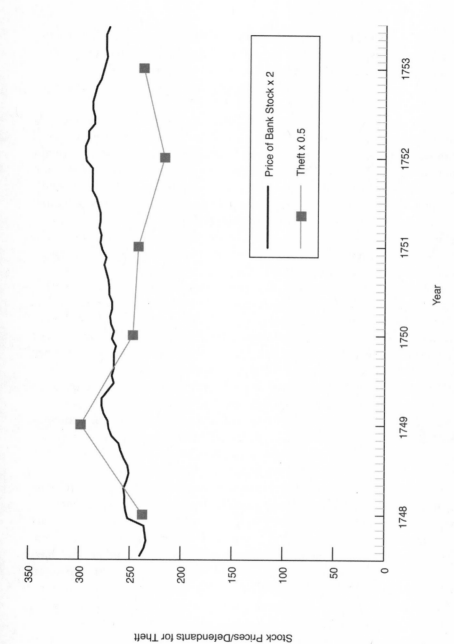

Graph 3: The movement of bank stock and theft in London, 1748–1753. *Source: Gentleman's Magazine*, 1748–53 (monthly figures); Old Bailey Proceedings Online, 1748–53.

workers. To rectify the situation, he advocated freer trade and a more restrictive franchise to curb the electoral treating and bribery that encouraged laziness amongst petty freeholders and craftsmen. He also proposed the creation of local industrial tribunals, presided over by employers, to discipline workers and bring them to a "proper subordination."[2]

Trade and debt undermined Britain's ability to remobilize its forces against the French, or so it was perceived. To compound matters, the gin craze sapped British energy, enterprise, martial spirit, and morale. Even a man as normally sanguine as the Reverend Doctor Stephen Hales could sound the alarm about gin addiction. In the 1751 postscript to his popular pamphlet, *A friendly admonition to the drinkers of gin,* Hales painted a picture of demographic and economic catastrophe at the hands of Madame Geneva, suggesting that "if the Number or good Condition of a People are the Strength and Security of a Nation" then Britain was in deep trouble, quite unable to provide the necessary muscle and economic vitality to take on the French.[3]

Gin impaired British competitiveness and martial spirit. It emboldened the common people to crime and aggravated the dislocations of demobilization. On this issue, such notable commentators as Isaac Maddox, the bishop of Worcester, Henry Fielding, the Bow Street magistrate, and the Royal Society luminary, Stephen Hales, could all agree. Maddox and Fielding went further, seeing the conjunction of crime and gin as generating a disturbing challenge to the property of the rich and perhaps even a sea change in plebeian-patrician relations, which had reached a rough-and-ready equilibrium after decades of relatively good harvests. Fielding's experience as a magistrate, in particular, led him to believe this was the case. He noted the way that the common people had evaded the Gin Acts and made a mockery of statutory law. He wrestled with the difficulty of regulating popular trades like tailoring and of curbing the impulse to collective action. He witnessed the way in which south coast smuggling gangs openly defied the leading patricians of the country and generated a virtual "civil war"[4] in contending with customs officers and their military auxiliaries. In the *Jacobite Journal* he reported the trial, execution, and gibbeting of the most important leader of the Hawkhurst gang.[5] And he must have been aware, as he began his new career as a magistrate, of the turnpike rioters who cut down the tollgates within twenty-five miles of where he was born. Openly defiant of the Bristol authorities, they showed little respect for the commercial innovations on which capitalist progress was predicated.

It was not simply the demobilization of some 80,000 soldiers and sailors that provoked alarm in the aftermath of the war. It was the larger conjuncture of patrician-plebeian relations that deepened the anxieties. Even so, in the immediate context, it was the palpable rise in class tensions on the streets of

London that registered the effects of the peace. Left to shift for themselves, soldiers and sailors provoked a crime wave noteworthy for its violence and, if the newspapers are to be believed, noteworthy for its assault on cash-laden tradesmen and well-dressed gentlemen and women. In the early years of the peace property theft rose conspicuously, but aggressive street robbery rose dramatically. In fact, it was arguably more dramatic than during the demobilization following the Seven Years' War. In that demobilization, the number of defendants charged with property theft at the Old Bailey rose a little faster than during the years 1748–51, but the actual number of defendants prosecuted for violent theft was half of what it had been in 1749–51, at a time when the number of servicemen laid off was notably larger, 200,000 as opposed to 80,000.[6]

The surge in the volume of violent crime was certainly acknowledged by contemporaries after Aix-la-Chapelle. "The frequency of audacious Street Robberies repeated every Night in this great Metropolis," declared the *Whitehall Evening Post,* "call aloud on our Magistrates to think of some Redress; for, as the Case is now, there is no Possibility of stirring from our Habitations after dark without the Hazard of a fractured Skull, or the Danger of losing that Property People are sometimes obliged to carry about them, which an honest industrious Family may be some Months, if not Years, working for again. These Villains now go in Bodies, armed in such a Manner that our Watchmen . . . absolutely declare, they dare not oppose them."[7]

What made the crime wave especially disturbing was the vulnerability of the wealthy and, indeed, of men and women high in the echelons of polite society. The newspapers certainly stressed this and helped produce something of a moral panic in London. They did not demonize one particular group in society, as often happens in moral panics. Contemporary attitudes toward seamen, for example, were too ambiguous for this to happen. Their bravery and fortitude was acknowledged even if their recklessness was feared. But some of the other conditions constituting a moral panic were met. The fear generated by violent street crime was disproportionate to the reality. Crime did seem to strike at the very sinews of society.[8] Compared to other demobilization crises in the eighteenth century, the one after 1748 was not associated with some obvious political crisis. It was not politically overdetermined in the manner of 1713, when Britons were absorbed with the succession crisis, or of 1763, when court favoritism overshadowed the politics of the peace in the figure of Lord Bute. Paradoxically the very stability of parliamentary politics in 1750 served only to emphasize the instability of civil society. This explains in part why Parliament devoted an unprecedented amount of time to investigating the crime wave, the seemingly intractable problem of gin, and associated social problems. On three occasions between 1751 and 1753, the king's opening speech to Parliament emphasized to need to suppress "those outrages and violences which are inconsistent with all good order and Government," to quote from the very first.[9] The committees assigned to this task predictably interpreted this mandate broadly. They not only elected to investigate the causes of rising crime and the laws pertaining to stolen goods, but as early as March 1751 they extended their inquiry into social policing. This involved a review of the poor laws and more generally matters of moral reform. In addition to a new Gin Act, such reform involved regulating places of popular entertainment and disorderly houses. These came under the spotlight in response to the government's injunction to curb "that profligate spirit of Irreligion, Idleness, Gaming and Extravagance" that "had extended itself, in an uncommon degree, to the Dishonour of the Nation."[10]

Historians who have explored this legislative program have tended to zone in on the laws relating to crime, following lines of inquiry first set down by Sir Leon Radzinowicz. There are obvious reasons why this might be so, most notably because the issue of whether the Bloody Code was functioning as a form of judicial terror was openly questioned in public discourse, and indeed it was made problematic by the struggles to recover the bodies of the condemned at Tyburn from the clutches of the surgeons. Such struggles undermined to solemnity of the law, so it was thought. They prompted demands to eliminate the procession to Tyburn altogether and to consider alternative punishments that might strike terror in the condemned and those who took stealing lightly, among them the establishment of galleys, where convicts could serve out life sentences policing the coasts and improving harbors. "Death" has become "too familiar to our Profligates" claimed one advocate of galleys; it was a "Jubilee for our Butchers Apprentices and loose fellows of that Class to attend a Dozen or a Score of the most unhappy wretches at Tyburn. The condemned are made a public Spectacle in our Jails, and suffered to Carouze not only there, but in their Passage to the Gallows. The only Emulations [*sic*] among them is who shall go out of the World with the least Remorse, Sense of Shame, or Token of Repentance."[11]

Without doubt the demobilization crisis dramatized the difficulties of finding the right balance between judicial terror and mercy that characterized the Bloody Code.[12] In a more general way, it highlighted the problem of calibrating sentences to offenses. Alternatives to transportation were contemplated, for there was a troubling uneasiness that transportation was not working in the light of the distressing number of convicts who managed to return to Britain before the expiration of their sentence. In 1752, hard labor in the dockyards nearly became a sanctioned punishment for felony and grand larceny. Even so, transportation continued to be a major source of punishment for major felonies, a critical backup to the few but exemplary hangings that judges still found necessary to ensure respect for the law. And Tyburn was retained as a theater of death, despite all the countercultural rituals that had grown up around it. Contemporaries remained confident that dutiful sheriffs could control the gallows crowd without resorting to military intervention and the most explicit forms of naked power. All that changed in the way of major punishments was extra severity for murderers, both in following up sentences with swift executions and adding the extra sanction of the gibbet. Murderers would henceforth be exposed to the full panoply of judicial terror and in circumstances that would make it difficult for newspapers to sensationalize their crimes.

As we have seen, the Murder Act of 1752 was one of three statutes that flowed from the social reform initiative. The others pertained to the stricter regulation of places of entertainment and disorderly houses, and to the removal of benefit of clergy from convictions for riverside theft, a matter that probably owed more to the efforts of City merchants who had been financing the prosecution of Thameside theft than to the MPs on social reform committees.[13] Taken together these statutes were a poor harvest from such a frenzy of legislative activity, disposing one to write off the postwar initiatives as a failure. Yet the failures themselves are noteworthy for what they reveal of the parameters of the debate over social reform and the disagreements they generated.

The social reform project was not entirely reactive, a response to a spiraling crime wave and associated social tensions. It was implicitly preventive as much as coercive, designed to create a higher degree of consensus in civil society and to curb the leisure preferences of the poor and any semblance of what we might now call a "welfare culture." The proposed reform of the poor laws should be seen in this light. There was a call to discipline the roving poor with hard labor in bridewells; to "stop Wickedness in the Bud," declared Thomas Alcock, and to keep them "a longer, or shorter time, according to the Degree of the Offence and the Appearance of Reformation."[14] There was a renewed disposition to penalize able-bodied welfare recipients, to inure them to a discipline of work, and above all, to save pauper children from a life of indolence and welfare dependence so that they could be of "universal Service to the Nation."[15] There was nothing especially new about this. Similar sentiments were voiced around the Workhouse Act of 1723, and even earlier around bridewells,[16] although this time the reform of the poor laws was subjected to extensive review in order to find what Alcock described as "better Methods of Cultivation and Management."[17] The central problem was that contemporaries could not agree on whether the poor laws should be comprehensively dismantled or simply tinkered with. Should the laws of settlement be abolished? Would larger work-houses prove more efficient and less costly than smaller? To what degree should there be a network of strategies to deal with the different forms of dependency and need that contemporaries encountered? To what degree should market forces rather than old-style paternalism determine plebeian opportunity, and how would plebeian workers respond to higher-wage incentives? These issues surfaced in a debate that proved inconclusive because in the end there was a residual inclination for the known rather than unknown. Contemporaries continued to prefer local discretionary regimes to grander carceral structures for fear that larger institutions would prove difficult to control, both in terms of patronage and expense. Only where local elites could agree on parish unions would larger institutions be entertained.

One of the issues that hampered the debate over the poor laws, at least for those with a vested interest in more radical solutions, was the absence of any reliable data about poor-law dependence. One of the objectives of the proposed 1753 census was to resolve this state of affairs. The other was to develop reliable demographic data about the state of the nation, especially in light of the fears generated by the gin craze and, in the conjuncture of 1748, of Britain's ability to compete economically with the French and to arrest her imperial ambitions. Perhaps one of the most striking aspects of the debate for social reform at mid-century was the push for governmentality, to develop new sites of knowledge on which social reform might be based and to micromanage target populations. Certainly, a few social reformers saw the need to develop new technologies of rule capable of mobilizing the populations required to raise Britain's competitive capacity in an age of war, commerce, and empire. Conventionally these developments are considered to be characteristic of the nineteenth century, when the prison, the school, and the census provided the machinery for mapping and coordinating the parameters of national growth, and when the prevailing ethic of political economy spawned new ideas of subjectivity, of how subjects might order themselves.

Clearly the mid-eighteenth century was a long way from this terrain of governmentality.[18] Yet a case could be made that filaments of this development had appeared by 1750 when fears of national degeneration and Anglo-French rivalry pushed social critics to consider new deployments of power and power/knowledge. To be sure, mid-eighteenth-century contemporaries lacked the infrastructural capacity and necessary expertise to put them into effect. They were amateurs compared to people like Edwin Chadwick, the Victorian welfare and sanitation reformer. And they inevitably came up against an ingrained suspicion of intrusive government. MPs thought the census an unpardonable interference in the liberties of the subject, a state too redolent of Britain's archenemy France. Similarly, critics decried any institutional reform that would enhance big or impersonal government at the expense of those informal reciprocities that had characterized patron-client relations and paternalist styles of rule in the first half of the century. Governmentality was not on; but it was imagined as one possible solution to the mid-century crisis brought on by gin, demobilization, crime, and the uncertainties of peace. Foucault was right in believing that modern notions of governmentality were grounded in eighteenth-century developments, making considerable headway with the invention of political economy; but he was too interested in the articulation of its discourse to detail the precise social contexts in which it occurred. And he problematically contrasted his notion of governmentality to Marxist notions of power, on the grounds that the diffusions of power in modern societies inhibited and complicated political revolutions by insurgent classes or coalitions.[19] Yet the elision of class from notions of governmentality is unnecessary, for historically the search for new strategies of rule in Britain occurred at a moment when patrician-plebeian relations had entered a new phase of contestation. New ideas about governmentality surfaced in the context of an uncertain peace when Britain feared for its commercial progress and imperial grip on British North America. It occurred during a prolonged gin epidemic, a smugglers' war, amid troublesome labor relations and the demobilization of thousands of servicemen who had few opportunities once their wages and prize money were gone. The moment of 1748–53 was momentous in its own way. A Fielding moment, to be sure, but more than that. Although the mid-century critics were unaware of it, their efforts to resolve the demobilization crisis after Aix-la-Chapelle anticipated the multiple strategies of good order and government that characterized the next century, when Britain was more urban, more industrial, but no less expansive in its imperial ambitions.

Notes

Introduction

1. Horace Walpole, *The Yale Edition of Horace Walpole's Correspondence*, ed. W. S. Lewis, 48 vols. (New Haven: Yale University Press, 1937–83), 20:48.

2. *General Evening Post*, 20 October 1748. All newspaper references, including tri-weeklies, are dated from the first day of issue. This allows readers to access the Burney newspapers online more efficiently.

3. *Gentleman's Magazine* 19 (April 1749): 185; Newman Flower, *George Frideric Handel* (London: Cassell, 1959), 325–27; Martin C. Battesin with Ruthe R. Battestin, *Henry Fielding: A Life* (London: Routledge, 1989), 466–67.

4. *London Evening Post*, 27 April 1749; *Old England*, 29 April 1749. The first talks of the "left wing," the latter the "right side." Charles Frederic, MP for New Shoreham 1741–54, was controller of the Woolwich depot and in 1750 surveyor-general of the Ordnance.

5. *The Private Journal and Literary Remains of John Byrom*, ed. Richard Parkinson (Manchester: Chetham Society, vol. 44, 1857), 485n; *General Advertiser*, 2 May 1749; *London Evening Post*, 27 April 1749; *Whitehall Evening Post*, 27 April 1749.

6. *Chester Courant*, 2 May 1749; *An alarm to the patriots* (London, 1749), 50.

7. *London Evening Post*, 2 May 1749. At the end of the war in 1748, 40 percent of tax revenues had to be devoted to paying down the national debt. In 1748, 14 percent (over £8 million) of the debt was unfunded. See John Brewer, *The Sinews of Power: War, Money and the English State, 1688–1783* (New York: Alfred A. Knopf, 1989), 117–19.

8. *London Evening Post*, 13–15 December 1748.

9. Marc Vigié, *Dupleix* (Paris: Fayard, 1993), 504, cited by Robert and Isabelle Tombs, *That Sweet Enemy: Britain and France* (New York: Vintage Books, 2006), 113.

10. J. H. Plumb, *The Growth of Political Stability in England, 1675–1725* (London: MacMillan, 1967), 13.

11. Pierra Nora, "The Return of the Event," in *Histories: French Constructions of the Past,* ed. Jacques Revel and Lynn Hunt (New York: New Press, 1995), 427–36.

12. See Joanna Innes, *Inferior Politics: Social Problems and Social Policies in Eighteenth-Century Britain* (Oxford: Oxford University Press, 2009), 109–78.

13. For a reassessment of the role of Parliament, in particular, in the making of domestic legislation, see Innes, *Inferior Politics,* chs. 1–3.

14. Innes, *Inferior Politics.*

15. Bob Harris, *Politics and the Nation: Britain in the Mid-Eighteenth Century* (Oxford: Oxford University Press, 2002).

16. Ibid., 20.

Chapter 1. The Trials of Admiral Knowles

1. John Charnock, *Biographia Navalis,* 6 vols. (London, 1794), 4:349.

2. See entries 3 and 5 April 1741 in HMS *Weymouth* logbook, The National Archives, London (hereafter TNA), Adm 51/1058.

3. Thomas Wentworth, *Authentic papers relating to the expedition to Carthagena* (London, 2nd ed., 1744), 77–84.

4. TNA, Adm 1/2006, see letter from Vernon dated 20 November 1741, and also Knowles's letters for February 1742.

5. Charles Knowles, *An Account of the Expedition to Carthagena* (London, 3rd ed., 1743), 7.

6. Ibid., 8n.

7. Ibid., 15n.

8. Ibid., 56. This caricature was disputed. See *A Journal of the expedition to Carthagena* (in answer to a pamphlet *An Account of the Expedition to Carthagena*), (London, 1744), 53–55.

9. *Old England, or the Constitutional Journal,* 16 April 1743, reprinted in the *Gentleman's Magazine* 13 (April 1743): 207.

10. The pamphlet was published around 12 April 1743 and was into its third edition by June. See *Daily Gazetteer,* 12 April, 8 June 1743.

11. [Charles Knowles], *An Account of the Expedition,* 55. Knowles called them "raw, new raised, undisciplined men."

12. TNA, Adm 1/2006, letter of 18 March 1743.

13. Ibid.

14. In these two raids, 603 men were killed or wounded out of a total complement of 3,045. See William Laird Clowes, *The Royal Navy,* 7 vols. (London: Low and Marston, 1897–1903), 3:86–88.

15. TNA, Adm 1/2006, 18 March 1743. See also letter of 3 February 1743 regarding the punishment of deserters.

16. TNA, Adm 1/2006, Knowles's memorial, dated 21 September 1743. See also

Daniel Baugh, ed., *Naval Adminsitration, 1715–1750* (London: Navy Records Society, 1977), 131–32.

17. See *Bath Journal,* 10 December 1744.

18. For newspaper accounts of this incident in Britain, see *Whitehall Evening Post,* 16 January 1748, *Westminster Journal,* 23 January 1748, *Old England,* 23 January 1748.

19. Baugh, *Naval Administration,* 132.

20. *Ipswich Journal,* 23 January 1748. See also *Whitehall Evening Post,* 16 January 1748.

21. *Boston Evening Post,* 21 December 1747.

22. *General Evening Post,* 14 April 1748.

23. *Penny London Post,* 2 May 1748; *London Evening Post,* 10 May 1748.

24. *Ipswich Journal,* 11 June 1748.

25. TNA, Adm 1/5293, court-martial of Capt. Digby Dent, 26 February–1 March 1750.

26. TNA, Adm 1/234/98, 122v.

27. TNA, Adm 1/234/149–50.

28. TNA, Adm 1/234/149–50.

29. TNA, Adm 1/234/158.

30. For an account of the battle that is favorable to Knowles, see H. W. Richmond, *The Navy in the War of 1739–48* (Cambridge, 1920), 133–44.

31. The news that the war was over disappointed others, too, for much the same reasons. One correspondent in the *Jamaica Gazette* wrote: "I cursed him [the Spanish vessel] for coming in our Way, for we should have gone and taken all the galleons else, and been as rich as Princes." Cited in *Ipswich Journal,* 4 February 1749.

32. TNA, Adm 1/234/175.

33. Charles Fearne, *Minutes of the Proceedings at the trial of Rear-Admiral Knowles . . . held on board his Majesty's yacht, the* Charlotte, *at Deptford* (London, 1750), 215–17.

34. TNA, Adm 1/5293, court-martial of Captain Charles Powlett of the *Tilbury,* 22–26 January 1750.

35. TNA, Adm 1/5293, court-martial of Captain Charles Holmes of the *Lenox,* 15–18 January 1750.

36. TNA, Adm 1/234/297.

37. TNA, Adm 1/234/181.

38. *Ipswich Journal,* 3 December 1748.

39. TNA, Adm 1/234/345.

40. TNA, Adm 1/234/347.

41. TNA, Adm 1/234/361.

42. TNA, Adm 1/234/304.

43. TNA, Adm 1/234/347.

44. TNA, Adm 1/5293, court-martial of Captain Robert Erskine, 10 November 1749.

45. The trial was reported in the *Ipswich Journal,* 30 December 1749, for example.

46. *London Evening Post,* 10 May 1748.

47. Reprinted in the *Whitehall Evening Post* and the *Ipswich Journal,* 4 February 1749.

48. See *Minutes of the proceedings of the trial of Captain Holmes* (London, 1751), esp. p. 115, which summarizes the charges against Holmes.

49. Fearne, *Minutes of the Proceedings at the trial of Rear-Admiral Knowles,* 215.

50. TNA, Adm 1/5293, court-martial of Captain Charles Powlett, 22–26 January 1750.

51. TNA, Adm 1/5293, court-martial of Captain Thomas Innes, 12–16 February 1750.

52. James P. Gilchrist, *A brief display of the origin and history of ordeals* (London: Bulmer & Nicol, 1821), 65–346. V. G. Kiernan, *The Duel in European History* (Oxford: Oxford University Press, 1989), is exceptional in acknowledging the importance of duels among army and navy officers.

53. Robert Shoemaker, "The Taming of the Duel: Masculinity, Honour and Ritual Violence in London, 1660–1800," *Historical Journal* 45/3 (2002): 528, claims that pistols were not common until the 1760s, but my sample suggests otherwise.

54. *Whitehall Evening Post,* 3 March 1750; *General Advertiser,* 7 March 1750, *Read's Evening Post,* 10 March 1750.

55. *Remembrancer,* 10 March 1750.

56. Shoemaker, "Taming of the Duel," 528, suggests that pistol duels were less lethal than swords, but in this period this is not the case.

57. Stephen Banks, "Killing with Courtesy: The English Duellist, 1785–1845," *Journal of British Studies* 47/3 (2008): 552–53. Figures offered by Andrew Steinmetz, drawing on Gilchrist, suggest that during the reign of George III, 48 percent of all combatants were killed or wounded, with 34 percent sustaining fatal or seriously disabling wounds. See Andrew Steinmetz, *The Romance of Duelling* (London: Chapman & Hall, 1868), 1:38, cited by Kiernan, *Duel in European History,* 102.

58. As in the case of a duel between two persons of distinction, reported in *Old England,* 1 September 1750. See also the account of a duel in Hyde Park noted in the *Whitehall Evening Post,* 13 March 1750.

59. *Ipswich Journal,* 1 October 1748. This was true of an anticipated duel between two naval captains in September 1748, one of whom could not remember the appointed location, Hyde Park.

60. TNA, Adm 1/5293, Innes's court-martial, 12–16 February 1750.

61. *The Trial of Captain Edward Clark* (London, 1750), 10–11.

62. *General Advertiser,* 16 March 1750.

63. On these protocols, see Shoemaker, "Taming of the Duel," 532, and Banks, "Killing with Courtesy," 552.

64. Old Bailey Proceedings Online (hereafter OBP; www.oldbaileyonline.org), April 1750, trial of Edward Clark (t17500425–19).

65. Banks, "Killing with Courtesy," 557. For the etiquette of duels, see also Donna Andrew, "The Code of Honour and Its Critics: The Opposition to Duelling in England, 1700–1850," *Social History* 5/3 (1980): 412–15.

66. *Trial of Edward Clark,* 14.

67. Reported in *Old England,* 12 May 1750, and the *Boston Evening Post,* 6 August 1750.

68. *Gentleman's Magazine* 11 (May 1750): 247.

69. *Derby Mercury,* 8–15 June 1750.

70. Kiernan, *Duel in European History,* 101; see also George Thomas Keppel, Earl of Albemarle, *Fifty Years of My Life* (London: Macmillan, 1876), 350.

71. *General Advertiser*, 26 May, 1750, *Penny London Post*, 2 July 1750, *Read's Weekly Journal*, 7 July 1750.

72. *London Daily Advertiser*, 30 September 1751

73. *General Evening Post*, 29 June 1751; see also the *London Daily Advertiser*, 19 June 1751.

74. Jonas Hanway, *An historical account of the British trade over the Caspian sea*, 4 vols. (London, 1753), 2:265.

75. Donna Andrew suggests this critique did not proceed apace until after 1770, but there are clearly intimations of it in 1750. See Andrew, "Code of Honour,"420–34.

76. For the rumor of a bill, see *Westminster Journal*, 15 November 1746; on the parliamentarians' attitude, see *London Daily Advertiser*, 12 June 1751.

77. Markku Peltonen, *The Duel in Early Modern England* (Cambridge: Cambridge University Press, 2003), ch. 4; David Hayton, "Moral Reform and Country Politics in the Late Seventeenth Century House of Commons," *Past and Present* 128 (August 1990): 88.

78. *A hint on duelling, in a letter to a friend* (London, 1752), 7.

79. Peltonen, *Duel in Early Modern England*, chs. 3–4. Jonas Hanway made this argument in *An historical account*, 2:255–66.

80. For examples, see *The trial of Mr George Timewell, late secretary to Commodore Mitchell, who was tried on board the Katherine yacht at Deptford, Wednesday 20 July 1748* (London, 1748). This duel took place because a commodore's secretary had been peremptorily ordered off the quarter deck by a captain. For a duel over the reputation of a women, see that of Dalton and Paul in May 1751. See *Whitehall Evening Post*, 23, 28 May 1751; *London Evening Post*, 1 June 1751; *London Daily Advertiser*, 6 June 1751; *Read's Weekly Journal*, 8 June 1751. For a duel that arose from a night's inebriety, see that of Captain Richard Sowle and George Paschal, OBP, July 1751, Richard Sowle (t17510703–18).

81. *Old England*, 12 May 1750, reprinted in the *Bath Journal*, 21 May 1750 and the *Boston Evening Post*, 6 August 1750.

82. *Old England*, 12 May 1750; *London Daily Advertiser*, 12 June 1751.

83. See *London Daily Advertiser*, 29 April 1750; *Whitehall Evening Post*, 2 June 1750, *Read's Weekly Journal*, 23 June 1750, *London Daily Advertiser*, 28 August 1751. On non-elite dueling, see Steven C. Hughes, *Politics of the Sword: Dueling, Honor and Masculinity in Modern Italy* (Columbus: Ohio State University Press, 2007). On Mandeville's views, see Peltonen, *Duel in Early Modern England*, ch. 5.

84. *London Daily Advertiser*, 12 June 1751.

85. On this, see Ronald Findlay and Kevin H. O'Rourke, *Power and Plenty: Trade, War and the World Economy in the Second Millenium* (Princeton: Princeton University Press, 2007), ch. 5.

86. Hanway, *An historical account of the British trade*, 2:263

87. Abraham Bosquett, *The young man of honour's vade mecum, being a salutary treatise on duelling* (London, 1819), 88, cited in Peltonen, *Duel in Early Modern England*, 310.

88. *London Gazette*, 12 June 1744.

89. Richard Pares, *War and Trade in the West Indies, 1739–1763* (Oxford: Clarendon Press, 1936), 183–84.

90. Philalethes, *The Profit and Loss of Great Britain* (London 1742), 12.

91. Julian Gwyn, *The Enterprising Admiral: the personal fortune of Admiral Sir Peter Warren* (Montreal: McGill–Queen's University Press, 1974), 19; *Profit and Loss,* 30, 35.

92. TNA, Adm 1/2007 (Knowles) 12 June 1744, *London Gazette,* 4–7 August 1744.

93. The *Daily Post* reported that Knowles's bride, Mary Allen or Alleyne, came with a "great fortune." *Daily Post,* 19 February 1741

94. *General Advertiser,* 10 February 1749.

95. *Whitehall Evening Post,* 13 June 1749, reported that the Spanish had demanded a return of the prize.

96. George Metcalf, *Royal Government and Political Conflict in Jamaica, 1729–1783* (London, Longmans, 1965), 111.

97. *Boston Evening Post,* 21 December 1747.

Chapter 2. The Sailors' Return

1. TNA, Adm 1/5293, trials of Captains Holmes, Powlett, and Toll, 15 January–8 February 1750.

2. For a report of seamen entering the Russian navy, see *London Evening Post,* 8 April 1749.

3. Baugh, *British Naval Administration,* 287.

4. *Ipswich Journal,* 12, 19 August 1749; *Old England,* 12 May 1750; *Read's Weekly Journal,* 12 May 1750; *General Advertiser,* 22 January 1751.

5. OBP, Ordinary of Newgate's *Account,* 18 November 1749 (OA17491118).

6. OBP, December 1750, Catherine Connor (t17501205-76), February 1751, Richard Butler (t17510227-30).

7. *Cobbett's Parliamentary History,* 14 (1747–51): 401.

8. Curiously, naval historians sometimes overlook this vital information. For references to withholding pay, see Christopher Lloyd, *The British Seaman, 1200–1860* (London: Collins, 1968), 251, and Dudley Pope, *Life in Nelson's Navy* (London: Allen and Unwin, 1981), 94–95.

9. *Penny London Post,* 14 December 1748.

10. *Whitehall Evening Post,* 25 January 1750.

11. Baugh, *British Naval Administration,* app.1, 509–14.

12. TNA, SP 36/114/49–50.

13. National Maritime Museum, Greenwich, CHA L/23, 7 February 1749, cited in Baugh, *British Naval Administration,* 479.

14. Clowes, *Royal Navy,* 3:138; N. A. M. Rodger, *The Command of the Ocean* (New York: W. W. Norton, 2005), appendix 2. In 1745 there were 104 ships of the line and 67 cruisers.

15. *The military prophet's apology* (London, 1750), 7.

16. *London Evening Post,* 17 January 1751.

17. *Bath Journal,* 18 January 1748; *Whitehall Evening Post,* 13 February 1748.

18. *Penny London Post,* 23 December 1748; *London Gazetteer,* 23 December 1748.

19. *General Advertiser,* 12 June 1749, 26 June 1749; *Whitehall Evening Post,* 24 June 1749.

20. *Old England,* 15 July 1749.

21. Jack Nastyface, *Nautical Economy* (London, 1936), 63.

22. *Ipswich Journal*, 24 December 1748. The paper reported that a sailor in Norton Falgate became so drunk and unruly he had to be tied down to a bed, only to suffocate in his own vomit.

23. OBP, *Ordinary's Account*, November 1750 (OA17501107).

24. *Whitehall Evening Post*, 23–25 February 1749.

25. *Worcester Journal*, 30 July 1752; *Whitehall Evening Post*, 14–16 June 1748. Some whores were committed to Bridewell in September 1748 for trying to steal from "roistering" tars. *General Evening Post*, *Whitehall Evening Post*, 8 September 1748.

26. *London Evening Post*, 5 August 1749.

27. *Whitehall Evening Post*, 20 February 1750. For an example of streetwalkers attempting to pickpocket tars and being committed to Bridewell, see *General Evening Post*, *Whitehall Evening Post*, 8 September 1748.

28. *Whitehall Evening Post*, 2 January 1748, 16 July 1749.

29. *Whitehall Evening Post*, 16 November 1749.

30. *Ipswich Journal*, 29 January 1748; *Bath Journal*, 16 January 1748.

31. *Gentleman's Magazine* 18 (1748): 293.

32. *General Evening Post*, 3 November 1748; *London Magazine* 17 (July 1748): 292–93.

33. *Boston Evening Post*, 26 September 1748, citing *London Daily Advertiser*, 14 July 1748.

34. For examples, see *Whitehall Evening Post*, 25 October 1748, 24 January, 9 February 1749, *General Advertiser*, 18 July 1748, *Remembrancer*, 17 September 1748, *Old England*, 22 July 1749, *Worcester Journal*, 2 August, 27 September, 1750.

35. *Penny London Post*, 10, 12, 17, 29 August, 5, 9 September 1748, *General Advertiser*, 27 August 1748, *General Evening Post*, 6, 10 September 1748, *Old England*, 3 September 1748, *Whitehall Evening Post*, 10, 15 September 1748.

36. *Old England*, 3 June 1749.

37. *Whitehall Evening Post*, 15 October 1748.

38. *General Evening Post*, 2 August 1748, *Remembrancer*, 6 August 1748.

39. *General Advertiser*, 23 January 1749.

40. *Whitehall Evening Post*, 4 December 1750

41. *General Advertiser*, 10 July 1749, *Penny London Post*, 13 August 1750.

42. *Remembrancer*, 17 September 1748; *Westminster Journal*, 29 July 1749.

43. *London Morning Penny Post*, 4 September 1751

44. On the reporting of crime, see Patrick Pringle, *Hue and Cry: The Story of Henry and John Fielding and Their Bow Street Runners* (London: Museum Press, 1955), 100–102; Leon Radzinowicz, *A History of English Criminal Law*, 5 vols. (London: Stevens & Sons, 1948–86), 3:11–62; John Styles, "Sir John Fielding and the Problem of Criminal Investigation in Eighteenth-Century England," *Trans. Royal Historical Society* 33 (1983): 127–49.

45. *Whitehall Evening Post*, 25 July 1749

46. *General Advertiser*, 10 August 1751. See also *London Evening Post*, 2 February 1751, where the highwayman holds up a coach but gives the coachman 2 shillings to drink his health.

47. *Whitehall Evening Post*, 7 January 1749.

48. *Whitehall Evening Post,* 6 February 1750.

49. *Whitehall Evening Post,* 6 July 1751; *London Evening Post,* 10 January 1751.

50. For examples, see *London Evening Post,* 6 April 1749, *Whitehall Evening Post,* 27 July, 16 November 1749.

51. OBP, *Ordinary's Account,* May, 1750 (OA17500516).

52. Henry Fielding, *A Proposal for Making an Effectual Provision for the Poor* (1753) in *Complete Works,* ed. William E. Henley (London: W. Heinemann, 1903), xiii, 141. Also Henry Fielding, *An Enquiry into the Causes of the late Increase of Robbers and Related Writings,* ed. Malvin R. Zirker (Middletown, CT: Wesleyan University Press, 1988), 231.

53. Walpole, *Correspondence,* 20:114

54. *Whitehall Evening Post,* 16 June 1748, 25 Janury 1750; *London Evening Post,* 2 February 1751; *General Evening Post,* 9 October 1750.

55. Walpole, *Correspondence,* 20:99, 101, 106, 199.

56. This is a crude measure, because newspapers replicated each other's stories, and the survival of London newspapers in this era is uneven. But the figures derived from the Burney collection are as follows: 1747, 269; 1748, 214; 1749, 280; 1750, 319; 1751, 542; 1752, 350; 1753, 462; 1754, 333; 1755, 231.

57. London Metropolitan Archives (hereafter LMA), MJ/SR, 2879, 2920, 2940, 2942, 2947.

58. Burglary offences rose from nineteen in the years 1746–47 to sixty-one in the years 1751–52.

59. OBP, *Ordinary's Account,* October 1748 (OA17481028).

60. OBP, *Ordinary's Account,* April 1749 (OA17490426).

61. OBP, *Ordinary's Account,* March 1750 (OA17500326).

62. OBP, *Ordinary's Account,* November 1750 (OA17501107).

63. Peter Linebaugh, *The London Hanged* (London: Allen Lane, 1991), 95, 97. Linebaugh calculates that 18 percent of the Irish hanged at Tyburn were seamen and also 6 percent of the English born outside of London. Combining the two ($N = 793$) we come up with a figure of 10 percent.

64. OBP, *Ordinary's Account,* August 1750 (OA17500808), February 1751 (OA17510211), February 1749 (OA17490220), July 1751 (OA17510729).

65. OBP, July 1751, William Brown (t17510703–50).

66. OBP, July 1750, Thomas Wallis (t17500711–28); OBP, *Ordinary's Account,* August 1750 (OA17500808); TNA, SP 44/85/227–8, SP 36/114/70.

67. OBP, September 1750, William Watson (t17500912–32); TNA, SP 44/85/241–2, SP 36/114/153–164.

68. OBP, December 1750, John Newcomb (t17501205–22); OBP, *Ordinary's Account,* January 1750 (OA17501231); TNA, SP 36/115/112–4.

69. OBP, *Ordinary's Account,* October 1749 (OA17491018).

70. OBP, *Ordinary's Account,* February 1750 (OA17500207).

71. OBP, *Ordinary's Account,* February 1750 (OA17500207), August 1750 (OA17500808).

72. *Proposals to the legislature for Preventing the Frequent Executions and Exportations of Convicts* (London, 1754), 15, cited in Randall McGowen, "'Making Examples'

and the Crisis of Punishment in Mid-Eighteenth Century England," in David Lemmings, ed., *The British and Their Laws in the Eighteenth Century* (Rochester, NY: Boydell Press, 2005), 182–205.

73. OBP, *Ordinary's Account,* June 1751 (OA17510617).

74. OBP, *Ordinary's Account,* October 1751 (OA17511023).

75. Ibid.

76. Bernard Mandeville, *An Enquiry into the Causes of the Frequent Executions at Tyburn* (London, 1725), 20–23.

77. Ibid., 24.

78. [Philonomos], *The Right Method of Maintaining Security in Person and Property to all Subjects of Great Britain* (London, 1751), 47–48.

79. Peter Linebaugh, "The Tyburn Riot against the Surgeons," in *Albion's Fatal Tree: Crime and Society in Eighteenth-Century England,* ed. Douglas Hay et al. (London: Allen Lane, 1975), 66. For an author who sees Tyburn as a carnival of misrule, see T. W. Laqueur, "Crowds, Carnivals and the English State in English Executions, 1604–1868," in A. Beier et al., eds., *The First Modern Society: Essays in Honour of Lawrence Stone* (Cambridge: Cambridge University Press, 1989), 305–99. See also V. A. C. Gatrell, *The Hanging Tree: Execution and the English People, 1770–1868* (Oxford: Oxford University Press, 1994), 56–105; Andrea McKenzie, *Tyburn's Martyrs: Execution in England, 1675–1775* (London: Hambledon Continuum, 2007), 7–30, 191–223.

80. Laqueur, "Crowds, Carnivals and the English State," 305–99.

81. [Philonomos], *Right Method of Maintaining Security,* 44.

82. *Covent Garden Journal,* 28 March 1752.

83. Fielding, *Enquiry,* ed. Zirker, 169. The pamphlet was first published in 1751. *Covent Garden Journal,* 28 March 1752.

84. Ruth Richardson, *Death, Dissection and the Destitute* (London: Routledge & Kegan Paul, 1987).

85. Radzinowicz, *English Criminal Law,* 1:191; Gatrell, *Hanging Tree,* 87; McKenzie, *Tyburn's Martyrs,* 19–21.

86. Mandeville, *Enquiry into the Causes of the Frequent Executions at Tyburn,* 26.

87. Cited by Linebaugh, "Tyburn Riot," 74.

88. *Daily Post,* 15 March 1739.

89. Linebaugh, "Tyburn Riot," 86–88; Radzinowicz, *English Criminal Law,* 1:191.

90. *Whitehall Evening Post,* 18 February 1749.

91. OBP, *Ordinary's Account,* March 1749 (OA17490317).

92. *The Liberty of the Subject and the Dignity of the Crown* (London, 1780), 54. This pamphlet is a reprint of *The Right Method of Maintaining Security* (London, 1751). *General Advertiser,* 23 October 1749.

93. *Remembrancer,* 21 October 1749.

94. *Whitehall Evening Post,* 19 October 1749; *Penny London Post,* 20 October 1749.

95. *Penny London Post,* 11 June 1750; *General Evening Post,* 2 October 1750; OBP, *Ordinary's Account,* May 1750 (OA17500516), October 1750 (OA17501003).

96. OBP, *Ordinary's Account,* March 1751 (OA17510325), March 1752 (OA17520325); *London Daily Advertiser,* 26 March 1751; *General Advertiser,* 25 March 1752.

97. *Covent Garden Journal*, 28 April 1752.

98. For contrasting views, see *London Magazine*, 19 (October 1750), 435, 453. Cf. Randall McGowen, "'Making Examples,'" 201–3.

99. *London Magazine*, 19 (October, 1750), 453.

100. "Publicus" in the *General Advertiser*, 12 February 1751.

101. [*Philonomos*], *Right Method of Maintaining Security*, 57–8, reprinted in *The Liberty of the Subject and Dignity of the Crown* (London, 1780), 57–58.

102. *London Evening Post*, 29 March 1750.

103. *London Evening Post*, 25 September 1750; *Whitehall Evening Post*, 25 September 1750.

104. These figures are derived from a search of the Burney newspapers, 1743–52.

105. This was the fate of John Hammond and John Cobby, condemned at the Special Commission in Chichester in January 1749.

106. *London Evening Post*, 11 November 1749, 23 August 1750, 28 August 1750, 2 April 1751.

107. *London Evening Post*, 3 August 1751, *General Advertiser*, 19 August 1751; *General Evening Post*, 24 August 1751. For a full account of the witch hunt, see James Sharpe, *Instruments of Darkness: Witchcraft in Early Modern England* (Philadelphia: University of Pennsylvania Press, 1996), 1–4.

108. *British Parliamentary Papers*, 17 (1819): 295–99.

109. See John Beattie, *Crime and the Courts*, 213–30, 525–30.

110. *London Evening Post*, 17 January 1751; *General Advertiser*, 23 October 1749.

111. For an excellent account of contemporary explanations of crime, see Andrea McKenzie, *Tyburn's Martyrs*, ch. 3.

112. *Cobbett's Parliamentary History*, 14 (1747–53): 611–12, 832–34, 841–62. Only Robert Nugent referred to the vulnerability of demobilized sailors to debt and capital crime. See columns 834–35.

113. Innes, *Inferior Politics*, 71–72.

114. John Lockman, *The vast importance of the herring industry . . . to these kingdoms* (London, 1750), 25–29.

Chapter 3. The Sailors' Revenge

1. *Bath Journal*, 10 July 1749; *Ipswich Journal*, 8 July 1749; *Worcester Journal*, 6 July 1749. See also John Byrom, *Private Journal*, 2:495.

2. [John Cleland], *The Case of the unfortunate Bosavern Penlez* (London, 1749), 22.

3. Henry Fielding, *The True State of the Case of Bosavern Penlez* (London, 1749), in *Complete Works*, 13:276–79.

4. Fielding to Bedford, 3 July 1749, Bedford Estate Office, Bloomsbury, Butcher Papers, IV/9/9, cited in Battestin, *Henry Fielding*, 474.

5. LMA, Middlesex sessions, SR 2924, Newgate Gaol Calendar, 11 May–5 July 1749. See also Entry book, SP/44/85/152–3

6. *Remembrancer*, 16 June 1750.

7. Hugh Phillips, *Mid-Georgian London* (London: Collins, 1964), 183.

8. Cleland, *Case of the unfortunate Bosavern Penlez*, 11.

9. Ibid., 14–15.

10. *London Evening Post*, 9 April 1748, referring to the escape on 30 March 1748. As the Ordinary of Newgate's *Account* reveals, armed guards routinely reinforced the Tyburn procession when smugglers were to be executed. See, for example, OBP, *Ordinary's Account*, May 1748 (OA17480511). Another prominent member of the Hawkhurst gang, William Pollard, alias Jeremiah Curtis, had escaped from Newgate in 1747. See *General Evening Post*, 21 June 1747.

11. This line of argument was developed in *An Enquiry into the Causes of the late Increase of Robbers* (London, 1751).

12. Henry Fielding, *A Charge Delivered to the Grand Jury . . . Westminster. . . 29 June 1749* (London, 1749), in *Works*, 13:212–14, quote 213.

13. OBP, September 1749, Bosavern Pen Lez (t17490906–4).

14. Ibid.

15. *Old England*, 25 November 1749.

16. *Worcester Journal*, 5 October 1749, *Remembrancer*, 7 October 1749, *London Evening Post*, 5 October 1749; Fielding, *Enquiry*, ed. Zirker, xl. Some accounts of the St. Clements petitioners numbered them as high as 300.

17. *The malefactor's register: or the Newgate and Tyburn calendar*, 5 vols. (London, 1779), 3:239.

18. OBP, September 1749, John Willson, Bosavern Pen Lez (t17490906–4).

19. R. Campbell, *The London Tradesman* (London 1747), 204–5.

20. *General Advertiser*, 1 January 1747.

21. *Remembrancer*, 21 October 1749.

22. [Philonomos], *Right Method of Maintaining Security*, 53.

23. Nine of the fourteen men hanged at Tyburn (besides Penlez) had some maritime experience, although some of them had subsequently come ashore, set up shop, and joined local gangs of thieves. See OBP, *Ordinary's Account*, October 1748 (OA17481128). Cf. Linebaugh, "Tyburn Riot," 98.

24. [Philonomos], *Right Method of Maintaining Security*, 53–54. The newspapers at the time played down Janssen's firm but tough address, saying that the "vast body of sailors" behaved towards the sheriff "with all imaginable Respect." See *Whitehall Evening Post*, 17 October 1749.

25. *Worcester Journal*, 26 October 1749.

26. Trentham publicly denied he had been approached, but so very much after the fact that his word can hardly be trusted. See *General Advertiser*, 9 December 1749.

27. *A genuine and authentic account of the proceedings at the late election for the city and liberty of Westminster* (London, 1749), 11.

28. *T——t——m and V——d——t: A Collection of the Advertisements and Handbills . . . published on both sides during the Election for the City and Liberty of Westminster* (London, 1749), 47–48.

29. Cleland, *Case of the unfortunate Bosavern Penlez*, 5.

30. Ibid., 41–42, 47. See also John Cleland's review of his own anonymous pamphlet in the *Monthly Review* 2 (November 1749): 63, where he claims 900 people signed the petition on Penlez's behalf. For the theatrical hoax, see Phillips, *Mid-Georgian London*, 92–93.

31. *Bath Journal*, 10 July 1749; *Worcester Journal*, 13 July 1749.

32. See British Library (hereafter BL), Add MS 48,800, William Strachan's ledger for September 1749, cited by M. C. and R. R. Battestin, in "Bedford, Fielding and the Westminster Election of 1749," *Eighteenth Century Studies*, 11/2 (Winter 1977/78): 165.

33. LMA, Middlesex sessions, SR 2924, indictment 79.

34. Battestin, *Fielding*, 483.

35. TNA, PRO 30/29/1/1, no. 14, folios 304–5.

36. *London Evening Post*, 13–15 December 1748.

37. Poem "On the Peace" in the *Worcester Journal*, 18 May 1749.

38. *London Evening Post*, 26 October 1749.

39. For an account of the plays and the protests of subsequent nights, when a Lord G—— (Gower?) remonstrated with the gallery protesters, see BL, Add MS 47,614, folios 22–24. For the suggestion that Trentham could have produced a sworn affidavit of his innocence, had he been so inclined, see *A genuine and authentic account*, 44.

40. *Some considerations on the establishment of the French Strollers* (London, 1749), 25.

41. *A genuine and authentic account*, 20–21.

42. Anon., *Peg T——m's Invitation to the two shilling Voters of Westminster* [London, 1749]; *T——t——m and V——p——t*, 48; *The Two Candidates, or Charge and Discharge* (London, 1749), 6.

43. On the Middlesex by-election, see Nicholas Rogers, *Whigs and Cities: Popular Politics in the Age of Walpole and Pitt* (Oxford, 1989), 204–20.

44. Anon., *To the unprincipled Electors of Westminster* [London, 1749].

45. [Paul Whitehead], *The case of the Honourable Alexander Murray Esquire, in an appeal to the People of Great Britain* (London, 1751).

46. BL, Add MS 32737, folios 304–5; Add MS 32876, folios 31–34, cited in Bob Harris, *Politics and the Nation: Britain in the Mid-Eighteenth Century* (Oxford, 2002), 54n. On Johns's leadership of the Independents, see West Sussex Record Office, Goodwood MS 51, folio 72.

47. *General Advertiser*, 20 December 1749.

48. Rogers, *Whigs and Cities*, 231, table 7.1.

49. *A genuine and authentic account*, 20.

50. Romney Sedgwick, ed. *The History of Parliament: The House of Commons, 1715–1754*, 2 vols. (London: H.M.S.O., 1970), 2:211.

51. West Sussex Record Office, Goodwood MS 51, folio 13.

52. BL, Add MS 47098 (F), Egmont's electoral survey, April 1750. Egmont thought the size of the electorate was about 7,000, but it was certainly larger than this by 1750.

53. West Sussex Record Office, Goodwood MS 51, folio 60.

54. Nicholas Rogers, "Aristocratic Clientage, Trade and Independency: Popular Politics in Pre-Radical Westminster," *Past and Present*, no. 61 (November 1973): 78–83.

55. *The Two Candidates, or Charge and Discharge* (London, 1749), 9; *A True and Impartial Collection of Pieces in Prose and Verse . . . written and published on both sides . . . during the Contest for the Westminster Election* (London, 1749), 22.

56. See Walpole, *Correspondence*, 20:112–3.

57. Bedford Estate Office, Westminster election papers 1749, bundle 60.

58. On Cheere, see the *Oxford Dictionary of National Biography* entry by Matthew Craske and Malcolm Baker.

59. Battestin, "Bedford, Fielding and the Westminster election of 1749," 149–51.

60. Ibid., 156–58, 162–63, 167–68; for the "Ten Queries," see *T——t——m and V——d——t*, 11–12.

61. Bedford Estate Office, Westminster election papers, accounts and expenses bundle, affidavit of William Bayley, yeoman, of St. Martin-in-the-Fields, 14 December 1749.

62. Battestin, *Fielding*, 155–58; [Paul Whitehead], *The Case of the Hon Alexander Murray in an appeal to the People of Great Britain* (London, 1751), 5–11; *Old England*, 9 December 1749.

63. Bedford Estate Office, Westminster election papers, letter dated 26 Dec. 1749, among inspector's bills.

64. British Library (hereafter BL), Lansdowne MS 506a, folios 374v, 526–27.

65. Westminster Library, E 3078, pp. 5, 8. Objections made by the council for Sir George Vandeput on the poll for St. Margaret and St. John, Westminster.

66. BL, Landsdowne MS 509b, folio 521v.

67. BL, Landsdowne MS 509b, folios 516, 528–29.

68. BL, Landsdowne MS 509a, folios 332–33; 509b, folios 13, 39v, 459.

69. Bedford Estate Office, Westminster election papers, inspectors' bundle.

70. Bedford Estate Office, Election papers, 1749, accounts and expenses bundle.

71. *General Advertiser*, 26 November 1749; *Old England*, 3 February 1750.

72. The largest number previously cast was in 1708, when 7,237 polled. One newspaper calculated in December 1749 that there were 15,558 houses in Westminster of which 1,500 were inhabited by peers and widows, 2,500 were empty, and 2,500 were underrated. This left an electorate of 9,058. See University College, London, Parkes MS 29 "election papers"; *Northampton Mercury*, 11 December 1749.

73. Bedford Estate Office, Westminster election papers, estimate of Thomas Woodward, General Surveyor of the Duty on Houses, 29 November 1749; see also *Remembrancer*, 24 February 1750.

74. BL, Lansdowne MS 509b, folio 541.

75. For examples, see Westminster Public Library, E 3078, and BL, Lansdowne MS 509b, folios 42v, 54, 59, 386, 499, 507v.

76. West Sussex Record Office, Goodwood MS 51, folios 60, 66, 75.

77. Of the St. Clement Danes vestrymen who voted in the 1749 election, 10 voted for Vandeput and 7 for Trentham. There were 26 abstentions. For the list of vestrymen, see Westminster Public Library, B 1068.

78. For the numbers of objections and requalifications, see BL, Lansdowne MS 509b, folio 562.

79. BL, Add MS 47092, folio 115. Lord Egmont's notes on the Westminster election, 1750–51. Compound householders are those householders who paid taxes as part of their rent and not separately.

80. *London Evening Post*, 20 January 1750.

81. Walpole, *Correspondence*, 20:123, 156.

82. *Commons Journals*, 26 (1751): 18–21, 26–27, 31–33, 60–62.

83. Horace Walpole, *Memoirs of the reign of King George II*, 3 vols. (London: H. Colburn, 1846), 1:27.

84. *Whitehall Evening Post*, 25 June 1751; *London Evening Post*, 25 June 1751

85. *Cobbett's Parliamentary History,* 14 (1747–53): 1065.

86. *Whitehall Evening Post,* 29 June 1751, cited in Battestin, *Fielding,* 487–88.

87. *A Complete Collection of State Trials and Proceedings for High Treason,* 4th ed. (London, 1778), appendix 22, pp. 205–8.

88. Bedford Estate Office, Westminster election papers, printers' bundle. Altogether 227,500 handbills were produced for this election on the Court side alone, a phenomenal number.

89. Bedford Estate Office, Westminster election papers, inspectors' bundle; East Riding of Yorkshire Record Office, DDGR 41/6.

90. West Sussex Record Office, Goodwood MS 51, folio 75.

Chapter 4. Fire from Heaven

1. Walpole, *Correspondence,* 20:154.

2. *Whitehall Evening Post,* 8 February 1750, reprinted in *Derby Mercury,* 9 February 1750.

3. Contemporary accounts make no mention of substantial damage. Cf. G. S. Rousseau, "The London Earthquakes of 1750," *Cahiers d'histoire modiale* 11 (1968/9): 437.

4. Thomas Jackson, *The life of the Rev. Charles Wesley* (New York: Lane and Sandford, 1842), 424.

5. Walpole, *Correspondence,* 20:130.

6. *Whitehall Evening Post,* 6 March 1750, reprinted in the *Derby Mercury,* 9 March 1750.

7. *Whitehall Evening Post,* 8 March 1750, reprinted in the *Bath Journal,* 12 March 1750, *Ipswich Journal,* 17 March 1750, the *Derby Mercury,* 9 March 1750, *Newcastle Courant,* 3 March 1750.

8. See the advertisement for this in the *General Advertiser,* 22 March 1750. The letter was also extracted in the monthlies and provincial press, and advertisements were published offering the full version at 3d a copy. See, among others, *Scots Magazine* 12 (March 1750): 105–10, *Worcester Journal,* 22 March 1750, *Bath Journal,* 2 April 1750.

9. Philip Doddridge, *The guilt and doom of Capernaum, seriously recommended to the consideration of the inhabitants of London* (London, 1750), vi.

10. Walpole, *Correspondence,* 20:154–55.

11. John Allen, *The Nature and Danger of Despising Repeated Reproofs* (London, 1750), 1; John Milner, *The Duty of God's People under Apprehensions of Publick Judgments* (London, 1750), 8; Thomas Newman, *The Sin and Shame of disregarding alarming Providences: A sermon preached at Crosby Square, April 4, 1750* (London, 1750), 13; Charles Wesley, *The cause and cure of earthquakes* (London, 1750), 6.

12. See William E. Burns, *An Age of Wonders: Prodigies, Politics and Providence in England, 1657–1727* (Manchester: Manchester University Press, 2002), esp. ch. 4.

13. John Wesley, *Hymns occasioned by the earthquake March 8, 1750* (London, 1750), 22.

14. Ludowick Muggleton, *A true interpretation of the eleventh chapter of the Revelation of St. John* (London? 1753), 152.

15. Doddridge, *Capernaum,* iv.

16. Elizabeth Montagu, *Elizabeth Montagu, the Queen of the Blue Stockings: Her Correspondence from 1720 to 1761*, ed. Emily J. Climenson, 2 vols. (London: John Murray, 1906), 2:85.

17. *Whitehall Evening Post*, 31 March 1750; *Bath Journal*, 9 April 1750.

18. *Bath Journal*, 9 April 1750.

19. *Worcester Journal*, 12 April 1750.

20. *Whitehall Evening Post*, 3 April 1750; Walpole, *Correspondence*, 20:136–37.

21. *Derby Mercury*, 6 April, 1750.

22. Robert Hooke, *The posthumous works of Robert Hooke* (London, 1705), 432.

23. *London Evening Post*, 10 February 1750.

24. Walpole, *Correspondence*, 20:154–5.

25. *Philosophical Transactions of the Royal Society* 46 (1749–50): 643.

26. *A Letter from the Lord Bishop of London to the clergy and people of London and Westminster, on occasion of the late earthquakes* (London, 1750), 4.

27. *A serious and affectionate address to the Cities of London and Westminster occasioned by the late Earthquake*, 3rd ed. (London, 1750), 5.

28. Samuel Chandler, *The scripture account of the cause and intention of earthquakes, in a sermon preached at the Old-Jury, March 11, 1749/50* (London, 1750), 5.

29. See Stephen Hales, *Some considerations on the causes of earthquakes* (London, 1750) and William Stukeley, *The philosophy of earthquakes, natural and religious* (London, 1750). Stukeley divided his pamphlet into "material causes" and "moral uses," the first directed at the Royal Society, the second to his congregation at St. George's, Queen Square. Beyond doffing his hat to divine agency, Hales avoided talking about the religious angle on the grounds that Bishop Sherlock had dealt with it.

30. The words are Stukeley's. See Stukeley, *Philosophy of earthquakes*, 42.

31. *London Evening Post*, 29 March 1750, *Worcester Journal*, 5 April 1750.

32. [Citizen of London], *A letter from a citizen of London to his fellow citizens . . . occasioned by the late earthquakes* (London, 1750), 4.

33. *A serious and affectionate address to the Cities of London and Westminster*, 6. The price of this tract was 2d or twenty-five for 3s, gratis to the poor. It was reprinted in the *Scots Magazine* 12 (March 1750): 105–10, and in the *Derby Mercury*, 30 March 1750, among other newspapers.

34. *Derby Mercury*, 6 April 1750.

35. On this, see Matthias Georgi, "The Lisbon earthquake and scientific knowledge in the British public sphere," in *The Lisbon Earthquake of 1755: Representations and Reactions*, ed. Theodore E. D. Braun and John B. Radner (Oxford: Voltaire Foundation, 2005), 81–96.

36. It is now reckoned that there were eleven super earthquakes in the period 1641–1800: four in China, three in Iran, two in Sicily, one in India, and one in Japan. To be designated "super" requires a death list of 100,000 or more. British naturalists arguably knew about four of these, the two in Sicily, the 1737 quake in Calcutta, and the 1730 one in China. They also knew of the very devastating earthquakes that destroyed Port Royal in Jamaica in 1692 and Lima in 1746.

37. John Michell, *Conjectures concerning the cause and observations upon the phenomena of earthquakes* (London, 1760), 37.

38. *London Evening Post,* 3 February 1750.

39. The 1692 earthquake is mentioned in *A particular account of all the earthquakes that have happened in Great-Britain from the reign of King William the Conqueror to the present time* (London, 1750), 21.

40. Ibid., 27.

41. Charles Bulkley, *A sermon preached at the evening lecture in the Old Jewry, on Sunday, November 30, 1755, on occasion of the dreadful earthquake in Lisbon* (London, 1756), 17.

42. On the notion that London could be the next Lima, see Charles Wesley, *The cause and cure of earthquakes,* 21.

43. [Joseph Besse], *Aminadab, one of the people called Quakers, to the B——p of L——n on his letter to the clergy and inhabitants of London and Westminster concerning the late earthquakes* (London, 1750), 1; see also the expanded version by Joseph Besse, *Modest remarks upon the Bishop of London's letter concerning the late earthquakes By one of the people called Quakers* (London 1750).

44. Thomas Gordon, *Serious Expostulations with the Right Reverend the Lord Bishop of London,* in John Trenchard and Thomas Gordon, *A Collection of Tracts,* 2 vols. (London 1751), 2:260.

45. Thomas Gordon, *A letter of consolation and counsel to the good people of England . . . occasion'd by the late earthquakes* (London, 1750), 1–6.

46. *Remembrancer,* 7 April 1750, reprinted in the *London Magazine* 19 (1750): 179.

47. John Bristed, *A discourse on the nature and use of prophecy* (London, 1743). On 18 March 1750 he gave a sermon on the earthquakes at St. Michael, Lewes, which was published in early April 1750 as *The late two shocks of a Earthquake,* see *London Evening Post,* 5 April 1750.

48. William Warburton, *Works,* 7 vols. (London, 1788), 4:411, 433, 463.

49. Thomas Gordon, *Seasonal Expostulations,* 266.

50. See the article "On Credulity" in the *Worcester Journal,* 21 June 1750.

51. *Bath Journal,* 21 May 1750.

52. *London Evening Post,* 23 May 1745.

53. *Derby Mercury,* 21 December 1750.

54. Roger Pickering, *An address to those who have either retired, or intend to leave the town, under the imaginary apprehension of the approaching shock of another Earthquake* (London, 1750). See also "Queries, seasonably proposed to those Persons of Distinction who are gone, or going from Town, on Account of the last Earthquakes," *Bath Journal,* 26 March 1750.

55. *Old England,* 5 May 1750

56. *Universal Magazine* 6 (April 1750): 187; *Bath Journal,* 9 April 1750.

57. Walpole, *Correspondence,* 35:131.

58. Richard Bentley, *A full and true account of the dreadful and melancholy earthquake* (London 1750), 4, 6.

59. *Newcastle Courant,* 5 May 1750.

60. Cited in Terry Castle, "Eros and Liberty at the English Masquerade, 1710–1790," *Eighteenth-Century Studies* 17 (Winter 1983/4): 158.

61. See *London Evening Post,* 21 April 1750; *Jubilee masquerade balls, at Ranelagh*

Gardens, a bad return for the merciful deliverance from the late earthquakes (London, 1750); *Derby Mercury,* 27 April 1750.

62. See *Bath Journal,* 16 April 1750.

63. For the original account, see John Cleland, *Fanny Hill, or Memoirs of a Woman of Pleasure,* ed. Peter Wagner (London, 1985), 193–96. The elimination of the gay sex scene from the second edition was a strategy forced on him by his publisher, Ralph Griffiths. It was not prompted by any anticipated clerical attack

64. For cockfights, see *London Evening Post,* 27 March, 24 April 1750; for the advertisement for *Fanny Hill,* see *London Evening Post,* 8 March 1750, and in subsequent issues.

65. Gordon, *A letter of consolation and counsel,* 19–30. See also *Old England,* 5 May 1750.

66. W. M. Jacob, *Lay People and Religion in the Early Eighteenth Century* (Cambridge, 1996), 124–35; David Hayton, "Moral Reform and Country Politics," *Past and Present* 128 (1990): 48–91; on the London societies, see Robert B Shoemaker, "Reforming the City: The Reformation of Manners Campaign in London, 1690–1738," in *Stilling the Grumbling Hive: The Response to Social and Economic Problems in England, 1689–1750,* ed. Lee Davison et al. (New York: St. Martin's Press, 1992), 99–120.

67. Shoemaker, "Reforming the City," 105.

68. Tim Meldrum, "Defamation at the Bishop of London's Consistory Court, 1700–1745," *London Journal,* 19/1 (1994): 1–20; for the quarter sessions, see Robert B. Shoemaker, *Prosecution and Punishment: Petty Crime and the Law in London and Rural Middlesex, c. 1660–1725* (London: Cambridge University Press, 1991).

69. Viviane Barrie-Currien, "The clergy in the diocese of London in the eighteenth century," in *The Church of England, c. 1689–c. 1833: From Toleration to Tractarianism,* ed. John Walsh, Colin Haydon, and Stephen Taylor (Cambridge: Cambridge University Press, 1993), 86–107.

70. LMA, DL/C/253/122. The general observations here are based on DL/C/243, 248, 253, 258, 263, 268, 272.

71. Viviane Barrie-Currien, ibid.; see also her article, as Viviane Barrie, "The Church of England in the Diocese of London in the Eighteenth Century," in *The National Church in Local Perspective: The Church of England and the Regions, 1660–1800,* ed. Jeremy Gregory and Jeffrey S. Chamberlain (Woodbridge, Suffolk, 2003), 53–72.

72. Jessica Warner, *Craze: Gin and Debauchery in an Age of Reason* (New York: Random House, 2002), 109–13.

73. *Cobbett's Parliamentary History,* 12 (1741–43): 1236, 1362.

74. Samuel Hull, *The fluctuating condition of human life, and the absolute necessity of the preparation for the eternal world* (London, 1750), 5; Stukeley, *Philosophy of earthquakes,* 59.

75. [Citizen of London], *A letter to his fellow citizens,* 21, 23; [Foreigner], *An epistle to the Bishop of London* (London, 1750), 6–12, 19.

76. Chandler, *A scripture account,* 37; Besse, *Aminadab,* 7.

77. On the developing concept of public utility in philanthropic endeavor, especially by people such as Jonas Hanway, see Sarah Lloyd, *Charity and Poverty in England, c. 1680–1820* (Manchester: Manchester University Press, 2009), 36–76.

78. Isaac Maddox, *The expediency of preventive wisdom* (London, 1750), 15.

79. A point noted by Jessica Warner in her useful commentary on Maddox, save that she misdates the sermon and perhaps confuses the two pamphlets. See *Craze*, 199–202.

80. Isaac Maddox, *An epistle to the Right Honourable the Lord Mayor, aldermen and common council of the City of London, and governors of the several hospitals* (London, 1751).

81. Ibid., 9–10.

82. Ibid., 45.

83. Edmund Gibson, *A Sermon preached to the Societies for the Reformation of Manners at St. Mary le Bow . . . January 6th 1723,* 4th ed. (London, 1725).

84. Warner, *Craze*, 202–6. Warner makes the important point that by the time of the 1751 act gin consumption was dropping.

85. On the importance of the sermon in early eighteenth-century public debate, see Tony Claydon, "The Sermon, the 'Public Sphere' and the Political Culture of Late Seventeenth-Century England," in *The English Sermon Revised: Religion, Literature and History, 1660–1750,* ed. Lori Anne Ferrell and Peter McCullough (Manchester: Manchester University Press, 2000), 208–34; John Brewer, *The Pleasures of the Imagination* (London: HarperCollins, 1997).

86. See John Bell, *A new catalogue of Bell's circulating library, consisting of above fifty thousand volumes, . . . which are lent to read* [London], [1778]; William Bathoe, *A new catalogue of the curious and valuable collection of books: (both English and French) consisting of several thousand volumes* [London], [1767?]. Books devoted to theology in these catalogues comprised 4 and 2 percent, respectively. The exception appears to be the Circulating Library at Crane Court. See *An alphabetical catalogue of books and pamphlets, in English, French, and Latin, belonging to the Circulating Library, in Crane-Court,* vol. 1 (London, 1748). Here the first 100 pamphlets contained 32 percent with a religious theme, although we do not know the degree to which they were borrowed. At Bristol circulating library, 1773–84, 9 percent of the books were devoted to theology but those borrowed comprised only 4.5 percent of the total library transactions. Of all books borrowed, 45 percent were in the category of history, travel and geography, and 25 percent were in belles-lettres. See Brewer, *Pleasures of the Imagination,* 181.

87. Charles Taylor, *A Secular Age* (Cambridge: Belknap Press of Harvard University, 2005).

Chapter 5. Riots, Revels, and Reprisals

1. *Weekly Packet,* 15 January 1715, *Englishmen,* 21 January 1715.

2. *London Daily Advertiser,* 10 May 1751. For reports of pamphlets discussing Fielding's *Enquiry,* see *London Evening Post,* 7 February 1751, *London Gazetteer,* 7 March 1751, *Whitehall Evening Post,* 16 March 1751. On sales, see Battestin, *Fielding,* 512.

3. *Covent Garden Journal,* 13, 20 June 1753.

4. *Old England,* 8 August 1747.

5. Charles Sackville, *A treatise concerning the militia* (London, 1752), 66.

6. Harris, *Politics and the Nation,* ch. 4; Geoffrey Plank, *Rebellion and Savagery: the Jacobite rising of 1745 and the British Empire* (Philadelphia: University of Pennsylvania Press, 2006).

7. *London Evening Post,* 29 July 1746.

8. Paul Kléber Moonod, *Jacobitism and the English People, 1688–1788* (Cambridge: Cambridge University Press, 1989), 340–41.

9. William E. A. Axon, ed., *The Annals of Manchester* (Manchester: John Heywood, 1886), 48; Alexander Grosart, *English Jacobite Ballads, Songs and Satires* (Manchester: Charles E. Sims, 1877), 82–84; John Harland and T. T. Wilkinson, *Ballads and Songs of Lancashire, Ancient and Modern,* 3rd ed. (Manchester and London: John Heywood, 1882), 75–77.

10. Byron, *Private Journal,* 479–80; *Whitehall Evening Post,* 26 November 1748; Monod, *Jacobitism,* 293; Nicholas Rogers, *Crowds, Culture and Politics in Georgian Britain* (Oxford: Clarendon Press, 1998), 47.

11. TNA, SP 36/102/80; Rogers, *Crowds,* 46–47; Monod, *Jacobitism,* 199.

12. Accounts differed as to whether the effigy was George I or II. The turnips and cornuted head would suggest George I, but the motto implied the current king. One witness believed he saw a second paper pinned to the dummy with the words "George Rex the second" on it (SP 36/113/119). The effigy was clearly a composite representation of the Hanoverian monarchy.

13. TNA, SP 36/113/73–86.

14. TNA, SP 36/113/83, 121.

15. Monod, *Jacobitism,* 206

16. TNA, SP 36/113/168.

17. *Read's Weekly Journal,* 28 July 1750.

18. *London Daily Advertiser,* 26 June 1751; *Criminal Cases on the Crown Side of King's Bench: Staffordshire, 1740–1800,* ed. Douglas Hay (Stafford: Staffordshire Record Society, 2010), 291–300.

19. TNA, SP 36/113/157–59

20. TNA, TS 11/929/3268.

21. TNA, SP 36/113/158.

22. TNA, SP 36/113/159.

23. See the comments of Major Chaban and Captain Hamilton, TNA, SP 36/133/108–9, 157–59.

24. Nicholas Rogers, "Popular Jacobitism in Provincial Context: 18th-Century Bristol and Norwich," in Eveline Cruickshanks and Jeremy Black, eds., *The Jacobite Challenge* (Edinburgh: J. Donald, 1988), 123–41.

25. TNA, SP 36/1, 28 June 1727, Mayor of Bristol to the Duke of Newcastle, cited in Philip D. Jones, "The Bristol Bridge Riots and Its Antecedents: Eighteenth-Century Perception of the Crowd," *Journal of British Studies* 19/2 (Spring 1980): 77. See also Adrian Randall, *Riotous Assemblies: Popular Protest in Hanoverian England* (Oxford: Oxford University Press, 2006), 161–62, and Robert Malcolmson, "'A Set of Ungovernable People: The Kingswood Colliers in the Eighteenth Century," in John Brewer and John Styles, eds., *An Ungovernable People? The English and Their Law in the Seventeenth and Eighteenth Centuries* (London: Hutchinson, 1980), 110–11.

26. William Albert, "Popular Opposition to Turnpike Trusts in Early Eighteenth-Century England," *Journal of Transport History,* new series, 5/1 (February 1979), 4; *Commons Journals,* 25 (1745–1750): 737.

27. Albert, op. cit, 2, 8–9; see also 22 George 2, c. 28.

28. *Bath Journal,* 31 July 1749; *General Advertiser,* 1 August 1749; *Ipswich Journal,* 5 August 1749.

29. *Bath Journal,* 31 July 1749.

30. Ibid.

31. *London Evening Post,* 5 August 1749.

32. Ibid.

33. *London Evening Post,* 12 August 1749.

34. *Worcester Journal,* 10 August 1749.

35. *Ipswich Journal,* 12 August 1749.

36. *General Advertiser,* 8 August 1749; *Whitehall Evening Post,* 5 August 1749; *Worcester Journal,* 10 August 1749.

37. TNA, SP 36/111/14; Rogers, *Whigs and Cities,* 291.

38. TNA, SP 36/111, Weekes to Newcastle, 19 September 1749, cited in Jones, "Bristol Bridge Riots," 79.

39. *Bath Journal,* 14 August 1749.

40. TNA, SP 36/111/77–78.

41. *Worcester Journal,* 19 April 1749.

42. Ibid.; TNA, Western Circuit 1749–50, Assizes 23/6; Randall, *Riotous Assemblies,* 163; Jones, "Bristol Bridge Riot," 79.

43. *London Evening Post, Whitehall Evening Post,* 14 April 1749.

44. *London Evening Post, Whitehall Evening Post,* 21 April, 8 May 1749; *General Advertiser,* 10 May 1749; *Old England,* 21, 28 April 1749.

45. *London Evening Post,* 9 September 1749.

46. *Whitehall Evening Post,* 14 September, 21 October 1749.

47. *Bath Journal,* 18 September 1749.

48. *London Evening Post,* 23 September 1749; *Whitehall Evening Post,* 23 September 1749.

49. B. M. Short, "The De-industrialisation Process: A Case Study of the Weald, 1600–1850," in Pat Hudson, ed., *Regions and Industries* (Cambridge, Cambridge University Press, 1990), 169–73; David Ormrod "Industry, 1640–1800," in Walter A. Armstrong, ed., *The Economy of Kent, 1640–1914* (Woodbridge, Suffolk: Boydell Press, 1996), 85–109; M. J. Dobson, "The Last Hiccup of the Old Demographic Regime: Population Stagnation and Decline in Late 17th and Early 18th Century South-East England," *Continuity and Change* 4 (1989): 395–428.

50. On the changing tax base, see John Brewer, *The Sinews of Power: War, Money and the English State, 1688–1783* (New York: Alfred A. Knopf, 1989), 96–97, figure 4.2.

51. George Morley, *The Smugglers' War* (Stroud: Sutton, 1994), 84–86.

52. *A full and genuine history of the inhuman and unparallell'd murders of Mr. William Galley . . . and Mr Daniel Chater,* 3rd ed. (London, 1779), 183.

53. OBP, Ordinary of Newgate's *Account,* 29 July 1747 (OA17470729), 23 December 1747 (OA17471223), 18 March 1748 (OA17480318). See also the testimony of Henry

Sheerman, little Harry, who at his trial in East Grinstead, 1749, said, "The considerable Gains that were allow'd to those who were as Servants to the Master Smugglers seduced him to leave his honest Employment, and taken on with them." *A full and genuine history*, 181.

54. *Commons Journals*, 25 (1745–50): 102–3.

55. *The Journal of the Reverend John Wesley*, 4 vols. (London: J. Dent, 1938), 3:242; 4:3.

56. Robin Craig and John Whyman, "Kent and the Sea," in *The Economy of Kent, 1640–1914*, 180; F. F. Nicholls, *Honest Thieves: The Violent Heyday of English Smuggling* (London: Heinemann, 1973).

57. OBP, *Ordinary's Account*, November 1747 (OA17471116).

58. See James Earnshaw, *An abstract of various penal and other statutes relating to the revenue of customs*, 2 vols. (London, 1793–96). The regulation about boats with more than four oars, within two leagues of the sea, being vulnerable to search and confiscation is to be found in 8 George 1, c. 18. It was extended to boats with more than six oars under 19 George 3, c. 69.

59. Mary Waugh, *Smuggling in Kent and Sussex, 1700–1840* (Newbury, Berks.: Countryside Books, 1985), 30–31.

60. Leonard P. Thompson, *Smugglers of the Suffolk Coast* (Ipswich: Bret Valley, 1968), 12.

61. 9 George 2, c. 35.

62. To these main clauses were added a number of others rewarding informers, extending the surveillance of coastal craft, fortifying revenue officers in their use of force against smugglers, and reducing the number of potential actions against them in the courts.

63. *Daily Gazetteer*, 2 June 1736.

64. TNA, CUST 41/4, p. 65. There was an ongoing dispute as to whether the Customs officers were entitled to a third or a half of the seized cargoes.

65. West Sussex Record Office, Goodwood MS 115, folio 115.

66. East Sussex Record Office, Sayer MS, SAY 288.

67. See *Daily Post*, 29 March 1738. "Smugglers are so desperate and hardy, that the Civil Officers can hardly carry off any Seizure made in those Parts without the aid of the Military Power."

68. From the Customs Letter Book, port of Rochester, 1740, cited by David Phillipson, *Smuggling: A History, 1700–1970* (Newton Abbot: David & Charles, 1973), 78.

69. TNA, SP 36/61/118–21.

70. *Bath Journal*, 19 November 1744.

71. TNA, SP 36/61/119.

72. TNA, SP 36/62/120.

73. *Daily Post*, 16 June 1736, *Old Whig*, 17 June 1736, *Read's Weekly Journal*, 19 June 1736; *Bath Journal*, 7 January 1745.

74. For the Hawkhurst gang, see Cal Winslow, "Sussex Smugglers," in Hay et al., *Albion's Fatal Tree*, 119–66.

75. TNA, CUST 41/42, King v. John Macdonald, 1741.

76. *Bath Journal*, 18 February 1745.

77. George Bishop, *Observations, remarks and means to prevent Smuggling* (Maidstone, 1783), 5.

78. *A full and genuine history*, 2, 185–87; E. Keble Chatterton, *King's Cutters and*

Smugglers, 1700–1855 (London, 1912; reprint New York, B. Blom, 1971), 84–86; *General Evening Post*, 20 October 1747; OBP, April 1749, Thomas Kingsmill (t17490405); Geoffrey Morley, *Smuggling in Hampshire and Dorset, 1700–1850* (Newbury: Countryside Books, 1983), 156–60. Some accounts, and the reward notice in the *London Gazette*, suggest the smugglers numbered sixty, but forty seems more accurate from the account in the subsequent trial at the Old Bailey.

79. OBP, April 1749, Thomas Fairall (t17490405).

80. *A full and genuine history*, passim.

81. West Sussex Record Office, Goodwood MSS 155/H24, cited in Winslow, "Sussex Smugglers," 138.

82. *Bath Journal*, 23 January 1749.

83. West Sussex Record Office, Goodwood MS 115, folio 10.

84. *The Correspondence of the Dukes of Richmond and Newcastle, 1724–1750*, ed. Timothy J. McCann (Lewes: Sussex Record Society, vol. 73, 1984), no. 420.

85. TNA, KB 8/72 for the documents on the trial. For newspaper accounts, see *London Evening Post*, 19 January 1749, *Old England*, 21 January 1749, *Whitehall Evening Post*, 24 January 1749.

86. *A full and genuine history*, 148–56. H. N. Shere, Lord Teignmouth & Charles G. Harper, *The Smugglers*, 2 vols. (London: C. Palmer, 1923), 1:105–8.

87. TNA, ASSI 94/771, 772; Waugh, *Smuggling in Kent and Sussex*, 144.

88. Pring later turned in two other smugglers, Edward Brooke and John Carbald or Carhold, who were successfully indicted and hanged for running goods at Thwaite in Suffolk in 1747. See OBP, September 1751, Edward Brook and John Carbald (t17510911).

89. *Correspondence of the Dukes of Richmond and Newcastle*, nos. 433–34, pp. 285–86n. See also OBP, *Ordinary's Account*, April 1749 (OA17490426).

90. OBP, April 1749, Thomas Lillywhite (t17490405–36). 91. West Sussex Record Office, Goodwood MS 115, H86, H93, 6 and 17 February 1749, cited in Winslow, "Sussex Smugglers," 149.

92. *A full and genuine history*, 258.

93. OBP, October 1747, John Harvey (t17471014–6); December 1747, Peter Tickner and James Hodges (t17471209–52); May 1748, William Gray (t17480526–29); December 1749, Thomas Palmer and James Monday (t17491209–63).

94. OBP, December 1749, Thomas Palmer, James Monday (t17491209–63).

95. Arthur Lyon Cross, ed., *Eighteenth-Century Documents Relating to. . . . Smuggling: Selected from the Shelburne Manuscripts in the William L. Clements Library* (New York: Macmillan, 1928), 241.

96. OBP, February 1747, Edmund Henley (t17470225–19).

97. East Sussex Record Office, Sayer MSS, SAY 297. See also the legal and political diary of Dudley Ryder, 1747, entries for 23 January, 9, 30 April, 27 May 1747. I am grateful to Professor James Oldham of Georgetown University for these references.

Chapter 6. Tackling the Gin Craze

1. OBP, Judith Defour (t17340227–32); OA 17340308; *Daily Journal*, 6 March 1734.

2. "Quartern" in this context means a quarter of a pint.

3. *Daily Journal*, 9 March 1734; *London Journal*, 9 March 1734.

4. Thomas Wilson, *Distilled Spirituous Liquors, the bane of the Nation,* 2nd ed. (London, 1736) 10.

5. Wilson became a chaplain to George II and the rector of St. Stephen Walbrook in 1737. His pamphlet is sometimes ascribed to his father, the bishop of Sodor and Man, but all the evidence points toward Thomas Wilson junior. Cf. Jessica Warner, *Craze: Gin and Debauchery in an Age of Reason* (New York: Random House, 2002), xviii, 16.

6. Wilson, *Distilled Spirituous Liqours,* 31, 37.

7. Derived from the Dutch *jenever* (juniper) or the French *geniévre.*

8. The figures for beer and spirits output are to be found in T. S. Ashton, *An Economic History of England: The Eighteenth Century* (London: Methuen, 1964), tables IV and V, 242–43.

9. *Weekly Miscellany,* 17 July 1736.

10. *Gentleman's Magazine* 7 (1737): 214, cited in Peter Clark, "The 'Mother Gin' Controversy in the Early Eighteenth Century," *Transactions Royal Historical Society,* 5th ser., 38 (1988): 65.

11. Elias Bockett, *Blunt to Walpole* (London, 1730), 30, in Clark, "'Mother Gin,'" 65.

12. Maxine Berg and Elizabeth Eger, "The Rise and Fall of the Luxury Debates," in *Luxury in the Eighteenth Century: Debates, Desires and Delectable Goods,* ed. Maxine Berg and Elizabeth Eger (New York: Palgrave Macmillan, 2003), 7–27.

13. M. Dorothy George, *London Life in the Eighteenth Century* (New York: Harper and Row, 1965), 23; Bernard Mandeville, *A Letter to Dion* (London, 1732), 51.

14. Jacob Vanderlint, *Money Answers All Things* (London, 1734), 43; L. D. Schwarz, *London in the Age of Industrialization* (Cambridge: Cambridge University Press, 1992), 202–4.

15. On this see Robert Woods, "Mortality in Eighteenth-Century London: A New Look at the Bills," *Local Population Studies* 77 (Autumn 2006): 12–23.

16. [John Kelly], *The Fall of Bob, or the Oracle of Gin* (London, 1736), 13.

17. *Cobbett's Parliamentary History,* 12 (1741–43): 1193–94.

18. Erasmus Jones, *Luxury, pride, and vanity, the bane of the British nation* (London, 1750), 37.

19. *Daily Gazetteer,* 10 January 1736.

20. *London Daily Post,* 1 March 1736.

21. *Daily Gazetteer,* 23 March, 1736; *London Evening Post,* 27 March 1736.

22. *An elegy on the much lamented death of the most excellent, the more truly beloved and universally admired lady, Madam Geneva* (London, 1736).

23. *Daily Post,* 1 April 1736.

24. *A supplement to the impartial enquiry into the present state of the British distillery* (London, 1736), 17–25; *Daily Post,* 1 April 1736.

25. Some historians have argued that gin drinking was not a marker of despair but of "affluence"; that is to say that more affluent artisans were involved. See Clark, "'Mother Gin,'" 63–84; J. A. Chartres, "Spirits in the North-East? Gin and Other Vices in the Long Eighteenth-Century," in *Creating and Consuming Culture in North-East England, 1660–1830,* ed. Helen Berry and Jeremy Gregory (Aldershot: Ashgate, 2004), 37–56.

26. *Cobbett's Parliamentary History,* 9 (1733–37): 1094.

27. *London Evening Post,* 20 January 1736. The report took up the whole front page of the newspaper, and more.

28. Wilson, *Distilled Spirituous Liquors*, 7–8, 10.

29. Isaac Maddox, *An epistle to the Right Honourable the Lord Mayor, aldermen and common council of the City of London, and the governors of several hospitals* (London, 1751), 15; See also Erasmus Jones, *Luxury, pride, and vanity, the bane of the British nation*, 38–39.

30. Cited in Patrick Dillon, *Gin: The Much-Lamented Death of Madame Geneva* (Boston: Justin, Charles, 2003), 210.

31. Wilson, *Distilled Spirituous Liquors*, 32.

32. Ibid., 37.

33. Hales, *Friendly Admonition*, 20.

34. Roderick Floud et al., *Height, Health and History: Nutritional Status in the United Kingdom, 1750–1980* (Cambridge: Cambridge University Press, 1990), 165, 198.

35. Jonas Hanway, *An account of the Marine Society* (London, 1759), 72; Roland Pietsch, *The Real Jim Hawkins: Ships' Boys in the Georgian Navy* (Barnsley: Seaforth, 2010), 18–19.

36. For Hanway's thoughts on the perils and dimensions of gin drinking, see Jonas Hanway, *A Journal of eight days journey from Portsmouth to Kingston*, 2 vols. (London, 1757), 2:81–146.

37. On the manner in which similar genres of writing constructed the nineteenth-century criminal, see Marie-Christine Leps, *Apprehending the Criminal: The Production of Deviance in Nineteenth-Century Discourse* (Durham: Duke University Press, 1992).

38. St. George Hanover Square, Christchurch Spitalfields, St. George Ratcliff Highway, and St. George the Martyr were included in the 1720s. St. Ann Limehouse and St. George Bloomsbury were added in the next decade along with St. John Southwark and St. Luke Old Street. St. Mark Bethnal Green was added in the 1740s. In 1744, there were 146 parishes within the Bills. See William Maitland, *The history and survey of London*, 2 vols. (London, 1760), 2:737–46.

39. John Landers, *Death and the Metropolis: Studies in the Demographic History of London, 1670–1830* (Cambridge: Cambridge University Press, 1993), 91–93; M. Dorothy George, *London Life*, 21–22; A. B. Appleby, "Nutrition and Disease: The Case of London, 1550–1750," *Journal of Interdisciplinary History* 6/1 (1975): 1–22; Robert Woods, "Mortality in Eighteenth-Century London," 12–13.

40. Maddox, *The expediency of preventive wisdom* (London, 1751), postscript, xxvii.

41. George Cheyne, *An Essay on Heath and Long Life*, 8th ed. (London, 1734), 54, cited in Roy Porter, "Consumption: Disease of the Consumer Society?" in John Brewer and Roy Porter, *Consumption and the World of Goods* (London: Routledge, 1993), 61. Cheyne's pamphlet ran through eight editions in ten years.

42. Wilson, *Distilled Spirituous Liquors*, 44. See also Jessica Warner, "Faith in Numbers: Quantifying Gin and Sin in Eighteenth-Century England," *Journal of British Studies* 50/1 (2011): 76–99.

43. *A supplement to the impartial enquiry*, 30, 41–42.

44. Ibid., 61.

45. Maddox, *An epistle*, 22–25, see also his *The expediency of preventive wisdom*, postscript.

46. *General Advertiser*, 16 February 1751.

47. [Corbyn Morris], *Observations on the past growth and present state of the City of London* (London, 1751), intro.

48. Ibid., 2, 25.

49. Ibid., 25.

50. Ibid., 6

51. Landers, *Death and the Metropolis,* 136, 170. The age specific mortality rate for Quakers (1700–1750) was 342 per 1,000 at birth and 244 per 1,000 ages one to four years. Infant mortality among the general population was higher, and judging from figure 5.3 in Landers, particularly severe during the gin era (c. 1720–50). Adult mortality was high in London but not that exceptional. Woods offers two sets of figures for children under ten: 320 per 1,000 for London 1728–37, and 297 per 1,000 for the 1730s, 264 per 1,000 for 1740s, 278 per 1,000 for 1750s. The last set of figures included still births. See Woods, "Mortality in Eighteenth-Century London," 15, 17.

52. D. V. Glass, *Numbering the People* (Farnborough, Hants: D. C. Heath, 1973), 18.

53. *Cobbett's Parliamentary History,* 14 (1747–53): 1326.

54. For the passage through the two houses, see *Commons Journals,* 26 (1750–54): 731–32, 777–78, 795, 810, and *Lords Journals,* 28 (1753–56): 120, 132, 137, 153–54.

55. Josiah Tucker, *An Impartial Inquiry into the Benefits and Damages arising to the nation from the present very great use of low-priced Spirituous Liquors* (London, 1751), 24–31.

56. Josiah Tucker, *A discourse on the natural disposition of mankind with respect to commerce* (London, 1755?), 12. On Dangeul, see John Shovlin, *The Political Economy of Virtue: Luxury, Patriotism and the Origins of the French Revolution* (Ithaca: Cornell University Press, 2006), 45–47, 58–59, 84–85.

57. [Louis-Joseph Plumard de Dangeul] Sir John Nickolls, *Remarks on the advantages and disadvantages of France and Britain with respect to commerce, and to the other means of encreasing the wealth and power of the state* (London, 1754), 192.

58. On biopolitics, see Michel Foucault, *"Society must be defended": Lectures at the Collège de France, 1975–1976,* trans. David Macey (New York: Picador, 2003), 242–54.

59. Michel Foucault, *Power,* ed. James D. Faubion (New York: New Press, 1994), 201–22.

60. "Police" was defined by Samuel Johnson as "the regulation and government of a city or country, so far as regards the inhabitants." See his *A Dictionary of the English Language,* 2 vols. (London, 1755–56), vol. 2, unpaginated. For the broad usage of the term by Foucault, going back to the French notion of *gouvernement,* see Thomas Lemke, "Foucault, Governmentality and Critique," *Rethinking Marxism* 14/3 (2002): 49–64.

61. For an example of how governmentality might work in the late sixteenth and early seventeenth century, see Paul Griffiths, *Lost Londons: Change, Crime and Control in the Capital City, 1550–1660* (Cambridge: Cambridge University Press, 2008).

62. Arthur Young, *Proposals to the legislature for numbering the people* (London, 1771), 13.

63. Warner, *Craze,* 97–99. Only 453 licenses were taken out during the lifetime of the act, 1729–33, and more than half were purchased in the first six months.

64. *Gazetteer,* 5 October 1736.

65. *London Evening Post,* 25 September 1736; *Craftsman,* 2 October 1736; Warner, *Craze,* 129.

66. George Rudé, "'Mother Gin' and the London Riots of 1736," *Guildhall Miscellany* 10 (September 1959): 62.

67. *London Daily Post,* 4 October 1736.

68. Jessica Warner and Frank Ivis, "'Damn you, you informing bitch': Vox Populi and the Unmaking of the Gin Act of 1736," *Journal of Social History* 33/2 (1999): 304, figure 1, which tracks the prosecutions and attacks on informers.

69. *Craftsman,* 3 December 1737.

70. *London Evening Post,* 1 November 1737.

71. See E. P. Thompson, *Customs in Common* (London: Merlin Press, 1991), 467–538; Martin Ingram, "Ridings, Rough Music and the 'Reform of Popular Culture' in Early Modern England," *Past and Present* 105 (1984): 79–113.

72. *London Daily Post,* 5 August 1738, *London Evening Post,* 15 January 1737, cited in Warner and Ivis "'Damn you, you informing bitch,'" 310, 326n.

73. *London Evening Post,* 22 July 1738

74. *London Evening Post,* 30 December 1738; on Parker's activities, see *Daily Post,* 13, 16 October 1738, and *Common Sense,* 18 November 1738.

75. *London Daily Post,* 22 August 1738; *Common Sense,* 26 August 1738.

76. Cited by Warner, *Craze,* 151–52.

77. *Weekly Miscellany,* 12 May 1738.

78. Warner, *Craze,* 171.

79. *Daily Post,* 11 September 1738; *Weekly Miscellany,* 15 September 1738.

80. Warner, *Craze,* 171–76.

81. The tax was 6d a gallon on imported materials and 1d a gallon on domestic. See Lee Davison, "Experiments in the Social Regulation of Industry: Gin Legislation, 1729–1751," in *Stilling the Grumbling Hive,* 41.

82. *Cobbett's Parliamentary History,* 12 (1741–43): 1195–96, 1243, 1327–28.

83. Ibid., 12 (1741–43): 1236, 1362.

84. Ibid., 12 (1741–43): 1325.

85. Warner, *Craze,* 188–91.

86. Davison, "Gin Legislation," 42. These figures are based on the calendars for half the sessions between 1745 and 1751.

87. Fielding, *Enquiry,* ed. Zirker, lx–lxi, 89–92.

88. Ibid., 90.

89. Maddox, *An epistle,* 14–15.

90. Cf. Dorothy Marshall, *Dr. Johnson's London* (New York, 1968), 230, who describes *Gin Lane* as an "unexaggerated picture of the alleys and lanes with which the Doctor (Johnson) must have been familiar."

91. BL, Add MSS 27,991 folio 49b, transcribed in William Hogarth, *The Analysis of Beauty,* ed. Joseph Burke (Oxford: Clarendon Press, 1955), 226.

92. Ronald Paulson, *Hogarth,* 3 vols. (New Brunswick: Rutgers University Press, 1991–93), 3:21–27.

93. *A Dissertation on Mr. Hogarth's Six Prints* (London, 1751), 21–23.

94. *Commons Journals,* 26 (1750–54): 55, 84–85.

95. Wilson, *Distilled Spirituous Liquors,* 30,

96. *Covent Garden Journal,* 20 June 1752, cited in Bertrand Goldgar, ed., *The Covent-Garden Journal and A Plan of the Universal Register Office* (Middletown, CT: Wesleyan University Press, 1988), 268–69.

Chapter 7. Henry Fielding and Social Reform

1. *General Advertiser*, 21 February 1751; *Ipswich Journal*, 23 February 1751; *Old England*, 23 February 1751.

2. OBP, April 1750, Thomas Lewis (t17500425–14), *Ordinary's Account*, May 1750 (OA 17500516); *London Evening Post*, 20 February, 22 March, 1750; *Penny London Post*, 21 February 1750.

3. OBP, *Ordinary's Account*, May 1750 (OA 17500516); on Beard, see Thomas Davies, *Memoirs of the Life of David Garrick Esquire*, 2 vols. (Boston: Wells and Lilly, 1818), 2:20, 54.

4. Fielding's dependence on legal fees was not total, thanks to his novels and the patronage of Bedford, and he resented the insinuation that he was a corrupt, self-interested trading justice. See Battestin, "Fielding, Bedford and the Westminster Election of 1749," 150–52, 175; Battestin, *Fielding*, 459–60, 532; and B. M. Jones, *Henry Fielding: Novelist and Magistrate* (London: George Allen and Unwin, 1933), 119.

5. Battestin, *Fielding*, 420

6. Fielding, *Enquiry*, ed. Zirker, 25.

7. Ibid., 26

8. *London Evening Post*, 1 August 1749; *Old England*, 5 August 1749.

9. *Monthly Review* 1 (1749): 239–40.

10. Josiah Tucker, *An Impartial Inquiry into the Benefits and Dangers arising to the Nation from the very great use of low-priced Spirituous Liquors* (London, 1751), 4–5; William Hay, *Remarks on the laws relating to the poor* (London, 1751), vi; Charles Gray, *Considerations on several proposals lately made for the maintenance of the poor* (London 1751), 14.

11. Hugh Amory, "Henry Fielding and the Criminal Legislation of 1751–1752," *Philological Quarterly* 1 (1971): 175–92; Radzinowicz, *English Criminal Law*, 3:63–64.

12. Fielding, *Enquiry*, ed. Zirker, 75.

13. Ibid., 76

14. Ibid., 108.

15. Henry Fielding, *The Journal of a Voyage to Lisbon* (Cambridge: Cambridge University Press, 1902), 63, 120, 157–61.

16. *Whitehall Evening Post*, 23 March 1749.

17. John Lockman, *The vast importance of the herring industry . . . to these kingdoms* (London, 1750), 25.

18. A. J. Youngson, *After the Forty-Five* (Edinburgh, Edinburgh University Press, 1973), 104. For the British fishery as a patriotic venture, see Bob Harris, "Patriotic Commerce and National Revival: The Free British Fishery Society and British Politics, c. 1749–58," *English Historical Review* 114 (April 1996): 285–313.

19. Harris, *Politics and the Nation*, 254–55; for the manufacture of the nets, see Fielding's letter to Thomas Wilson, December 1750, cited by Harris, 255.

20. *Old England*, 4 May 1751.

21. Charles Moss, *A sermon preached before the Right Honourable the Lord Mayor and the Governors of the Several Hospitals of the City of London* (London, 1750), 6–7.

22. Fielding, *Enquiry*, ed. Zirker, 80.

23. Ibid., 89–90. Isaac Maddox, *An epistle to the . . . Lord Mayor, Aldermen and Common Council,* 2nd ed. (London, 1751) and *The expediency of preventive wisdom,* 3rd ed. (London, 1750).

24. Fielding, *Enquiry,* ed. Zirker, 98–117.

25. Malvin Zirker, *Fielding's Social Pamphlets* (Berkeley and Los Angeles: University of California Press, 1966). I would go further than Zirker in recognizing the reactionary, antique features of some of Fielding's proposals.

26. Joseph Massie, *A plan for the establishment of charity houses for exposed and deserted women or girls, and for penitent prostitutes* (London, 1758), 54–59.

27. On the decline of wage regulation, see R. Keith Kelsall, *Wage Regulation under the Statute of Artificers* (London: Methuen, 1938), ch. 7. Only a third of all English counties issued wage regulations after 1750, and some of these perfunctorily.

28. On the shift away from low wage theory, see A. W. Coats, "Changing Attitudes to Labour in the Mid-Eighteenth Century," *Economic History Review,* 2nd ser., 11/1 (1958): 35–51; Richard C. Wiles, "The Theory of Wages in Late English Mercantilism," *Economic History Review,* 2nd ser., 21/1 (1968): 113–26.

29. Vanderlint, *Money answers all things,* 83, 86; George Berkeley, *The Querist* (London, 1750), nos. 20, 355, pp. 3, 38. *The Querist* first published in 1735, was reprinted and expanded in 1750 and 1751.

30. Josiah Tucker, *A brief essay on the advantages and disadvantages which respectively attend England and France with respect to trade,* 2nd ed. (London, 1750), 37; *A discourse on the natural disposition of mankind with respect to commerce* (London, 1755?), 1–13.

31. Josiah Tucker, *An impartial inquiry into the benefits and damages arising to the Nation from the present very great use of Low-priced Spirituous Liquors* (London, 1751). On the importance of high wage theory to the mid-century debate over gin, see Jonathan White, "The 'Slow but Sure Poyson': The Representation of Gin and Its Drinkers, 1736–1751," *Journal of British Studies* 42 (January 2003): 35–64.

32. Kelsall, *Wage Regulation,* ch. 7.

33. C. R. Dobson, *Masters and Journeymen: A Prehistory of Industrial Relations, 1717–1800* (London: Croom Helm, 1980), 60–66.

34. Campbell, *London tradesman,* 193. See also *A General description of all trades, digested in alphabetical order: by which parents, guardians, and trustees, may . . . make choice of trades* (London, 1747), 206.

35. *London Evening Post,* 22, 24 January 1745.

36. *The Case of the Journeymen Taylors and Journey Staymakers residing within the Cities of London and Westminster and the Weekly Bills of Mortality* (1752).

37. *London Evening Post,* 24 January 1745.

38. *General Evening Post,* 25 May 1751.

39. *General Evening Post,* 30 May 1751; *London Daily Advertiser,* 31 May 1751.

40. *London Daily Advertiser,* 18 July 1751.

41. *London Gazette,* 15 October 1751.

42. *Whitehall Evening Post,* 24 October 1751; *General Advertiser,* 10 October 1751.

43. Henry Fielding, *A Journey from this World to the Next* (London, 1783), 51.

44. *London Evening Post,* 13 May 1749.

45. *An abstract of the Master Taylors Bill before the Honourable House of Commons, with the Journeymen's Observations* (London, 1721), which perceptively exposes the class bias of the "paternalist" regulation of the trade.

46. [Country Justice of the Peace], *Serious Thoughts in regard to the publick disorders* (London, 1750), 9–10.

47. Clark, "'Mother Gin,'" 63–84; Davison, "Gin Legislation, 1729–1751," 25–48; Warner and Ivis, "'Damn you, you informing bitch,'" 299–330.

48. See Warner and Ivis, "'Damn you, you informing bitch,'" 313–30.

49. Fielding, *Enquiry,* ed. Zirker, 73.

50. See Battestin, *Fielding,* 478–80, 706–11.

51. BL, Add MS 35603, folios 229–32, cited in *Justice in Eighteenth-Century Hackney,* ed. Ruth Paley (London: London Record Society, 1991), xvi.

52. See Radzinowicz, *English Criminal Law,* 3:71–2

53. Fielding, *Enquiry,* ed. Zirker, 152; Beattie, *Crime and the Courts,* 419.

54. Fielding, *Enquiry,* ed. Zirker, 168–69.

55. Ibid., 171

56. *Covent Garden Journal,* 13, 20 June 1753.

57. *Salisbury Journal,* 16, 21, 28 August 11, 25 September 1749, 14 May 1750; *Newcastle Courant,* 21–28 April 1750; For protests against the export of grain in Cornwall by tinners and others in October 1748, see TNA, WO 5/37/323, 344, and *Boston Evening Post,* 10 January 1749, citing a London report of 31 October 1748.

58. *London Morning Penny Post,* 28 August 1751.

59. *Monthy Review* 4 (January 1751) 229–39; *London Magazine* 20 (February 1751): 64–67.

60. William H. Draper, *The morning walk; or, city encompass'd* (London, 1751), v.

61. Maddox, *An epistle,* 36.

62. Ben Sedgly, *Observations on Mr. Fielding's Enquiry into the Causes of the late increase of robbers* (London, 1751), 11–17, 41–43, 82–83; *London Magazine* 20 (June 1751), 281.

63. Sedgly, *Observations,* 61.

64. Ibid., 17.

65. Ibid., 66.

66. Philo-Patria, *A letter to Henry Fielding, Esquire, occasioned by his Enquiry* (London, 1751?).

67. Norma Landau, *The Justices of the Peace, 1679–1760* (Berkeley and Los Angeles: University of California Press, 1984), 98–145.

68. *Commons Journals,* 26 (1750–54): 3.

69. See Richard Connors, "'The Grand Inquest of the Nation': Parliamentary Committees and Social Policy in Mid-Eighteenth-Century England," *Parliamentary History* 14/3 (1995): 285–313, and Joanna Innes, "Parliament and the Shaping of Eighteenth-Century Social Policy," *Trans. Royal Historical Society* 60 (1990): 63–92.

70. *Commons Journals,* 26 (1750–54): 159–160.

71. Ibid., 26:190.

72. Ibid., 26:289.

73. 24 George 2, c. 40.

74. *Commons Journals,* 26 (1750–54): 298.

75. Amory, "Henry Fielding and Criminal Legislation," 179.

76. Gwenda Morgan and Peter Rushton, *Eighteenth-Century Criminal Transportation* (Basingstoke, Hants: Palgrave Macmillan, 2004), 97; Beattie, *Crime and the Courts,* 522–23.

77. John Brooke, ed., *Walpole Memoirs,* 1:174–75, cited in Connors, " 'Grand Inquest of the Nation,' " 309.

78. Beattie, *Crime and the Courts,* 523.

79. Jonas Hanway, *The Defects of the Police, the Cause of Immorality* (London, 1775), 221; Amory, "Henry Fielding and Criminal Legislation," 422–23.

80. "Publicus" in a letter to Sir Richard Lloyd, in the *London Magazine* 20 (1751): 82–83.

81. Anon., *A Letter to a Member of Parliament* (London, 1752).

82. *Commons Journals,* 26 (1750–54): 381–82, 490.

83. 25 George 2, c. 36. It applied only to London. The Lords attempted to extend its application to England, and they wanted to extend the original bill to gaming houses as well as bawdy houses. The Commons rejected the first amendment but agreed to the second. *Lords Journals,* 27 (1749–52): 686–89; *Commons Journals,* 26 (1750–54): 515.

84. *London Magazine* 20 (1751): 82–3; [Student in Politics], *Proposals to the Legislature for Preventing the Frequent Executions and Exportations of Convicts* (London, 1754), 26–38.

85. Radzinowicz, *English Criminal Law,* 1:399–424.

86. Beattie, *Crime and the Courts,* 506–13, 548–52.

87. *Commons Journals,* 26 (1750–1754): 289.

88. Ibid, 289.

89. Joshua Fitzsimmonds, *Free and Candid Disquisitions on the Nature and Execution of the Laws of England* (London, 1751), 45.

90. William Hay, *Remarks on the Laws Relating to the Poor, With Proposals for Their Better Relief and Employment* (London, 1751), x. Massie, *A plan for the establishment of charity houses,* 53–62.

91. Hay, op. cit., xi.

92. Charles Gray, *Considerations on Several Proposals Lately Made for the Better Maintenance of the Poor* (London, 1751), 18. See also 3–5, 23.

93. Sir James Creed, *An Impartial Examination of a Pamphlet entitled Considerations* (London, 1751), 22; *London Magazine* 20 (1751): 502.

94. *Commons Journals,* 26 (1750–54): 500; *London Magazine* 21 (1752): 152–54. The bill was not finally abandoned until 1754, when Henry Pelham prevailed upon Lord Hillsborough not to pursue it any further, fearing a backlash of public opinion similar to the Jew Bill of 1753. See Innes, "Parliament and the Shaping of Eighteenth-Century Social Policy," 79.

95. *London Magazine* 21 (1752): 220–23.

96. Thomas Alcock, *Remarks on two Bills for the Better Maintenance of the Poor* (London, 1753), 4–7; *London Magazine* 22 (1753): 124.

97. Alcock, *Remarks on two Bills,* 18; *London Magazine* 22 (1753): 126.

98. *Commons Journal,* 26 (1750–54): 563, 643, 702.

99. Connors, "Grand Inquest of the Nation," 285–314.

100. Innes, "Parliament and the Shaping of Eighteenth-Century Social Policy," 63–92, and her *Inferior Politics;* John Beattie, *Crime and the Courts,* chs. 9–10; L. Davison et al., eds., *Stilling the Grumbling Hive.*

101. 26 George 2, c. 19 (1753), cited in John Rule, "Wrecking and Coastal Plunder," in *Albion's Fatal Tree,* 168. For wrecking incidents, see *London Evening Post,* 16 January 1746, TNA, SP 36/112 pt. 1, folios 89, 98, 119 (Dorset, February 1750); *Ipswich Journal,* 23 December 1749 (Cornwall).

102. On this change of heart, see Fielding, *Enquiry,* ed. Zirker, lxxiii. For the pamphlet, *A Proposal for Making an Effectual Provision for the Poor* (London, 1753), see Zirker, 219–78.

103. Emily E. Butcher, ed., *Bristol Corporation of the Poor, 1696–1834* (Bristol: J. W. Arrowsmith, 1932: Bristol Record Society Publications, vol. 3).

104. Fielding, *Enquiry,* ed. Zirker, 238.

105. Ibid., 249–51.

106. Ibid., 256. See Robin Evans, *The Fabrication of Virtue: English Prison Architecture, 1750–1840* (Cambridge: Cambridge University Press, 1982), 53–56; John Bender, *Imagining the Penitentiary: Fiction and the Architecture of Mind in Eighteenth-Century England* (Chicago: University of Chicago Press, 1987), 11–22, 147–50. The sale of spirituous liquors was banned from jails and workhouses by the 1751 Gin Act. See 24 George 2, c. 40.

107. Fielding, *Enquiry,* ed. Zirker, 275.

108. Ibid., 269.

109. For a useful summary of the prison before the penitentiary, see Bender, *Imagining the Penitentiary,* ch. 1.

110. Thomas Alcock, *Observations on the defects of the Poor Laws* (London, 1752), 55–71.

111. Joanna Innes, "Prisons for the Poor: English Bridewells, 1555–1800," in *Labour, Law and Crime,* ed. Francis Snyder and Douglas Hay (London: Tavistock, 1987), 42–122.

112. On the *Proposal*'s links to the penitentiary, see Michael Ignatieff, *A Just Measure of Pain: The Penitentiary in the Industrial Revolution, 1750–1850* (London: MacMillan, 1978), 46.

113. See Tony Henderson, *Disorderly Women in Eighteenth-Century London* (London: Longman, 1999), chs. 4–6.

114. See the *General Evening Post,* 17 October 1751; *Old England,* 14 December 1751; *General Advertiser,* 1 February 1752; *Covent Garden Journal,* 11 February 1752; *General Advertiser,* 6 June 1752; Henderson, *Disorderly Women,* 138–39.

115. *General Evening Post,* 24 October 1751.

116. Alcock, *Observations on the defects of the Poor Laws,* 71.

117. David Garland, *Punishment and Welfare: A History of Penal Strategies* (Aldershot: Gower, 1985).

118. Philonauta, *The sailor's happiness, A Scheme to prevent the impressing of seamen in time of war* (London, 1751), 24–25.

119. On this development, see Stephen Gradish, *The Manning of the British Navy during the Seven Years' War* (London: Royal Historical Society, 1980), 57–59, and Nicholas Rogers, *The Press Gang: Naval Impressment and Its opponents in Georgian Britain* (London: Continuum, 2007), 7.

120. Donna Andrew, *Philanthropy and Police: London Charity in the Eighteenth Century* (Princeton: Princeton University Press, 1989).

Chapter 8. From Havana to Halifax

1. John Grenier, *The Far Reaches of Empire: War in Nova Scotia, 1710–1760* (Norman: University of Oklahoma Press, 2008), 143.

2. The first official reference to the scheme is in the *London Gazette,* 4 March 1749.

3. *London Evening Post, General Evening Post,* 13 October 1748: Winthrop Pickard Bell, *The "Foreign Protestants" and the Settlement of Nova Scotia* (Toronto: University of Toronto Press, 1961), 336n.

4. *London Gazetteer,* 10 March 1749. One could also sign up before a commissioner in the navy at Plymouth and Portsmouth, as well as before the Board of Trade in Whitehall; see *Whitehall Evening Post,* 11 March 1749, *General Advertiser,* 13 March 1749.

5. John B. Brebner, *New England's Outpost: Acadia before the Conquest of Canada* (New York: Columbia University Press, 1927), 172.

6. Naomi E. S. Griffiths, *The Contexts of Acadian History, 1686–1784* (Montreal and Kingston: McGill–Queen's University Press, 1992), 66–68. The total Acadian population in French and British territory was about 15,000.

7. Ibid., 70n.

8. *Selections from the Public Documents of the Province of Nova Scotia,* ed. Thomas B. Akins (Halifax: Charles Annand, 1869), 162–63.

9. Mascarene to the Board of Trade, 17 October 1748, cited in Lawrence H. Gipson, *Zones of International Friction: The Great Lakes Frontier, Canada, the West Indies, India, 1748–1754* (New York: Alfred A. Knopf, 1942), 171.

10. See Governor Shirley's letters to the Admiralty, in TNA, Adm 1/3817, 27 March, 10 July 1745. See also *An accurate description of Cape Breton* (London 1755), 69–71.

11. Ibid., 179–80; John A. Schutz, *William Shirley: King's Governor of Massachusetts* (Chapel Hill: University of North Carolina Press, 1961), 117, 153; Geoffrey Plank, *An Unsettled Conquest: The British Campaign against the Peoples of Acadia* (Philadelphia: University of Pennsylvania Press, 2001), 117; George A. Rawlyk, *Nova Scotia's Massachusetts* (Montreal and Kingston: McGill–Queen's University Press, 1973), 193–212.

12. Plank, *Rebellion and Savagery,* 41, 66, 70.

13. Akins, *Public Documents,* 174.

14. TNA, CO 217/9, folios 67–68; Akins, *Public Documents,* 561; Beamish Murdoch, *A History of Nova Scotia or Acadie,* 2 vols. (Halifax: James Barnes, 1866), 2:138; Gipson, *Zones of International Friction,* 182.

15. Akins, *Public Documents,* 561, 563, 573–74. L. F. S. Upton, *Micmacs and Colonists: Indian-White Relations in the Maritimes, 1713–1867* (Vancouver: University of British Columbia Press, 1979), 51. Nova Scotia Archives, council minutes, RG1/209/ 14. I am grateful to Dr. Paul Craven of York University, Toronto, for allowing me access to his microfilm edition of this series.

16. *Ipswich Journal,* 14 October 1749; *London Magazine* 18 (1749): 471.

17. Brebner, *New England's Outpost,* 175.

18. William C. Wicken, *Mi'kmaq Treaties on Trial* (Toronto: University of Toronto Press, 2002), 174–76. For a recent reassessment of the power of aboriginals in the Northeast of America, including Mi'kmaq, see Emerson W. Baker and John G. Reid, "Amerindian Power in the Early Modern Northeast: A Reappraisal," *William and Mary Quarterly* 61/1 (2004): 77–106.

19. Richard White, *The Middle Ground: Indians, Empires and Republics in the Great Lakes Region, 1650–1815* (Cambridge: Cambridge University Press, 1991), ch. 2.

20. Murdoch, *Nova Scotia,* 2:161–62.

21. Pierra Maillard to Abbé du Fau, 18 Ocotber 1749, declaration printed in *Le Canada Français* 1 (1888): 17–19, cited in Upton, *Micmacs and Colonists,* 51–52. See also John Grenier, *Far Reaches of Empire,* 149. "L'endroit où tu es, où tu fais des habitations, où tu bâtis un fort, où tu veus maintenant comme t'inthroner, cette terre don't tu veux présentement te render maître absolu, cette terre m'appartient, j'en suis certes sorti comme l'herbe, c'est le proper lieu de ma naissance et de ma résistance, c'est ma terre à moy sauvage; oui, je le jure, c'est Dieu qui me l'a donnée pour être mon pais à perpetuité . . ." An English translation was published in *London Evening Post,* 30 December, 1749; *Old England,* 6 January 1750; *Ipswich Journal,* 6 January 1750.

22. TNA, CO 217/9, 108v. *Boston Evening Post,* 16 October 1749. According to the newspaper, two soldiers were scalped, although the report to the Board of Trade mentioned only one.

23. Nova Scotia Archives, RG1/209, 22.

24. "Letters and Other Papers Relating to the Early History of the Church of England in Nova Scotia," *Collections of the Nova Scotia Historical Society* 7 (1889–91): 101.

25. TNA, CO 217/9, 129v; "Letters and Other Papers," 101. Tutty suggested Cornwallis had some reservations, but this could well be a projection of his behalf, because he was always saccharine about Cornwallis's affability and moderation.

26. Akins, *Public Documents,* 506–57.

27. Ibid., 546.

28. *General Advertiser,* 7 September 1749; *Berrow's Worcester Journal,* 14 September 1749.

29. Akins counts 1,546 men, although I think he added servants into this category. See Thomas B Akins, "History of Halifax City," *Collections of the Nova Scotia Historical Society* 8 (1892–94): 5.

30. *London Gazette,* 4 March 1749.

31. TNA, Adm 1/2007 (Knowles), folio 283; Adm 1/2008 (Knowles), folio 57v.

32. *Whitehall Evening Post,* 25 July 1749.

33. TNA, Adm 36/4511 (Warwick), 36/2776 (Plymouth), 36/1730 (Lenox).

34. Richard Brinsley Sheridan, *School for Scandal,* act 2, scene 2.

35. See Richard Rolt, *An Impartial Representation of the Conduct of the Several Powers of Europe engaged in the late General War . . . 1739 to 1748,* 4 vols. (1749–50), 2:509–32.

36. *General Advertiser,* 13 June 1748.

37. *Ipswich Journal,* 9 September, 14 October 1749; *Berrow's Worcester Journal,* 14 September 1749.

38. *Westminster Journal,* 2 January 1748. On the Halifax yard, see Julian Gwyn, *Ashore and Afloat: The British Navy and the Halifax Naval Yard before 1820* (Ottawa: University of Ottawa Press, 2004). On trade with the French, see Rawlyk, *Nova Scotia's Massachusetts,* 194–95.

39. TNA, CO 217/9, folio 70.

40. TNA, Adm 36/4245 no. 1022 (Morgan); Adm 36/1730 no. 810 (Bickmore); 36/4711 no. 43 (Moore).

41. TNA, Adm 36/2882, nos. 91, 207, 508, 530.

42. TNA, Adm 51/655, see entries for 7 April, 10–16 August, 1748. TNA, Adm 36/3075, nos. 168, 261; Adm 51/813, 24 April 1747.

43. TNA, Adm 36/2776. Harbin entered in December 1743.

44. For the divorce degree, see Nova Scotia Archives, RG 1/209, 15 May 1750.

45. *Old England,* 1 April 1749.

46. For details of the trial, see *London Evening Post,* 23 February 1738, *Weekly Miscellany,* 3 March 1738.

47. John Oliphant, in the *Oxford National Dictionary of Biography.*

48. Akins, *Public Documents,* 565.

49. *Old England,* 1 April 1749.

50. TNA, CO 217/9, folio 68v; CO 217/40, folio 98v; Akins, *Public Documents,* 565.

51. Nova Scotia Archives, RG 1/29/43, 7 January 1750; *London Magazine* 18 (1749): 414.

52. Akins, *Public Documents,* 587

53. Ibid., 588.

54. For the ballads, see *Expeditions of Honour: the Journal of John Salusbury in Halifax, Nova Scotia, 1749–53,* ed. Ronald Rompkey (Newark: University of Delaware Press, 1982), 19–20; *Gentleman's Magazine* 20 (1750): 84; *The Nova Scotia's Garland* (Newcastle, 1750), 3–7.

55. Akins, *Public Documents,* 565.

56. *Old England,* 1 April 1749, where there is talk of the "weary veteran" getting a "competent tract of land" in return for "toils of his youth."

57. *Expeditions of Honour,* 96; TNA, CO 217/9, folio 70v.

58. *Ipswich Journal,* 28 October 1749.

59. *Expeditions of Honour,* 64, 73n.

60. *Remembrancer,* 14 October 1749; Allan Everett Marble, *Surgeons, Smallpox and the Poor: A History of Medicine and Social Conditions in Nova Scotia* (Kingston and Montreal: McGill–Queen's University Press, 1993), 25–28; *Boston Evening Post,* 3 December 1750.

61. Nova Scotia Archives, RG 1/209/41, 27 December 1749.

62. TNA, CO 217/33, folio 39; see also *Foreign Protestants,* 339.

63. *Boston Evening Post,* 5 November 1749; Murdoch, *Nova Scotia,* 2:163; *Gentleman's Magazine* 25 (1755): 261–64, suggested that 350 cabins had been built by October 1749.

64. See the letter from an officer lately arrived from Louisbourg, *Ipswich Journal,* 28 October 1749.

65. TNA, CO 217/9, folio 189.

66. *Boston Evening Post,* 30 July 1750, 24 December 1750.

67. *Read's Weekly Journal,* 2 March 1751,

68. *Boston Evening Post,* 2 July 1750.

69. Murdoch, *Nova Scotia,* 2:200–201; *London Magazine* 20 (1951): 341, 419; TNA, CO 217/33, folios 161–62; *London Morning Penny Post,* 9 September 1751, *Read's Weekly Journal,* 14 September 1751.

70. [Old and experienced traveler], *The American Traveller, or, Observations on the present state, culture and commerce of the British Colonies in America* (London, 1769), 53.

71. Murdoch, *Nova Scotia,* 2:166–67.

72. John Mack Faragher, *A Great and Noble Scheme* (New York: W. W. Norton, 2005), 262–65.

73. Ibid., 238–39, 265–67; Murdoch, *Nova Scotia,* 2:178–79.

74. TNA, CO 217/33, folio 124.

75. TNA, CO 217/33, folios 90–91.

76. See Grenier, *Far Reaches of Empire,* 162; see also *Gentleman's Magazine* 25 (1755): 264.

77. *Ipswich Journal,* 23 March 1751

78. For calculations of the numbers coming in 1750–51, see Bell, *Foreign Protestants,* 106, 284.

79. Akins, *Public Documents,* 632.

80. Nova Scotia Archives, RG 1/209/87, 89, 107–8, 11, 18 October 1750, 16 February 1751. For a wharfside brawl, see RG 1/209/167–68, 18 April 1752. On the intention to send German Protestants to Chinecto, RG 1/209/75, 2 September 1750.

81. Bell, *Foreign Protestants,* 350–51.

82. Harry Piers, "The Old Peninsular Blockhouses and Road at Halifax, 1751," *Collections of the Nova Scotia Historical Society* 22 (1933): 106–7.

83. See the letter in the *Ipswich Journal,* 9 September 1749.

84. Esther Clark Wright, *Planters and Pioneers in Nova Scotia, 1749–1775* (Hantsport, NS: Lancelot Press, 1982), 8; see also Marble, *Surgeons, Smallpox and the Poor,* 19.

85. Atkins, *Public Documents,* 667 for the fishermen.

86. Wright, *Planters and Pioneers,* passim. I have used this source and the two lists in Akins, *Public Documents,* to reconstruct the family histories of the mariners.

87. For the mutiny, see Clowes, *Royal Navy,* 3:287–88.

88. On the *Salamander*'s activities, see *London Evening Post,* 30 June 1744; *General Advertiser,* 2, 27 July 1744.

89. For details of the prizes, see *Daily Post,* 18 June 1744, *General Advertiser,* 27 July 1744, and the *London Evening Post,* 21 August 1744.

90. *Boston Evening Post,* 26 June 1749; *London Evening Post,* 5 July, 4 August 1750; *Read's Weekly Journal,* 2 March 1751.

91. *Old England,* 1 April 1749.

Conclusion

1. Henry St. John, Viscount Bolingbroke, *Some reflections on the Present State of the Nation* (London, 1753). Written in 1749, but published with *A letter to Sir William Windham* in 1753. The quote is on page 407. For its reception in France, see Michael Sonenscher, *Before the Deluge: Public Debt, Inequality, and the Intellectual Origins of the French Revolution* (Princeton: Princeton University Press, 2007), 182–83.

2. Josiah Tucker, *A brief essay on the advantages and disadvantages which respectively attend France and Great Britain, with regard to trade* (London, 1749). "Proper subordination" appears on pages 35 and 38.

3. Stephen Hales, *A friendly admonition to the drinkers of gin, Brandy and other Distilled Spirituous Liquors* (London, 1751), 33–34.

4. The phrase was used in describing smuggling affrays. See *London Evening Post,* 23 May 1747.

5. *Jacobite Journal,* 14 May 1748.

6. Douglas Hay, "War, Dearth and Theft in the Eighteenth Century: The Record of the English Courts," *Past and Present* 95 (May 1982): 139.

7. *Whitehall Evening Post,* 14 January 1749.

8. On moral panics, see Stanley Cohen, *Folk Devils and Moral Panics: The Creation of the Mods and Rockers* (London: MacGibbon and Kee, 1972) and Erich Goode and Nathan Ben Yeheuden, *Moral Panics: The Social Construction of Deviance* (Oxford: Wiley-Blackwell, 2009).

9. *Commons Journals,* 26 (1750–54): 4, 298, 841. The dates are 17 January 1751, 14 November 1751, 15 November 1753.

10. Ibid., 26:298, quoting from the second king's speech.

11. *General Evening Post,* 12 February 1751, see "Supplement to a Letter to Sir Richard Lloyd" by Publicus.

12. For the classic statement on this balance, see Douglas Hay, "Property, Authority and the Criminal Law," in *Albion's Fatal Tree,* 17–63.

13. For evidence of City merchants financing the prosecution of river theft, see *London Evening Post,* 17 January, 23 March 1751, and *Penny London Post,* 8 March 1751.

14. Alcock, *Observations on the defects of the Poor Laws,* 60, 68.

15. Ibid., 72.

16. Tim Hitchcock, "Paupers and Preachers: The SPCK and the Parochial Workhouse Movement," in *Stilling the Grumbling Hive,* 145–66; Joanna Innes, "Prison for the Poor: English Bridewells, 1555–1800," in *Labour, Law and Crime,* ed. Francis Snyder and Douglas Hay (London: Tavistock, 1987), 42–122.

17. Ibid., 71.

18. For a useful discussion of this issue, see Bruce Curtis, "Foucault on Governmentality and Population: An Impossible Discovery," *Canadian Journal of Sociology* 27/4 (2002): 503–33.

19. On this debate, see Simon Gunn "From Hegemony to Governmentality: Changing Conceptions of Power in Social History," *Journal of Social History* 39/3 (Spring 2006) 705–21.

Index